Praise for the Previous Edition of
Wea'

"Finally...sage advice, now tested by financ[...]
his own family's wealth every day. *Wealth i:* [...]
sonal financial management. You get straigh[...] [...]es like
entrepreneurship, fiscal prudence, and comn [...].ship from generation to
generation."

—**Penny Pritzker, Chairman and CEO, PSP Capital Partners and Pritzker Realty Group**

"Stuart Lucas has connected all the dots, from the first dollar you earn to the last dollar you give away. This book should be read and re-read by a large and growing audience."

—**Robert W. Doran, former Chairman and Chief Executive Officer, Wellington Management Company, LLP**

"Lucas draws from deep personal experience to offer us a rare look at the complex challenges for families who share ownership of assets. His eight strategic steps for managing assets provide unique insights of great value to other families who hope to pass wealth successfully to future generations. Even leading financial families will find this work essential to benchmarking their own financial process."

—**Sara Hamilton, Founder and Chief Executive Officer, Family Office Exchange**

"Lucas's unique background—as a financial manager and an heir to a significant family fortune—gives him valuable insights into the emotional as well as practical side of managing wealth. His concept of wealth stewardship will resonate with families who want to extend their legacies beyond the first generation."

—**Liz Weston, Columnist for MSN Money and author of *The 10 Commandments of Money***

"*Wealth* addresses all the right questions. It has already helped me and my family think through what is really important."

—**William J. Poorvu, Professor Emeritus, Harvard Business School**

"...a perceptive, engaging, and valuable guide to wealth management. This book will not only improve and protect your financial wealth, it will also help keep your family together."

—**Steven N. Kaplan, Neubauer Family Distinguished Service Professor of Entrepreneurship and Finance, University of Chicago Booth School of Business**

WEALTH

GROW IT AND PROTECT IT

UPDATED AND REVISED

Stuart E. Lucas

Vice President, Publisher: Tim Moore
Associate Publisher and Director of Marketing: Amy Neidlinger
Executive Editor: Jim Boyd
Editorial Assistant: Pamela Boland
Development Editor: Russ Hall
Operations Specialist: Jodi Kemper
Marketing Manager: Megan Graue
Cover Designer: Chuti Prasertsith
Managing Editor: Kristy Hart
Project Editor: Betsy Harris
Copy Editor: Cheri Clark
Proofreader: Sarah Kearns
Indexer: Heather McNeill
Senior Compositor: Gloria Schurick
Manufacturing Buyer: Dan Uhrig

© 2013 by Stuart E. Lucas

Published by Pearson Education, Inc.
Upper Saddle River, New Jersey 07458

This book is sold with the understanding that neither the author nor the publisher is engaged in rendering legal, investment, accounting, or other professional services or advice by publishing this book. Each individual situation is unique. Thus, if legal or financial advice or other expert assistance is required in a specific situation, the services of a competent professional should be sought to ensure that the situation has been evaluated carefully and appropriately. The author and the publisher disclaim any liability, loss, or risk resulting directly or indirectly, from the use or application of any of the contents of this book.

FT Press offers excellent discounts on this book when ordered in quantity for bulk purchases or special sales. For more information, please contact U.S. Corporate and Government Sales, 1-800-382-3419, corpsales@pearsontechgroup.com. For sales outside the U.S., please contact International Sales at international@pearsoned.com.

Company and product names mentioned herein are the trademarks or registered trademarks of their respective owners.

Printed in the United States of America

First Printing December 2012

ISBN-10: 0-13-419465-9
ISBN-13: 978-0-13-419465-3

Pearson Education LTD.
Pearson Education Australia PTY, Limited
Pearson Education Singapore, Pte. Ltd.
Pearson Education Asia, Ltd.
Pearson Education Canada, Ltd.
Pearson Educación de Mexico, S.A. de C.V.
Pearson Education—Japan
Pearson Education Malaysia, Pte. Ltd.

Library of Congress Cataloging-in-Publication Data is on file.

This product is printed digitally on demand. This book is the paperback version of an original hardcover book.

To Mom for being the glue,
To Dad for inspiration,
To Susan for her love,
And to our children for the future.

Contents

Foreword to the Second Edition

I joined my family's controlled public company in 1996, as a wine sales-man in New York City. I was 27 and newly married. The team there taught me a lot of things about our company, industry, and much more. There are stories from those days that I'll never forget. At the top of the list was a chat with a colleague, while we were stuck in traffic on the Pulaski Skyway, between Newark and Jersey City, trying to get to a sales call. It was ice cold, and, after too much time watching exhaust float into the steel ribs of the bridge, he eventually took me through the ups and downs of his own family's business before it was sold. Turning the cor-ners of his mouth down, he advised calmly, "Never mix family and busi-ness." There was an awkward silence. "But what if it's too late?" I asked.

Suffice it to say, the average person would agree with my friend. Holly-wood and the literary canon have had fun with the topic, too. So, if you meet someone who can grapple with this age-old subject, I recommend that you listen closely. Stuart Lucas is one of those people. Stuart has the rare and valuable mix of experience as both a professional investor and as a fourth-generation member of another business-owning family: His great-grandfather founded Carnation Company, which his family controlled until its sale to Nestlé in 1985. There just are not very many people like Stuart who "sit on both sides of the table," are able effectively to communicate their acquired knowledge, and who are also willing to share their family's experience with warmth and candor. He wears his wisdom lightly and is a joy to have in the mix. I have enjoyed working with and learned a lot from Stuart. I think you will, too.

For me, Stuart has brought yet another perspective on the value of hold-ing onto a long-term operating business. In our case, that business is Brown-Forman, the company founded by my great-great-grandfather, George Garvin Brown, in 1870. I am one of the many members of the fifth generation of the Brown family who are actively engaged in the governance of the company. More than a dozen of us have roles on the board, in the company, or on our family committee. Brown-Forman started with the creation of Old Forester Kentucky Straight Bourbon Whisky, America's first bottled and bonded whiskey. Since that time, the company has expanded with the acquisition and development of other brands, including, of course, Jack Daniel's Tennessee Whiskey.

When we acquired Jack Daniel's in 1956, it was smaller than Old Forester and scarcely known outside of its home state or beyond the circles of a few connoisseurs. Today, it is one of the most widely recognized and valuable spirits brands in the world. And yet, as we say...while it is sold in over 160 countries, it still comes from a town with one stop light: Lynchburg, Tennessee. Jack Daniel's is a global success story, but it hasn't lost its way. The challenge for Jack Daniel's is the same as the challenge for any multigenerational family. How does your family grow, evolve, and spread its wings across the world, without forgetting its roots? How are children raised in ever-changing circumstances, without forgetting who they are?

Stuart's chapter on entrepreneurial stewardship is at the heart of these questions. He talks about kids growing up, education, careers, and communities. He also does a good job at turning the family tree upside down and looking at it through the lens of today's multicultural kids rather than through the prism of ancestral oil paintings and portraits. I can't recommend this view enough. Like anyone, I venerate the old black-and-white photos. I've even caught my breath, looking at tombstones that bear my name. But Stuart reminds us that it's about the future, not the past. His message to any business-owning family is that it needs to think about its children first and foremost, at the start of every day. Long-term strategy and family governance get built by all generations, but its principal benefactor is tomorrow's generation. Happily for their parents, when the next generation is given a sense of purpose and direction, they'll never forget their way home.

We are all inundated with information, from an ever-increasing multitude of sources, about the critically important topic of family wealth management. I find that Stuart's is a rare voice in that deluge: genuine, deeply knowledgeable, credible, and pragmatic.

G. Garvin Brown IV
October 2012

Geo. Garvin Brown IV is part of the fifth generation of Brown family members engaged in the governance of their family's company. He is an Executive Vice President of the company, the Co-chair of the Brown-Forman/Brown Family Shareholder's Committee, and the Chairman of the Board of Directors.

The views expressed in this foreword are the personal views of the author and do not necessarily reflect those of his employer, Brown-Forman Corporation, or anyone else.

Foreword to the First Edition

I recently asked my wife who she would consult for advice about our financial situation if I were hit by the proverbial bus. Stuart Lucas was the first name she mentioned. I think I know why. Stuart is smart and savvy about wealth management. He engenders a high degree of trust. And he does everything in a measured, well-reasoned way. We have enjoyed getting to know Stuart and his family over the years. As you read this book, I believe you will share our appreciation.

Creating trust is essential for anyone who offers advice about wealth management. In an age where everyone seems to be selling something, how do you know who will really put your interests first? More than ever, investors want independent and unbiased sources of advice. As head of Morningstar, I realize that the trust we've built over the years is essential to our success. You'll also discover that Stuart is a person of high integrity who is out to do his best for every reader.

As a fourth-generation heir of E. A. Stuart, the man who founded the Carnation Company back in the late 1800s, Stuart knows firsthand the privileges, challenges, and responsibilities of wealth. His family's approach to wealth management is a backdrop to this book—a peek through the window that you rarely experience. This gives *Wealth* unusual credibility. The author is practicing day-to-day—with real dollars—the lessons he prescribes. That seldom happens in the world of investment advice, where recommendations tend to be offered enthusiastically by those who have little at stake in the outcome. The hands-on examples here are useful for everyone, regardless of the size of your fortune.

Stuart and I share many basic beliefs about wealth management. Most important, we both have an investor's perspective. "Investors come first" is Morningstar's mantra, and you'll see in this book that Stuart approaches investing in exactly the same way. He offers insightful and practical advice. He seeks to empower investors and to give them the knowledge and tools they need to make wise decisions.

The first of the eight principles that Stuart uses as guideposts is the need to "take charge." He explains the importance of accepting responsibility—both for setting strategy and for making sure that things stay on course. Then, and only then, can wealthy individuals delegate to the experts effectively. Stuart shows, through personal experience, how his own family learned the importance of this insight. Even with access to elite professional talent, simply delegating to the experts turned out to be a mistake.

Another piece of advice that I love is Stuart's suggestion that wealth owners send an "RFP" or "request for proposal" to wealth management firms. This can trigger a competitive bidding process, which will help you understand the services you're receiving. It also ensures that things are competitively priced. This is a simple idea and something that's rarely done. But it's grandly empowering for investors.

I also applaud Stuart's holistic approach. He articulates a comprehensive, strategic view of wealth management that integrates all the issues that individuals (and their advisors) need to think about. This requires knowledge across many disciplines—investment, asset allocation, risk assessment, taxes, philanthropy, and estate planning. Many authors focus on just one aspect of the process. Their readers must figure out how to integrate and manage everything. Because he's done all this, real-time, Stuart packages advice for his readers in an understandable, cohesive *framework*. That's highly valuable.

One of our goals at Morningstar is to bring greater transparency to the mutual fund industry. I see *Wealth* as a clarion call to do the same thing in the world of wealth management. Compared to the mutual fund industry, clients of wealth management firms have much less data available to help them make informed decisions about which firms to retain. There are no benchmarks that customers can use to gauge how well they're being served. There are, of course, superb wealth advisors in the marketplace. Many are Morningstar customers. But it's tough to compare one with another in a way that allows you to identify with confidence who has the best record. Reading *Wealth* will help you do this with greater confidence.

I expect that the top wealth management advisors will read this book and share it with their clients. Better-informed investors will choose better advisors, and they'll hold advisors to a higher standard. In turn, the advisors who do the best jobs of serving their clients will see their businesses prosper. It's a win-win situation.

Stuart's life revolves around his family and so does his approach to wealth management. Most books deal with this subject from an individual's perspective. It's much more difficult when a family is involved. Stuart explores the often complicated interplay between family members and family wealth, and he stresses the importance of creating a wealth plan that reflects a family's values and purpose. He also offers solid advice about family-related topics that touch on wealth management, such as parenting, education, and careers—all the while generously sharing his own family's experience.

I find it refreshing that Stuart offers a broad definition of wealth. To him, it means far more than how much one has in a bank account or the stock market. Being wealthy is about being productive, giving to others, serving society, and creating a legacy. Perhaps, most important, though, it's about taking the risks and responsibilities necessary to manage one's assets and teach one's children to do the same. Wealth, in other words, is a tool to help people across generations live more productive and fulfilling lives, and to be good citizens. To me, that's a more exciting and fulfilling proposition than merely worrying about being able to buy your next yacht.

I believe that this book will help you manage your assets more effectively. But it just might inspire you, too—and help you see the full potential that your wealth can provide. The thing I admire most about *Wealth* is that Stuart places values squarely at the center of things. That notion is sadly missing from most investment planning discussions. Without values, you don't have wealth, just money.

Enjoy!

Joe Mansueto
Founder, Chairman, and CEO
Morningstar, Inc.

Acknowledgments

The experience of writing *Wealth* has been more rewarding than I could have imagined. Perhaps its greatest rewards come from the help, support, and encouragement I have received from so many people because they believe in the book's purpose and they trust me to do the subject matter justice. To all of you I owe a great debt of thanks.

In the early days of the project, Howard Stevenson at Harvard Business School encouraged me to use my family as a case study for the book and stimulated my thinking on a number of issues, many of which tie back to his own fine book on success and significance, *Just Enough.* Paul Sturm, an experienced journalist and Director of Morningstar, helped me to navigate the publishing world and led me to my wonderful agent, Doris Michaels, and ultimately to Jim Boyd at FT Press. Both Doris and Jim had strong hands in shaping the book's tone and defining its audience, and I deeply appreciate their support and encouragement of me in the book writing process. Jim has also assembled a superb team. Kayla Dugger and her production team, Dan DePascuale, Jim Schachterle, and others have worked many hours to perfect and promote the book. Plus, they have been professional and a real pleasure to work with. I can only say the same of Lisa Berkowitz, my publicist. She has been tireless in getting the word out.

Doris also introduced me to Richard Koonce. Rick and I worked intensively together over 18 months to bring my dream to life. As my editor, he has been a great partner. We bring different skills and perspectives to the table, and Rick has never been shy about expressing his views clearly and professionally. It was when we didn't agree that the partnership was at its strongest. We pushed each other, sometimes hard, until we found the right solutions. Rick handled these debates with great professionalism and grace, and without ego. He's also a darn good writer.

Numerous people in the financial business have been a great help along the way. Bob Doran at Wellington Management Company showed me by example how a great investment business is managed, and I am grateful for his continuing advocacy on my behalf. Jeff Thomasson, Jon Hirtle, and Shelby Notkin personify professionalism, integrity, and best practices in everything they do. Lorraine Tsavaris, Ralph Rittenour, Andy Eberhart, Susan Johnston, Karen Harding, and other folks at U.S. Trust and CTC Consulting have been strong supporters and suppliers of data that help to reinforce my message. Mark Augenstein, my wonderful accountant, was also kind enough to read through several chapters and impart his wisdom.

Joe Mansueto, tennis maestro and the soft-spoken founder and CEO of Morningstar, is a busy guy. Yet he believes so strongly in this project that he was willing to carve out the time to read the manuscript and write a compelling foreword to this book. Thank you.

I also want to thank my friend Garvin Brown for being an inspiration to me as I watch him work with his large multigenerational family and their family business. He also generously agreed to write the foreword to the second edition.

Others I want to thank include Tim Dolan, because he always makes me think; Scott Dille, my friend and former boss at Bank One; Cynthia Wambold, for making the graphics comprehensible; and Jim Eckstein, for a real-time case study. My gratitude goes also to my friends Martin Alderson Smith, Etienne Boillot, Ted Hibben, Tracy Weisman, Brian Miner, Lyle Logan, the Rosenbergs Senior and Junior, Alex DuBuclet, and Linda Litner. All of them read drafts of various chapters, contributed ideas, and offered praise that helped me convince FT Press to take on this project. I also want to thank the members of the Harvard Business School personal finance group in Chicago for reading an early draft of my work and providing both useful feedback and solid encouragement.

From the start, my friend and esteemed professor of finance Steve Kaplan encouraged me to keep refining the processes I use for setting wealth management financial strategy; he was always there to help with tactical introductions, the right answers to my technical questions, and the leadership to start the Private Wealth Management Program at Chicago Booth.

Bob McDermott and his late wife (and legal partner), Jane, have had a profound effect on my family that goes far beyond my book. Their professional and practical advice has been enormously valuable to us over the decades. I got help of a different sort from Jack Lanphar. Starting more than ten years ago, Jack figured out how to make things happen that seemed impossible.

I received valuable input from still others in the writing of this book. They include Ken and Peter Lehman, Penny Pritzker, John Manley, Jack Polsky, Lenny Gail and Robin Steans, Peter Goulds, Matt and Kay Bucksbaum, and Will Doheny. Each generously added his or her perspective, shared ideas, and kept me thinking broadly about the issues that wealthy individuals and families face.

Three other friends with experience in publishing and media, Christopher Ainsley, Gary Lucido, and Bob Reichblum, spent hours brainstorming with me about how to hone this book's message and create a breakthrough model for the strategic management of wealth across multiple generations. Sara Hamilton at Family Office Exchange and I have had numerous conversations about wealthy families and their needs, and she has been a strong supporter of the book and my ideas.

One of my toughest critics is my mentor, friend, and fellow NPR Foundation Board member Bill Poorvu. Bill has taught me so much about investing, managing meetings, philanthropy, and values. His wisdom about business and also about life is truly inspirational to me.

José Ramon Sanz has become a close friend, inspiration, and fellow educator. We've worked together for five years building the Spanish Private Wealth Management Program, including families from Latin America. He has taught me many things, but maybe the most important is the obsession with "continuous improvement" mixed with "Don't worry, be happy."

No doubt, the bravest supporters of this project have been members of my family. Eight years ago, a group of about 12 people—cousins, parents, and siblings—came together at my request to learn about my desire to write this book and to highlight the family's experience. Many in the group were tentative about the idea of incorporating our family's story into this book. Despite their reservations, they trusted and supported me 100%. It's my firm hope that this book does justice both to their faith in me, and to our family's heritage and values.

There are three family members to whom I owe a special debt of gratitude. Dad, my brother William, my sister-in-law Melissa, and I built our family office. Although the office and our roles have evolved, their thinking touches every aspect of this book.

A special thank-you goes to my wife, Susan, and to our three children. At times, this project consumed me. You have taken it all in stride and been supportive throughout. You are the very best that I could ever hope for!

About the Author

Living with wealth, managing its complexities, investing it for the long run, using it to advance worthy causes, and perpetuating his family's legacy are all topics **Stuart E. Lucas** knows a great deal about. For over 30 years, he's lived a double life, both as a member of one of America's wealthy families and as a senior executive in prestigious wealth management and investment firms.

Lucas is a fourth-generation heir of E. A. Stuart, founder of the Carnation Company, best known as the maker of such all-American food products as Carnation evaporated milk, Friskies pet food, Coffee-Mate nondairy creamer, and Contadina food products. In 1985, the Stuart family sold Carnation to Nestlé, the Swiss-based global food giant.

Today, Lucas is Chairman of Wealth Strategist Partners LLC, an investment advisory firm that provides an outsourced Chief Investment Officer service for individuals and families (including his own) of significant net worth. An accomplished speaker and educator, Lucas designed and teaches the Private Wealth Management program, exclusively for wealth owners, at the University of Chicago Booth School of Business.

Lucas has a long-standing commitment to public service. He serves as a Director of the Stuart Foundation, which supports public education and child welfare programs in California and Washington. He also serves on the Investment Committee of National Public Radio in Washington, D.C.

Lucas was formerly Senior Managing Director of the Ultra-high Net Worth Group within Private Client Services at Chicago-based Bank One. During the 1980s, Lucas worked for Wellington Management Company, serving for three years as General Manager of the firm's European business operations and before that as Assistant Portfolio Manager of a Forbes Honor Roll mutual fund.

Lucas has a bachelor's degree with high honors from Dartmouth College, has an M.B.A. from Harvard Business School, and is a Chartered Financial Analyst. He is married with three children.

Introduction

Question: What's the best way to make a small fortune?
Answer: Start with a big one.

This book focuses on what an individual like you and families like yours can do to protect and grow your wealth, share it with others, and build lasting personal and family legacies based on it. The lessons learned and shared here come from my many years as a wealth industry professional combined with the experience of representing my family as longtime clients of the industry. There is value in having sat on both sides of the table, and I want to share that value with you.

Whether you are building your wealth over time or acquired it suddenly, whether you have a few hundred thousand in assets or a few hundred million, whether your family situation is simple or complex, the principles discussed in this book will help you sustain, grow, and, most important, enjoy your wealth.

Everyone dreams of striking it rich—by selling a business, scoring a great investment, receiving an inheritance, or winning the lottery. In fact, most people generate their wealth, small or large, by patiently accumulating and nurturing their asset base. Either way, integrating all the components of wealth management into a coherent, satisfying whole is the challenge we have before us.

I was one of the lucky ones because I was born into a wealthy family. For me, the dream began with $25,000 and the founding of what became the Carnation Company by my great-grandfather E. A. Stuart in 1899.

Eighty-six years later, the company was sold to the Nestlé Corporation for $3 billion, and I am a beneficiary of that wealth. But I am even luckier because I've drawn perspective from a thoughtful family legacy and over a quarter century of working in financial services.

I've used this perspective to build a flexible framework that can be customized to the unique circumstances of anyone who cares about managing their wealth. That's what this book is about. My hope is that you'll use this framework to protect and grow your own wealth, share it constructively with those you love, enjoy financial security, and build a lasting personal and family legacy.

But first, I will share a little personal and family history so that you can see firsthand where I'm coming from.

Good Idea, Bad Start

The story of Carnation's founding and of E. A. Stuart's pluck and grit in revolutionizing the production of fresh, safe milk products at the turn of the 20th century is the stuff of American history. So too is the fortune he amassed in bringing these products to your grandparents, your parents, and now your kitchen table.

Back in the late 19th century, E. A. Stuart had a dream of making wholesome, good-tasting milk as available to the Americans of his day as sugar and salt. So in 1899, he co-founded the Pacific Coast Condensed Milk Company and spent $25,000 to buy the rights to a process for producing evaporated milk.

The circumstances surrounding E. A. Stuart's purchase of his new milk production process were hardly auspicious. In fact, in the beginning, they had all the markings of a business disaster. At first, poorly sealed cans of evaporated milk spoiled by the wagonload after leaving Stuart's plant near modern-day Seattle, Washington. Making matters worse, local customers in those days weren't convinced they needed his product anyway, not in a region where cows dotted the lush local countryside and fresh milk flowed as plentifully from local pastures as cold, clear water did from local mountain streams.

But my great-grandfather persisted. "Pluck wins. It always wins," he used to say in those challenging and sometimes dark early days. Showing flinty resolve, he perfected his milk evaporation process and improved his canning procedures.

When Opportunity Comes Face to Face with Hard Work and Preparation

Then luck struck. Or as some might say, "Opportunity came face to face with hard work and a lot of preparation." Just as Stuart perfected his production techniques, demand for evaporated milk skyrocketed as gold prospectors swept through Seattle on their way to Alaska to join the great Klondike Gold Rush. Prospectors started buying it off the shelves as fast as my great-grandfather produced it. By 1909, Carnation had grown from one plant to seven, and sales had gone from nothing to over $4 million a year. At 10 cents a can, that meant 40 million cans of evaporated milk were being produced each year.

Stuart's production process was extraordinary because it took about 60% of the water content out of dairy milk, thus making it easy to transport and store without refrigeration. Stuart, it seems, was in the right place at the right time. His perseverance, discipline, hard work, and faith—plus a little luck—launched the Carnation Company on the path to becoming a multibillion-dollar global food company.

Three generations later, the Stuart family hit pay dirt again. In 1985, international food giant Nestlé bought Carnation for $83 a share, or about $3 billion in cash. That price was nearly double the stated value of the company just a few years earlier and, at the time, was the highest price ever paid for a food company. Our extended family, which had much of its wealth tied up in the nearly 27 percent of Carnation stock it controlled at that time, suddenly landed on the Forbes 400 list of the wealthiest families in America, with close to $1 billion in collective assets!

It was an exciting time for us. We had achieved the American dream. In one fell swoop, we became wealthy beyond our wildest hopes and expectations. But therein lay the seeds of a problem.

Since Carnation's founding in 1899, members of my family had always identified closely with the company and all it stood for. The company had five presidents, three of whom were Stuarts. And even though H. Everett Olson, Carnation's CEO and the Chairman at the time of the sale, wasn't a family member, Wall Street and the business press always described the Carnation Company as "a tight-knit family enterprise."

End of an Era

The day that company executives sold Carnation to Nestlé, all of that changed. Our family's wealth, most of which was tied up for almost a century in Carnation stock, suddenly became liquid. And the family's ties to Carnation, the company that for years prided itself on giving Americans "better milk from contented cows," were suddenly severed.

The aftermath of Carnation's sale to Nestlé offered my family a unique opportunity to decide how its members would relate to one another now that they no longer had a day-to-day business to run. But that also posed some unique challenges: challenges of identity, purpose, leadership, and family legacy. Carnation had been my family's life and work for 86 years. Now that it was gone, what would we do? In the early 1900s, when my great-grandfather had first thought about selling Carnation, his son, E. H. Stuart, Carnation's second president, pleaded with him not to. "If you do, I won't know what to do with myself," he said. Now that reality had come to pass. And we, E. A's descendants, had to deal with it.

No Strategic Approach to Wealth Management

Carnation's sale to Nestlé precipitated a crisis for our family in three ways.

First, our family never anticipated the sale of Carnation. So our family never adopted a coordinated approach to managing our wealth, should that eventuality arise. Thus, in early 1985, when Carnation's sale was consummated, assets of nearly $1 billion suddenly got divided among a large number of Stuart family members. Less than a decade later, there were at least seven different Stuart family branches, each pursuing its own investment goals and strategies—with widely varied results.

Second, after the company's sale, our family no longer had a single focal point for its identity. So our common family heritage and history began to slip away. My great-grandfather and Carnation's founder, E. A. Stuart, died in 1940. His son, E. H. Stuart (my mother's father), passed away in the early 1970s. Within a year of the company's sale, not a single Stuart family member worked for Nestlé. The last family member who worked there quipped to me, "The Stuart family connection went from being an asset to a liability."

Third, after Carnation was sold, our family's wealth was reinvested in mixed stock/bond portfolios that yielded yearly dividends. But these new investment funds couldn't begin to match the average annual growth rate of 13% that Carnation stock had enjoyed from 1899 to 1985. In fact, income distributions to Stuart family beneficiaries started to decline in the early 1990s. Soon, some members of my family, who were dependent on investment income for their lifestyles, began to emphasize fixed income investments more than in years past—a move that was destined to further erode our wealth if we weren't careful.

All of this caused me to look at the Lucas branch of the family—my parents, my siblings, and our children—with a great deal of concern. By this time, I had spent more than ten years in the investment and wealth management industries. After graduating from Dartmouth in 1981, I had gone to work for Wellington Management Company, an investment management firm that manages hundreds of billions of dollars in assets. Over the years, I also became deeply involved in our family's financial and investment affairs as part of the Lucas family office.

My experience at Wellington Management gave me superb on-the-job training as an investment analyst, and as I looked over the state of our investments, I didn't like what I saw. The performance of our funds under the trustee who oversaw our family's assets was mediocre at best—to the limited extent I could measure it.

Alarm Bells

Between 1987 and 1994, the U.S. stock market grew a whopping 133% while the bond market grew 92.4% in value. That meant that a portfolio of 60% stocks and 40% bonds like ours should have grown 117% over that same seven-year period. But to my shock, my family's portfolio had not. In fact, my research showed that during the roaring bull market from the late 1980s into the mid-1990s, the value of our main portfolio grew only 31%. Taking inflation into account, this meant we hadn't really increased the value of our wealth at all.

It's Hard to Grow Assets AND Enjoy the Fruits of Success at the Same Time!

So where was the problem? First, I discovered that there were significant "costs" associated with our wealth that were continuously dragging down the value of our assets. To maintain the existing value of our assets—after distributing roughly 4% a year to family members, paying taxes, paying our investment advisor, paying brokerage fees, and adjusting for inflation—we had to generate roughly 9.5% a year in asset value growth. But because 40% of our assets were invested in bonds, the value of our stock holdings actually had to grow at an annual rate closer to 12%, almost the same 13% average annual growth rate that Carnation stock enjoyed year after year, decade after decade!

But that wasn't all.

Over time, to enjoy the same level of investment income from family trusts that my parents enjoyed, I realized it wouldn't be enough for us just to maintain the value of our assets. We had to increase their value because our family was getting bigger. I have three siblings, and among us we have nine children. If we wanted to live as well as my parents, we would have to generate not 12%, but nearly 17% growth in our stock portfolio year after year for the next 50 years. That's impressive even for someone like Warren Buffett to achieve!

My fellow family members and I always assumed that there would be plenty of money to pass on to our children and grandchildren. But that assumption, I realized, wasn't accurate. Even if we maintained our family's assets in the coming years, spending what we earned net of fees, taxes, and inflation, it became clear that each of my children would have nearly 90% less wealth than my parents simply because the family was increasing in numbers. Growing up, I'd often heard the expression, "from shirtsleeves to shirtsleeves in three generations." Now, I realized what that expression really meant. And I didn't like its implications.

Clearly, none of us was about to starve or see a significant near-term change in our lifestyle. But with an eye toward the future, and on what each of us wanted to do next in our lives, my family and I realized that the fortune my great-grandfather and grandfather built, which had been lovingly preserved in family trusts, wouldn't last another 86 years. My generation would have to work just as hard and be just as entrepreneurial to build our family's assets for the future as our forebears had done in the past if we didn't want to preside over a crumbling legacy.

Our Wealth Represented More Than Cash

I realized something else too. Our family's money represented more than just cash. It represented risk taking, serving customers well, perseverance, history, love, and aspirations for a better future—a tangible gift from past generations of Stuarts to my own. It was meant to last a long time and to be used in ways that would benefit not just my family and me, but also society and generations of Stuarts yet unborn.

We Needed to Get a Handle on Our Investment Portfolio

My family and I needed to get a handle on the long-term management of our wealth. Otherwise, we wouldn't have a family fortune anymore—only the memory of it. What could we do to reverse the tide of our financial fortunes? Crafting a solution demanded the use of all the financial and business training I was fortunate to get at the Harvard Business School and in the volatile business of investment management. When I understood the extent of our family's long-term asset-erosion problems, I presented the facts of our situation to my family. Talk about breaking a family taboo! Can you imagine convening a meeting of your family members to discuss the family's financial health? I can and did, and by reading this book, you'll be able to do it as well.

Introducing Strategic Wealth Management

I persuaded my family that we needed to take a disciplined and coordinated approach to what I call "strategic wealth management." Strategic wealth management is a philosophy and approach to wealth building that involves a number of key components: defining family purpose; setting goals for investments, family businesses, and individual careers; deciding on a time horizon for wealth management planning (your lifetime or multiple generations); asset, liability, and cash flow management; control of spending; wealth transfer; and tax and risk mitigation—all coordinated in a strategic, synchronized way that results in the whole being worth more than the sum of the parts. Strategic wealth management is a comprehensive approach to managing wealth productively in which synergies come from careful planning and from leveraging a family's assets in purposeful ways, not just for a lifetime, but, in our case, for multiple generations. It's also about respecting each individual family member and committing ourselves as a family to helping each one of them to lead productive, happy lives. Remember our American Declaration of Independence; what has made our country great is respect for life, liberty, and the pursuit of happiness. If each one of us is useful, each of us will be productive and our family will be stronger. Being useful is a very broad concept. It's about much more than making money or being the smartest guy in the room. Business success and intellect are important, but being useful is also about being honest, taking care of customers, inspiring children to learn in school or designing someone's dream home. I learned an important lesson from a friend named Charlie. You can be an inspiration to countless numbers simply with a radiant smile and a "can do" attitude.

The Lucases are far from perfect as a family. We are all flawed as individuals, too. It really irritates me when people tell me how wonderful my family is and then woefully say, "if only you understood my situation," as if to excuse their own passive acceptance of their circumstances. Making any family function well takes determined resolve and serious compromise, and there are occasions when no amount of resolve will make a family functional. What may differentiate my family somewhat is that, as a group, we focus on the values that we think should drive the future management of our family enterprise. We talk about our family's shared heritage—a heritage built on "pluck," persistence, personal flint, and private Quaker faith (plus a few other religions)—and our individuality. We also discuss our tolerance for entrepreneurial risk taking, our expectations for earned income, our desire for investment income, and our long-term goals for the future, as individuals, as nuclear families, as the Lucas family, and as descendents of E. A. Stuart. The overriding question in all these discussions is, How do we take measured and educated risks, with the potential benefit of growing our human capital over multiple generations? Family is a work in progress; it always will be. To Joe Mansueto's point in his Foreword, if we manage the work successfully, we will have true wealth, not just money.

We Are Stewards, Not Owners, of Our Wealth

As the Lucas family wrestles with the work of strategic wealth management, several things have happened.

We have begun to see ourselves not as owners of our wealth, but as stewards of it. We spoke of the drifting apart of various branches of the Stuart family after Carnation's sale and agreed we didn't want our family to fracture further. So we decided to reverse the splintering of the Lucas family assets and, together, manage our inherited wealth so that the bulk of it is passed on to future generations, along with the skills and governance to manage it wisely.

We decided to base future wealth management decisions and strategies on core family and individual values. Why focus on values first? Values help to define family purpose and to construct a framework for establishing your wealth management priorities.

We realized it was critical to foster family harmony, strong communications, and wealth management leadership. Wealth management and wealth creation are difficult, distinct tasks. They require high-order management and leadership competencies, whether the preponderance of your assets are concentrated in one family business or diversified in a portfolio of financial assets. We recognized that effective governance was critical to the successful long-term management of our family's assets, and you will also.

Taking Control for the First Time

As a result of our discussions, my family and I pulled our family trusts out of the Midwestern bank that had managed them for years. In an ironic twist, however, the bank didn't try to retaliate for this move or hold a grudge against our family. Instead, the bank hired me in 2001 to manage its high-net-worth business and to implement for its clients many of the strategic wealth management practices and approaches that my family and I decided to put in place.

The decision my family and I made to replace our existing trustee and to take proactive control of our family's wealth management activities had profoundly powerful effects that I want to share with you throughout the book. You will also learn how to enhance your own financial and family successes, given your own circumstances and objectives.

The Power and Purpose of Entrepreneurial Stewardship

Successful business owners wake up every day thinking, "How can I serve my customers better?" They have a mind-set of continuous improvement. They know that loyalty goes only so far and that if they don't get better their competition will. They also know the satisfaction that comes from being useful to others.

I will show that the math of wealth management requires you to re-create the wealth in each generation if you want to keep it. But the core concept behind entrepreneurial stewardship is about building human capital in your family. With the passage of time and generations, many people worry that wealth can be demotivating. A culture of entrepreneurial stewardship inspires people to lead fulfilling and productive lives, and its spirit can give families a sense of purpose and shared identity that transcends the family business. It's more rewarding than growing investment portfolios. It's more flexible than a family company. It's more effective than family philanthropy.

Our family has teachers, doctors, and clinicians who express a spirit of entrepreneurship and service in their work. You might have scientists, politicians, philanthropists, environmental advocates, or artists in yours. In a world of constant change, entrepreneurial stewardship is the best way to preserve common family purpose while helping each individual family member to flourish.

Philanthropy Has Emerged as a Shared Interest Among Many Family Members

Besides strengthening our bottom-line financial results, improved family communication and financial coordination has yielded other benefits. As our extended family has reconnected in recent years, we've rediscovered much about the wonderful Stuart family legacy and have come to appreciate our common family roots.

We found that many of us share a common interest in philanthropy. E. A. Stuart first set up a foundation back in 1937, and additional foundations have been established by virtually every generation of Stuarts since then. Today, these foundations focus the attention of family members on the needs of disadvantaged children, the elderly, at-risk urban youth, schools, and other social issues. Stuart family members quietly give away millions each year in their capacities as foundation trustees and directors. Following in E. A. Stuart's footsteps, many of us also give substantial sums to charity from our own pockets and spend countless hours working with nonprofit organizations both large and small. Some of these causes are well known and prestigious, whereas others are small and support some of society's neediest people. I'll have much more to say about philanthropy as a family bonding agent and component of wealth management in subsequent chapters.

Closer Family Ties

Since the members of my immediate family today coordinate our wealth management activities, it has brought my siblings, parents, and me closer together emotionally than in years past. You should know that growing diversified wealth is not easy. It requires cutting-edge investment and/or business knowledge, a competitive spirit, shared vision, education, and effective governance. It also requires a commitment to communicating openly, honestly, and respectfully with other family members—even when you don't always agree with them. In the Lucas clan today, that's not always easy to do. As our family continues to grow, we must each consider the concerns and interests of all family members in setting wealth management goals and making other critical wealth management decisions.

The Value of Family Lore

Growing up, my siblings and I were raised on stories of E. A. Stuart's persistence in the face of repeated setbacks in starting the Carnation Company. Those lessons resonate in us to this day, and I hope that our family stories make this discussion of wealth management less academic and more tangible to you, regardless of your financial or familial situation.

There's a delivery drop box from one of E. A.'s notable business failures—a dry goods business that flopped before he founded Carnation—that we keep in the kitchen of our Cape Cod summer house. We keep this drop box around for an important and symbolic reason: to emphasize that wealth isn't to be taken for granted and isn't easily attained. "You may have inherited wealth, but in this family you are expected to work hard" is the message my siblings and I got from our parents growing up.

The story of how E. A. Stuart ran Carnation in its early years contains important lessons—not just for running a business, but also for managing the wealth that a business creates. Many of his ideas, in fact, form the core principles espoused in this book:

- **Consistent profits are critical to successful growth.** In its 86 years as an independent company, through two world wars and the Great Depression, Carnation lost money in only three years. The keys to this remarkable track record were prudent diversification, modest leverage, recurring cash flow, empowerment of people, and careful measurement of results.

- **Take measured and informed risks.** The entrepreneurial risks he took and his well-honed intuition were always grounded in his deep knowledge of his business.

- **Align your interests with customers and suppliers.** E. A. Stuart was always looking to partner with people, not to gain the upper hand as an adversary.

- **Conserve your wealth.** He worked hard and was frugal. To this day, my mother takes real pride in describing her family as "understated people."

- **Be useful.** This was E. A. Stuart's ultimate measure of success.

How My Dad Taught Me the Value of Money

A quick story from my childhood illustrates just how large a role prudence and "financial modesty" played in my family's household when I was growing up. In 1965, when my family and I moved back to the U.S. following a three-year job stint for my father in Europe, Dad bought a brand-new red Plymouth Valiant. Over the next 17 years, as he rose through job ranks at Carnation, ultimately to become President of the International Division, this car remained his preferred form of transportation for virtually all business and family activities. Even when the presidents of overseas divisions turned up in Los Angeles to meet with Dad to conduct business, they always drove to company dinners not in some shiny Lincoln Continental or Cadillac, but in my father's red Valiant!

My father so loved this Valiant that for its 25th anniversary in 1990, we bought a vanity license plate for it that read, "65 JUNK." When 65 JUNK finally gave up the ghost, my father pulled the Mercedes that my grandmother had bequeathed him years before out of storage and began to drive it. By then, it was only 20 years old. "Still has many years of useful service in it," he told us.

The lesson my father taught us by keeping that less-than-fashionable Plymouth Valiant around for so long was clear: "Image isn't everything. Don't squander your assets. Preserve your wealth and use it for worthwhile pursuits no matter how much of it you might have." The message he sent to his division presidents was equally clear: "Cost control is important, and I lead by example."

A Book About Strategic Wealth Management

Today, my family's value system regarding money is based both on personal prudence and on an aggressive and shrewd approach to the long-term strategic stewardship and growth of wealth. You'll read a lot about these values—and others—throughout the pages of this book.

But I don't assume that my values are your values. I've learned many lessons about wealth management, as a member of a wealthy family, as an industry professional advising others, and in my years of teaching the Private Wealth Management program at University of Chicago Booth School of Business. One of the most important things I've learned is that each individual and each family has its own values and unique circumstances relating to managing wealth. This book discusses many roads to effective wealth management, not just the ones used by my family. You can explore the options and then decide which ones are right for you.

This book deals with how you can manage your wealth, be it for your lifetime or for multiple generations, using proven wealth management principles to do so. What I say here is directed to anyone concerned about wealth creation, wealth management, family business, retirement planning, and multigenerational estate management. The book will be of value to wealth industry professionals who are interested in providing their clients with fresh investment insights. It will also help upwardly affluent professionals and successful entrepreneurs who are interested in adopting a strategic, focused, and disciplined approach to growing and diversifying their financial assets.

With an insider's perspective, I wrote this book to share the lessons that my family and I have learned, and hopefully to spare you from some of our mistakes. Most of these lessons apply whether you are worth a few hundred thousand dollars or a few hundred million.

As you turn to Chapter 1, "Protecting and Growing Your Wealth," remember this: Wealth management isn't just about money. It's also about people, relationships, values, doing well by doing good, and, of course, family. Enjoy this book for the tools and insights it provides you. Use it as a guide to more strategic and insightful stewardship of your personal and family wealth and to the achievement of a more fulfilling life. Wealth is a gift you should safeguard, nurture, and share productively with others. This book will show you how.

Stuart Lucas

August 2012

1

Protecting and Growing Your Wealth

"Solve your problems. Don't let them lick you."

—E. A. Stuart

hat can an individual like you and families like yours do to protect and grow your wealth, share it with others, enjoy financial security, and build lasting personal and family legacies?

Over the past 30 years, I have learned that effective wealth management has little to do with how much money you have or how you accumulated it. Effective wealth management is much more about how well you manage than it is about how much you manage. The hard lessons that I've learned as a financial industry insider and from managing substantial wealth for my family and other wealthy families are the focus of this book. These lessons are applicable to anyone willing to meet the challenge of managing wealth.

Since the first edition of *Wealth,* I've also had the opportunity to design and teach an executive education program for wealth owners at the University of Chicago Booth School of Business. Over the past five years, more than 400 people from around the world, with wealth from millions to billions, have taken this four-day course. They have generously shared their wisdom in the classroom and in private with me. Many are first-generation entrepreneurs who often attend with their spouses, and sometimes their grown children, laying the groundwork for a multigenerational family legacy. Others are business owners who want to manage their excess cash flow more productively, or who've just sold and need to navigate the labyrinth of wealth management. Every class has a group of second-, third-, and fourth-generation inheritors (one Asian participant claimed more than 50 generations, and another Latin American family has lived continuously in the New World since before Cortez landed in 1519). These people have a different, equally valid, and often more informed perspective on multigenerational wealth than do the first-generation entrepreneurs. It gets rather complicated to manage a family business, financial assets, and multiple generations when your family numbers more than 100 people!

By sharing the lessons I've learned firsthand and from the wisdom of other wealth owners, and using real-life illustrations, I'm confident you can avoid many of the pitfalls inherent in managing your personal wealth, whether you're a business-owning entrepreneur, in the aftermath of a liquidity event, or a fourth-generation heir.

Wealth management is about more than deploying capital effectively, though that is an important part. Money, business, family, and community are invariably bound together. People pay taxes, save, spend, support philanthropic causes, and transfer wealth to their heirs. Successful wealth management involves the integrated and effective management of all these components.

Transitions

Some people build their wealth by saving money a little bit each month and managing it with the goal of having financial security in retirement. Even after years of accumulating financial assets, working with advisors, and experiencing the volatility of financial markets, they are still uncomfortable with how their assets are managed and are looking for better ways to achieve their goals.

Others focus on building equity capital in their business for years, decades, even generations. As the business matures, excess cash flow might be used to diversify into financial and other assets, requiring the development of new financial and investment skills. Most business owners are ill-prepared to deal with the abrupt and often stressful circumstances associated with managing their accumulated savings in the wake of selling their business. In the aftermath, their wealth takes on a completely new character.

The same can be said for those who work hard at their careers for many years and retire with a pension that they are now responsible for managing, or those who receive assets as a result of divorce or loss of a spouse. One of the biggest sudden and high-stress circumstances for coming into wealth is the death of a parent. Over the next 50 years, the United States will see the greatest transfer of wealth in its history. Boston College researchers John J. Havens and Paul G. Schervish estimate that, over this period, total bequests to heirs will total more than $41 trillion.[1] In many of these circumstances, people will not be prepared to take on the responsibility of their new wealth, and the event itself will often come as a surprise.

Building and conserving wealth takes time, and it demands considered action. The key is to not do something prematurely that results in a significant loss of capital. For that reason, resist the impulse to act quickly or to retain outside wealth advisors before you are ready to act. Do your homework first and plan ahead. Carefully consider how you will continue to manage and grow your wealth and help your family to flourish, whether you are most concerned about managing in your golden years or you want to create and/or manage a multigenerational legacy of strong human and economic capital.

How the Wealth Management Industry Works

Why is it important to plan before engaging wealth management advisors to manage your assets? You need knowledge to protect your interests. Unless you are a proactive, thoughtful, and informed client, the structure of the wealth management industry today actually works against your interests in three ways:

1. The wealth management goals of clients and their financial advisors can easily diverge. When conflicts of interest arise, advisors might put their own interests ahead of those of their clients.

2. Advisors are unlikely to fully understand or appreciate your business, personal, and family dynamics. These dynamics are key drivers of wealth management priorities, goals, risk factors, and strategies in families, and they influence many business and investment decisions—frequently behind the scenes.

3. Very few wealth management professionals have enough breadth of skill and experience to operate across multiple disciplines or to anticipate how advice offered by one expert can potentially affect that offered by another. The advice of one advisor should, ideally, complement and reinforce the value of another advisor's input. But the siloed nature of professional fields such as estate and tax law, financial planning, investment management, and banking often works against this desired outcome.

Wealth management firms that are waiting to make money (from your money) include brokers, mutual fund companies, life insurers, money managers and hedge funds, law firms, banks, independent financial planners, accounting firms, and multifamily offices. The organizational culture in most firms focuses on finding a balance between getting acceptable results for the client and achieving the firms' profit goals. As with any market-driven business, the financial rewards and recognition that wealth management practitioners enjoy are based on the amount of business they bring in the door. A premium is placed on generating revenue. It's easy to measure and is tied directly to firm profitability. But larger revenues and bigger profits don't always mean better service.

By contrast, it's not easy to measure the added value that a wealth management firm or advisor actually generates for a client. Thus, clients are often left in the position of having to trust their advisors without an accurate yardstick to measure their effectiveness. This is a big reason why numerous studies of the wealth management industry show a high level of customer dissatisfaction.

This state of affairs hasn't been in the long-term interests of either party. Fortunately, the problems are not insurmountable. That's why America's wealth management industry is in a state of dynamic transition, in which old business models are competing with new ones in a struggle between service and profit. No one knows which will be the winner. There is no better system than a competitive marketplace to resolve industry problems, but the process is messy and clients can get hurt. For that reason, I say: "Buyer beware!" and "Keep reading this book!"

Classic Approach to Wealth Management

Many people rush to retain wealth management advisors in whom they desire to place their trust. Clients are busy, and most are anxious to have professional oversight in place. They either look to a trusted advisor who has helped them before (maybe with issues unrelated to current wealth management challenges) or respond to inquiries from enterprising advisors who identify them as new business prospects. In either case, people often choose one firm immediately or decide to have multiple firms compete for their business before they really know what they want or how to assess accurately the characteristics and quality of each firm's offering. During the course of the selection process, prospective advisors are asked to explain the strengths of their firm and their own background and to describe how they would manage the assets if the prospective client chose them. The prospective client tries to absorb this information with limited relevant experience and typically chooses the most attractive-sounding sales pitch without a thorough understanding of what they want to achieve or the likelihood of doing so.

Sidebar 1.1:   Learning the Language of Wealth Management

Many people's experience with wealth management advisors is minimal at best. Making matters worse, the language of the wealth management industry is often mysterious and intimidating.

I am regularly reminded (usually by one of my children) of just how much a "language barrier" can incite feelings of misgiving and uncertainty. One notable reminder of this barrier came in the form of Pokémon, the hugely successful Japanese trading card game based on mythical creatures pitted against one another in combat. Pokémon is a game at which my then eight-year-old son excelled, but at which I was at best an outmatched opponent. The complex world of Pokémon is filled with hundreds of creatures—some that evolve into others—with myriad powers and weaknesses and all with unpronounceable names. Besides trading cards, there are also stuffed animals, television shows, how-to books, and Pokémon

T-shirts. My son was both an expert at Pokémon and a supremely confident Pokémon salesman. Here's a typical exchange that we might have had in the course of playing a round of Pokémon:

Son: Daddy, why don't you battle this Cyndaquil against my Feraligatr? Cyndaquil is really cool; he has singe attack and an HP of 50!

Dad: What attacks does Alligator have?

Son: Not alligator, Daddy, Feraligatr! He has slash attack.

Dad: Oh, okay. Well, can I use slash attack instead of singe attack with my Cindyquill?

Son: No, Dad. You have to play by the rules. You should know that...

As you can see, this conversation is already a slippery slope. After five minutes of talking with my son about the arcane details of Pokémon, my head was spinning. I couldn't remember what HP is, let alone whether 50 is good or bad. Singe attack didn't mean anything more to me than slash attack. As I played the game, I never quite knew when the rules changed, and even if I did, my facility with the vocabulary of Pokémon was too rudimentary to argue my case. (My son, of course, knew this.) In addition, I hadn't read the small print at the bottom of the Cyndaquil trading card, which states that its weakness is slash attack. After my inevitable loss, I didn't have to ponder very long whether my son had systematically memorized all the small print this game has to offer, with the intention of clobbering me every time we engaged in battle.

Although my son is now 15 and has moved on from Pokémon to other games of wit, power, and deception, the story still seems to resonate.

When faced with managing their wealth, many individuals find themselves in situations similar to those I faced when I played Pokémon with my son. They must operate in alien territory, trying to understand the parameters of an unfamiliar game while being outmaneuvered by complex rules and a vocabulary they don't understand.

After the new client chooses an advisor, both client and advisor are limited to solutions that the advisor can provide, whether or not they are advantageous to the client. Because most private wealth advisors don't generate revenue from a client until they have sold one or more products, and because many clients want the security of knowing that their assets have been invested, there's often an unspoken urgency on both parties' parts to consummate investment arrangements and to lock the client into specific solutions, often with long-term consequences.

When they rush to action, most clients have not thought deeply about their financial, personal, or family goals, how to realistically achieve them, or their comfort with financial risk. So their financial advisors end up driving the agenda. Most advisors inquire about the client's financial situation and learn something about his or her goals, family situation, and personality. This classic approach leaves little incentive for advisors to explain the pros and cons of all the financial options available, especially low-cost, high-value ones. After interviewing a client, the advisor interprets the client's expression of need and selects the firm's available products that most closely match that interpretation, regardless of whether they are optimal for the client. For example, a standard asset allocation is constructed, it is divided by major category or asset class—stocks, bonds, cash, private equity, hedge funds, real estate—and a target allocation is assigned to each category so that the total equals 100%. Then the advisor reviews his firm's stable of available investment managers and recommends a subset that represents each asset class. The client then reviews the list, approves the recommendations, and invests the target amounts.

Within a month or two, and sometimes faster, the client's strategy is set, the assets are fully invested, and the revenues are flowing to the advisor's firm. From here on out, the advisor meets periodically with the client to review the performance of the portfolio, to offer suggestions for improvement, and to make any agreed-upon changes. This classic approach is standard across the industry, and it happens time after time.

Strategic Wealth Management of Your Family Enterprise

You can see that the classic approach equates wealth management with investing. This book focuses on a new way to structure your wealth management affairs. I call it "strategic wealth management." Strategic wealth management is a holistic approach to wealth management that focuses on your entire family enterprise. At its heart, family enterprise is about human capital, not just money. The complete enterprise integrates your family purpose with your business, financial assets, careers, estate plans, and other aspects of your personal and family circumstances. It explores all of your strategic options and puts you in the driver's seat while showing you how to employ your advisors to greatest effect. Your values, your skills and resources, and how you relate to your business, career, and family are at the core of the strategic wealth management approach and are key elements of what I call the "Strategic Wealth Management Framework."

Figure 1.1 diagrams a new Strategic Wealth Management Framework, updated from the first edition of *Wealth*. This new framework is based on hundreds of detailed interactions I've had with other wealth owners since this book was first published. I've learned a lot from them and I'm grateful for the wisdom they've shared. Their insights have broadened my thinking and given me increased confidence that wealth effectively managed is proactively managed. The Strategic Wealth Management Framework is now more action oriented than its predecessor, highlighting the key value drivers for success. Effective governance of your key value drivers—family purpose, your economic engine, and your management of leakages—is the heart of the framework and the lifeblood of your family enterprise.

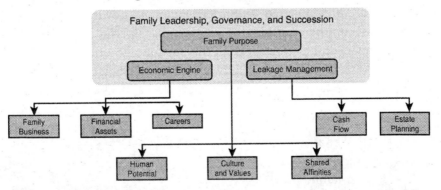

Strategic Wealth Management Framework

Figure 1.1 Use the new Strategic Wealth Management Framework to create a fully integrated plan that meets your objectives.[2]

Using this framework requires more time and effort to implement than the classic model. It is a more comprehensive, systematic approach designed to help you manage your wealth according to your personal and family goals, whether for your lifetime, or for multiple generations. If you work with this framework, you will spark greater focus for your family and will generate better performance from your advisors. Fortunately, there are many surprisingly simple elements of managing wealth, especially financial assets, effectively. Many are even simpler than the classic approach implies. I will highlight these simple, pragmatic, responsible solutions throughout the book. Take them to heart, especially if your core interests lie elsewhere than investing, tax, or complex estate planning.

Figure 1.1 shows that flourishing family enterprises require a clear and shared family purpose, a strong economic engine, and effective management of leakages. Sometimes these key value drivers work in harmony, but conflicts among them regularly arise and must be resolved. If your family is executing well in all three areas, you can make business decisions for the success of the business, invest financial assets prudently for long-term appreciation, and support family members to realize their individual potential while strengthening family ties. In well-managed families, success and stability in any one sphere influence and strengthen the other spheres and the whole system, creating a virtuous circle.

For the virtuous circle to prevail, effective leadership and governance are necessary, within and across the three key value drivers. Governance structures must be aligned, values and rules of engagement must be shared and understood, and leaders must be credible and empowered.

- **Family purpose.** The family's leadership, operating within the governance structure, is responsible for shaping, communicating, and advancing the family's purpose. Family purpose is supported by three commitments:

    - *Maximize the human potential of each family member.* When each individual is encouraged to flourish and be productive your family benefits, regardless of the way in which each individual meets his or her potential.

    - *Adapt and evolve the family's culture and values over time.* In an ever-changing context that is our world today, a stagnant family culture and value set will likely become irrelevant and be ignored.

- ◆ *Identify and invest in shared affinities.* What brings family members together with purpose or fun? What builds a sense of shared identity and purpose? Invest in these affinities just like you do your economic engine.

In catalyzing connections and common identity beyond your family's economic ties, a shared purpose provides the platform for stronger interpersonal relationships and more effective decision making. The strength and value of shared family purpose become particularly evident during times of transition: of leadership, of generational ownership, and during the complex transition from business-owning family to financial family.

- ■ **Economic engine.** Your lifestyle is fundamentally tied to the strength of your economic engine. In the wealthiest families, this link might seem trite—but even in these families, eventually reality bites.

The math is clear, though not widely understood. Your family's economic engine—businesses and/or financial assets—must generate annual returns of at least 10% just to cover the combined weight of taxes, fees, inflation, (modest) distributions, and the "law of compounding children" (the growth in the number of family members from one generation to the next). Over a generation or two, only exceptional businesses and investment portfolios generate returns at this level. The strength of your family's overall economic engine depends on the robustness of each of the following: your business, the performance of your financial assets, and your family members' careers.

- ◆ *Your family business.* Businesses are typically the primary engine of wealth creation. Most businesses start out undiversified, illiquid, and subject to powerful operational, economic, and competitive factors that can lead to wealth creation and, just as rapidly, wealth destruction. If your fledgling business survives to maturity, your family will face new challenges. Mature family enterprises control businesses that generate stable excess cash flow—although they still entail considerable risk. Families in this enviable situation face additional challenges. How do you maintain a family culture of entrepreneurship as the wealth grows? What should be your family's continuing operational involvement in the business? How should your operational involvement affect your governance structure? How do you diversify if you don't want to sell your business? How do the cash flow requirements of the business, financial assets, and family members relate to each other?

Most families eventually choose to sell the core family business. For any number of reasons—perceived risk in the business, lack of family business leadership, animosity within the family, inadequate returns—a family might determine that the benefits of continuing to own the business are insufficient relative to the value achievable from selling. You want to maximize the probability that your family will control the disposition of your core asset, rather than having a decision forced upon you by externalities. For the optimal outcome, you want to evaluate the decision to hold or sell within the context of your family enterprise as a whole. What would be your net-net result, after the sale causes you to realize what might be decades or generations of deferred capital gain on your company shares? What will you do with the cash? Where will you reinvest the proceeds not earmarked for spending? Are you prepared—organizationally, culturally, and in terms of financial infrastructure—to be a financial family? The transition from a business-owning family to a financial family is a radical and risky transformation of the family enterprise. You want to be prepared.

+ *Financial assets.* Excess cash flow generated by your business and salary can be used to diversify into financial assets. Effective conservation and management of your financial assets is crucial to the functioning of your family enterprise, especially as they become substantial asset pools in their own right. Well-managed financial assets bring your family greater economic security by diversifying the family enterprise without having to sell the core business. They also give the family financial management experience that grows exponentially in value when there is a liquidity event. On the other hand, I've seen poorly managed financial assets, sometimes by just one individual, bring unanticipated liabilities to bear on entire families (for example, when a cousin uses shares in the family business to collateralize a risky loan).

Some families distribute excess cash flow to each family member, leaving it up to individual family members to manage their capital as they see fit. Other families make a concerted effort to commingle financial assets, develop a common investment strategy, and retain highly experienced investment professionals.

Considerable benefits come from managing financial assets with scale and focus, especially if your collective assets exceed $100 million or more. First and most important, you can attract better investment talent, specifically a chief investment officer (CIO), with a single large asset pool than with a series of much smaller, independently managed pools. A CIO is a professional investor—not a client service representative or product salesperson—responsible for delivering investment performance and integrating that effort with the strategy for the entire family enterprise. Second, your single, larger pool of capital will have access to more desirable investment opportunities, which often come with higher minimum investment requirements and lower management fees. Third, commingling assets allows your family to share the administration of estate planning and investment management, simplifying tasks and lowering administrative costs. Finally, with a commingled investment strategy, family members are mutually accountable. To make the strategy work, each family member must control his or her financial affairs within guidelines that are agreed upon through the family governance process. Although to some this all might feel constraining, the structure and discipline of pooled investing and leakage management can significantly increase your family's economic security, including the long-term security of your core business.

- *Careers.* Careers generate additional income and reduce your family's overall economic risk profile because they diversify family members' sources of cash flow. Careers carry a cultural benefit to your family, too. Over generations, wealthy families risk creating a culture in which family members are always valued customers but do not benefit from the discipline of having customers themselves. A culture of setting stretch goals, of prudent risk taking, of service to customers and community, and of having to make reasonable sacrifices in the pursuit of those goals is healthy. Again, we see the potential for a virtuous circle: The less each family member depends on the family's wealth for his or her lifestyle, the more risk you can collectively afford to take, and the more likely the family enterprise will flourish for generations to come.

- **Leakage management.** Think of the economic engine as having leaks—dividend or distribution payments, expenses, taxes, and inflation, to name a few. Leakages are an inevitable part of any family enterprise, and they are much more within the family's control than the value of a business or an investment portfolio. Over years and decades, leakages profoundly affect your family's wealth, but their importance to the long-term vitality of your family is often poorly understood. The larger and less well-managed your leakages are, the greater the risk to the family enterprise and the more likely it won't stand the test of time.

You can divide family leakage management into two areas. The first area is cash flow management. How much is distributed to family members and spent each year? What are family operating expenses above and beyond those of the business? How much does your family pay in taxes annually? The second area is estate planning, including governance, control, succession planning, and tax minimization. How much of your family wealth will be transferred to government coffers upon the death of family members? Are estate plans structured to help protect the family's assets from unwanted outside interference?

Good leakage management can mean the difference between maintaining control of your family business and leaving the fate of your family enterprise to chance, and seemingly small changes in the rate of leakage can have large consequences over ten, twenty, or fifty years.

- **Building a virtuous circle.** People wonder why family enterprises don't last. A healthy economic engine is necessary, but insufficient. For long-term vitality, you must manage your entire family enterprise as an integrated whole. Well-managed family enterprises are stable and strong with good governance, clear family purpose, diversified assets, and controlled leakages. Operating in this context, you can make prudent long-term investment decisions for your core family business, determine the most productive level of family involvement in the business, and control its destiny. Your family's financial assets, professionally managed to realize the benefits of scale and focus, are key contributors to your family's continuing economic vitality. Family members feel a strong positive connection to your family enterprise and are encouraged to thrive and contribute to an evolving, forward-looking family culture. When you build this virtuous circle, you are stewarding your good fortune and cultivating your family's valuable business, human, and financial resources. In doing so, you serve the family enterprise as a whole, as well as each family member.

The Eight Principles

The dynamism of today's wealth management industry, coupled with ever-changing business pressures and the complexity of family dynamics, can make managing a family enterprise difficult, even with the Strategic Wealth Management Framework. So, I devised Eight Principles of Strategic Wealth Management to help my family and my readers by bringing greater clarity and precision to our actions and activities. I use these eight principles as guideposts to keep me focused on the things that are most important when it comes to implementing a family enterprise strategy. When decisions get complicated, the Eight Principles help me narrow my choices while maximizing the impact of each decision I make. They can do the same for you. In the next chapter, I will discuss the Eight Principles in detail.

I know that the Strategic Wealth Management Framework and the Eight Principles of Strategic Wealth Management work because they have worked very well for my family and for many others. By using them,

- You'll make sound wealth management decisions based on purposeful reflection, planning, and action.

- You'll select advisors whose skills and experience best match your financial objectives and family enterprise strategy.

- You'll make sound capital allocation decisions that are closely aligned with your business outlook, investment skills, interests, and risk tolerance.

- You'll integrate cash flow, tax management, and estate planning with your asset growth strategies.

- For those with a multigenerational perspective, you'll build your sense of shared family purpose and a culture to enable each individual to flourish.

By embracing the Strategic Wealth Management Framework and the Eight Principles of Strategic Wealth Management, you'll be able to project your values and ambitions (and those of your family) outward into the external environment to achieve specific and concrete goals. When your strategy is a success, you create a legacy that improves your satisfaction and significance, and that benefits your family and society.

The Family as a Cultural System

No two families are alike. All families, wealthy or not, are complex, dynamic organisms that are forever-changing cultural systems. The culture of a family consists of the beliefs, values, attitudes, norms, and behaviors of its members. Each family's history affects its current culture. Individual family members influence one another in countless, complex ways. Numerous external forces influence the life, identity, and norms of a family as well. Marriages bring "outsiders" into a family, and death and divorce can shatter families and shift lines of power and influence. The extended families of spouses who marry into a family exert their influence too, bringing with them new issues of culture, heritage, business success, family dysfunction, and social prominence.

The very presence of wealth colors the dynamics in any family. Money can be tremendously empowering and can afford its owners extraordinary opportunities. At the same time, money can complicate family relationships, foster resentment, and create dependency. At the extreme, poorly managed wealth can lead to disenfranchisement, degeneracy, and even corruption.

I believe that wealthy parents—like all parents—need to be intentional about instilling values of accountability and responsibility in their children when it comes to the use of money. Indeed, doing so can be critical to the family's long-term survival! Many wealthy parents indulge their children financially. In so doing, they often foster economic dependency and create a generation of children that feels entitled to the benefits of wealth but that is ill-prepared to manage the responsibilities that wealth entails. Such children often become reliant on their parents for their lifestyles and often lack the discipline, education or even experience to use money wisely. It's no wonder that some people believe that passing wealth from one generation to the next is doing their heirs and society a disservice.

Not surprisingly, financial dependency can affect a family in significant ways. Just how do you go about raising a generation to be empowered by its wealth, not filled with a sense of overentitlement because of it? I don't know of a single wealthy parent who doesn't worry about this issue a great deal.

That's one more reason why wealth management is about so much more than money. True family wealth comes not from money but from maximizing each individual's human capital and by nurturing a culture of collective goodwill and personal responsibility within the family. Doing this can ensure the health of families (and their money) for multiple generations. The failure to do it leads to family dysfunction and the rapid loss of wealth.

Taking Control of the Wealth Management Process

Using the Strategic Wealth Management Framework requires leadership. Leadership is necessary to define and reinforce your family purpose, govern your business, and manage your family's leakages. You must accept personal accountability for managing your wealth, regardless of whether you want to manage simply and conservatively or with focus and risk. It doesn't matter whether your goal is to build the next Rockefeller dynasty, launch a new start-up business, save for retirement, or hand over day-to-day responsibilities for wealth management to an advisor who has earned the moniker "trusted." In all cases, you, as the wealth owner, must take personal charge of your wealth management by assuming a role I refer to throughout the book as the "Wealth Strategist."

Sometimes the Wealth Strategist is an individual. Sometimes several, or better yet, all adult family members work as a team to play the role. Typically, a first-generation wealth creator takes on the role himself or herself. In a multigenerational context, either model can operate successfully. However, if you still have a family business, business leadership is often separated from the Wealth Strategist role. The Wealth Strategist's role is governance and succession planning for the entire family enterprise, of which the business is one critical component. Managing a complex multigenerational family and managing a successful business are just too much for one person to manage effectively, and the required skills are different.

In the multigenerational context, just as it is important for business leadership and financial managers to be accountable to the owners, it is important for Wealth Strategists to serve at the pleasure of the family. Autocratic leadership is a characteristic of many successful entrepreneurs, but as an American family governance structure it tends to be fundamentally unstable, even when the position is earned through merit and sanctioned by the previous generation! One of the big challenges for second-generation leaders of family enterprises is in shifting the culture from autocracy to a more democratic form of family governance, even as your family business might continue to need strong, autocratic executive leadership. As families plan succession from one generation to the next, it's important to think about the characteristics required to be a successful leader in the next generation, not just the preceding one. Business-owning families have another transition that they often have to struggle through: shifting the family's involvement from business leadership and governance to business governance that relies on nonfamily professional senior management.

Successful Wealth Strategists have a skillful hand in leading their families through these transitions. For those with substantial wealth and a multigenerational timeframe, a managed transition of the Wealth Strategist role from one generation to the next is a critical task. In turn, my great-grandfather, my grandfather, and then my father played the role of Wealth Strategist. Today, I share the Wealth Strategist role with my brothers William and John and our sister, Nori. My sister-in-law, Melissa, my wife, Susan, and I also lead Wealth Strategist Partners, serving as Chief Investment Officer to our family and a handful of others. As a rule, our family believes in gradual generational transitions, not as a delaying tactic by the older generation to retain power, but to give ourselves time to diligently work through the inevitable issues that arise. Time has been our ally in working out complex family and financial dynamics. I hope it can be yours too.

You and your family stand to benefit greatly from having designated Wealth Strategists in place to work closely with advisors and family business leaders. As a chief investment officer to a handful of wealthy families and a teacher of wealth management, I know that the relationships I've built with designated Wealth Strategists from other families over the years make wealth management activities a lot easier and more efficient for everybody. If I'm able to work with a designated Wealth Strategist, we can optimize our working relationship in numerous ways. We use our time more efficiently, we make better investment decisions during times of stress, and our decisions are based on a clearly understood set of operating principles and investment goals. As an educated client, you'll delegate responsibility more effectively, and you will distinguish confidently and accurately between good and mediocre performance.

The Nature of the Wealth Strategist's Role

Wealth Strategists play the critical role in developing and executing a family's wealth management strategy. They work closely with their family to define plans and goals for the family enterprise and then oversee implementation, coordinating the involvement of family members, business executives, and professional financial advisors as needs require. The Wealth Strategists' main governance functions are to manage the key value drivers of family purpose, the economic engine, and leakage management, and to integrate the advice and activities of various professional advisors with the overall wealth management strategy and with the dynamics and priorities of the family. Wealth Strategists in multigenerational families must also take responsibility for leading smooth succession transitions. Without careful planning and effective execution, entropy will pull at your family, just as it has mine. The family will fragment, even when there is no animosity among family members. Without the collective will to fight entropy, as your family grows and matures, the allure of money plus individual autonomy is just too great. The cost becomes apparent only later. Believe me, I've seen it firsthand.

Becoming a Wealth Strategist doesn't require detailed knowledge of business management, investment theory, estate law, or the tax code. However, it does require the following:

- Patience and a long-term perspective
- The ability to foster good communication among family members
- Accurate assessment of your own skills, those of family members, and those of prospective advisors
- An informed layperson's understanding of how the wealth industry works
- Reasonable financial and managerial discipline

I'll have much more to say later in this book about the critical role of the Wealth Strategist. Suffice it to say for now that the Wealth Strategist is in fact the leadership within your family, and it is the job of this individual or team to ensure effective wealth management over time.

Conclusion

This chapter introduced a new Strategic Wealth Management Framework and explained why it's so important for you, the wealth owner, to grasp the reins of control when it comes to implementation. Exercising strong leadership as a Wealth Strategist while following the Framework significantly enhances the productivity of your advisors, and puts you on a track to fully execute your family enterprise strategy and realize your wealth management goals.

Let's go on now to Chapter 2, "Eight Principles of Strategic Wealth Management," where I talk in depth about the principles that are central to the effective management of wealth.

Chapter 1: Issues to Discuss with Your Family

1. Do you find the subject of wealth management intimidating? If so, why?

2. Does your family communicate well about business and money? How might communication be improved?

3. How would you describe the "culture" of your family? In what ways do your family's beliefs, values, attitudes, and norms shape behavior when it comes to risk, growth, spending, and saving? Is there "a presumption of good will" among its members? How can you repair distrust if it exists?

4. Has your family taken time to articulate its "purpose" and how that purpose should drive future wealth management planning efforts?

5. Is "doing your homework" and planning ahead before hiring your wealth management advisors a reasonable approach to take? If not, what forces compel you to act now? What are the long-term costs or advantages of taking your time?

6. Do you have a personal interest in closely managing your finances? If so, how much time are you willing to devote to this activity? If you do not have interest in closely managing your finances, can you structure your wealth management strategy accordingly?

7. Who are the logical Wealth Strategists for your family? Why? What if there isn't a logical choice or a consensus pick?

8. Have you ever hired someone to manage your finances? Was it a positive or negative experience? If it was negative, how can you improve things in the future?

9. Do you know how to assess the relative merits of prospective advisors? How do you know you've assembled the best alternatives to choose among instead of a middling pool of talent? (Hint: Brand alone is not the answer.) After you've hired an advisor, how and when will you know they're doing a good job?

10. What advantages do you see in using the Strategic Wealth Management Framework as a tool in family enterprise planning instead of the classic approach?

Endnotes

1. John Havens, Boston College Center for Wealth and Philanthropy, 2012.

2. The new Strategic Wealth Management Framework was first published in the July/August 2012 issue of *Family Business Magazine*, published by the Family Business Publishing Company, and is reprinted with the permission of the publisher. For more information, go to www.familybusinessmagazine.com.

2

Eight Principles of
Strategic Wealth Management

"Each generation that discovers something from its experience must pass that on, but it must pass that on with a delicate balance of respect and disrespect, so that the [human] race...does not inflict its errors too rigidly on its youth, but it does pass on the accumulated wisdom, plus the wisdom that it may not be wisdom."

—Richard P. Feynman, Nobel Laureate, Physics (1965)

Over the past 30 years of managing other people's money, my personal finances, and our family's wealth, I have developed a useful set of principles for effective long-term wealth management. They apply equally well whether you're managing a nest egg of $1 million or $1 billion. They apply regardless of time horizon and family complexity, and they apply whether your ambitions are aggressive or conservative. For anyone concerned about managing wealth, they provide a source of stability and a critical frame of reference.

Although I've learned a lot from teaching and experience since *Wealth* was initially published, the same Eight Principles of Strategic Wealth Management continue at the heart of what I do every day:

1. Take charge and do it early.

2. Align family and business interests around wealth-building goals and strategies.

3. Create a culture of accountability.

4. Capitalize on your family's combined resources.

5. Delegate, empower, and respect independence.

6. Diversify but focus.

7. Err on the side of simplicity when possible.

8. Develop future family leaders with strong wealth management skills.

Every decision I make, whether it involves managing Wealth Strategist Partners, choosing investment managers, thinking about tax strategy, or working with my family or other clients to set goals, gets filtered through these principles. Let's examine them now in detail.

Principle #1: Take Charge and Do It Early

I discussed this principle in some depth when introducing the role of Wealth Strategist in the preceding chapter. The Strategic Wealth Management Framework requires that you, as Wealth Strategist, articulate—and in a larger family, build consensus around—a set of values and a purpose that will be the foundation of your family enterprise. You must educate yourself about your family finances, existing assets, spending patterns, expected rates of return, and current estate plans. Finally, you must decide how to structure long-term family, business, and financial goals so that they become integrated and can positively reinforce one another. Without following this first principle, you cannot go further in the wealth management process.

Managing wealth effectively requires that you take charge of the process early. Doing so even before you have many financial assets like stocks, bonds, and excess cash is highly advisable. And if you have had wealth for some time, there's no time like the present to start. You probably sense the costs of not engaging earlier. There are insidious forces such as taxes, fees, and inflation that can accelerate wealth erosion and eat away at your net worth even in upward-moving markets. It's also easy to get complacent. For these reasons, wealthy individuals and families need to exercise disciplined leadership of the wealth-building process, particularly at certain critical points in time and around key decisions that can have implications for multiple generations.

The time horizon you set for your wealth management process can be a single lifetime, a single generation, or multiple generations. Making a few good decisions early on can have an impact for decades, building a culture of hard work, service to others, and stewardship within your family. If you simply wait for your advisors to guide you, it's likely that you will get incomplete advice, or advice that tends to fragment rather than coalesce family goals. You might wind up with good products but without an integrated strategy or the resources to implement it over time.

Principle #2: Align Family and Business Interests Around Wealth-Building Goals and Strategies

Creating strong alignment of family members around common goals is critical to ensuring successful implementation of wealth management strategies—especially when they are multigenerational. Aligning interests among family members helps define a family's identity. It leads you to invest in shared affinities and it creates economies of scale. If a family is united around wealth management goals, for example, it has collectively more power and focus in business, philanthropy, or even politics than would individual family members alone.

To align family members around wealth management goals, a Wealth Strategist must articulate and build consensus around family purpose and establish a legitimate rationale for people to want to work together. It helps if he or she is an adept facilitator who is a good listener and is able to mediate conflicts, drive consensus, and ensure regular review of wealth management goals and results. Wealth Strategists will be lightning rods for vigorous and lively family discourse at times because family members don't always see eye to eye. Wealth Strategists must focus constructively on surfacing and resolving contentious issues, separating operational or strategic differences from personal confrontation, and highlighting the shared benefits of cooperation and consensus. It's not easy.

A Wealth Strategist must be able to frame family conversations around critical objectives. He or she must ask powerful questions, recognize the psychological and financial positions from which different family members come, and be adept at shepherding discussions toward consensus resolutions. When opportunities arise to reinforce the presumption of good will among family members, even when they disagree about a specific issue, use them! Sometimes discussions and dynamics get stuck in "history." If you get into this rut, try to shift discussions from a focus on the past (nostalgia, festering hurt, or demands of continued obedience) to the opportunities and challenges presented by the future (social and business entrepreneurship, community involvement, legacy building, and a shift from professional success to "personal/life significance"). The key to building a successful future is in aligning individual interests, not imposing a collective straightjacket. Families that make this shift, whether they are wealthy or not, go on to be successful for multiple generations because the family and its individual members are able to reinvent themselves.

Alignment, of course, also means structuring professional relationships with advisors so that everyone benefits or suffers proportionately from the financial decisions you make together. Wealth managers and their firms are usually smart, aggressive, and ambitious, and have their own internal measures of success that might or might not include customer service and high rates of return for clients. As you go about selecting advisors and money managers, you'll want to make "alignment of interests" a key element of the hiring process and a key filter through which you negotiate and configure working relationships. The more closely advisor interests are aligned with yours, the more likely the relationship will succeed long term.

Principle #3: Create a Culture of Accountability

Although family dynamics are always intertwined in family wealth management activities, the wealth management process itself is fundamentally a business activity. To successfully implement your strategies, you need to put accountability systems and performance metrics in place. Doing so helps to reinforce objective business goals and performance expectations. It also helps drive implementation of wealth-creation strategies and provides a reliable benchmark by which to judge the performance of a Wealth Strategist and his or her team of wealth management advisors, including accountants, lawyers, investment managers, and others.

Individuals and families should measure financial performance on the basis of *overall* investment return. Most financial advisors are measured by the performance of individual products and by the profits they contribute to their firms. Because these metrics are very different and sometimes in opposition, the roles and responsibilities of the Wealth Strategist and key advisors need to be clearly defined. It's also important to establish a timeline for regular review of the Wealth Strategist's and advisors' job performance as well as the financial performance of investment portfolios, trusts, and other components of the family's financial portfolio. Achieving good accountability is tough to do. Even highly sophisticated family offices that manage hundreds of millions of dollars complain about the inadequacy of the available performance measurement systems and the challenge of accurate accounting.

Creating a "culture of accountability" within the family becomes increasingly important as the number of family members involved in the wealth building process grows. Using objective performance measures can help depersonalize criticism of individuals in cases in which family members are not performing. In other words, a good system of accountability makes the message "I love you, but you are not performing" more palatable for all parties involved.

Principle #4: Capitalize on Your Family's Combined Resources

In science, one of the basic laws of thermodynamics is the Law of Entropy. It states that there is a strong tendency in our universe to move toward randomness. I sometimes think that families are subject to entropy because, so often, they seem to fly apart, much as parts of our family did decades ago. But families can overcome this tendency toward randomness.

In families of any size, resources become distributed across the membership with the passage of time. Distributed resources stimulate individual autonomy, a seductive but potentially dangerous power in wealth management. The challenge is to figure out how—and how much—to reassemble these distributed resources so that they function more effectively. The tools for reversing entropy lie in capitalizing on the family's financial scale and the combined strength of family members' personalities, experience, skills, affiliations, networks, and governance, all within a meritocratic culture.

Sidebar 2.1: Understanding Your Family's "Cumulative Advantages"

The Wealth Strategist must be concerned with the family's resources—both economic and human. Taken together, these things constitute a wealthy family's "cumulative advantages" vis-à-vis other families and individuals. Cumulative advantage can be measured by the degree to which a family is able to leverage the economic assets, business skills, investment acumen, social prominence, and personal influence of individual members to help the family collectively achieve its wealth management goals.

As part of clarifying a family's cumulative advantage, here are typical questions a Wealth Strategist might ask members of his or her family:

- Do some family members possess talents or business skills that have a direct bearing on the preservation and future growth of the family's assets?

- If so, how can we leverage the entrepreneurial or professional talents of family members to maintain or improve our family's competitive advantage in the marketplace?

- How should we think about leveraging the scale of our wealth to investment advantage? What will be required of us as individuals in ensuring success here?

- How do we share the responsibilities of governing the family enterprise? How should governance of the family enterprise differ from governance of the family business? How do we hold family leaders accountable to all family members?

- What are the benefits of family control of a business? Do you view family ownership as a competitive advantage? Why? How does business ownership reinforce family's purpose? What criteria should be used for selecting family members to work in the business?

- If you have career passions that aren't very remunerative, can the family structure its wealth in such a way that you don't have to sacrifice the quality of your children's education and healthcare?

- How do we want to leverage family prominence and personal influence in matters of philanthropy? What are our goals in these areas?

Putting family talents, skills, and resources to good use is every bit as important to sound wealth management as shrewd investing, strategic thinking, and the clear enunciation of values. For one thing, it fosters a sense of responsibility, ownership, commitment, and accountability among family members insofar as the wealth management process is concerned. It also helps reinforce values such as education, civic responsibility, personal empowerment, and collective stewardship (rather than ownership) of wealth. All of these values are tremendously important to the Lucas family.

As financial assets become distributed among family members, there's a tendency to manage them separately. Sometimes legal restrictions or personal relationships make other solutions impossible. But you should recognize that there are costs associated with the distributed model. Simply put, a pool of capital with $100 million in assets has more potential investment options open to it than does a pool with $10 million or $1 million due to the following factors:

- Premier money managers often exclude investors who can't commit at least $5 million to that manager's current fund.

- There are legally imposed minimums to gain access to most hedge funds and private equity pools that start at $1 million per entity and go up from there.[1]

- Mutual funds, annuities, and life insurance products that impose sales charges usually charge small investors a larger percentage of assets than large ones.

- Most investment managers discount their annual management fees for large clients.

- Fewer, larger pools of capital will get more attention from both the family and financial services providers.

- Pooling arrangements can be used to help a family member launch a successful start-up business. (A qualified investment might be risky for one individual to finance, but in the context of a whole family's assets, it might be prudent diversification.[2])

Large business-owning families have the additional challenge of managing ownership and control of the company, whether the company is private or public. By the third or fourth generation, ownership interests may vary a lot from branch to branch. In addition, estate taxes and varying spending patterns can cause individuals to sell stock in the family business. Each individual decision may not appear material, but collectively the impact can threaten the family's control of the business. If you don't monitor and coordinate your ownership, purchases and sales can cause unintended consequences that might be enormous.

The benefits of effective coordination and collaboration to improve control, access, fees, and focus can translate to several percentage points of additional return per year!

Inherited Wealth Can Be a Good Thing

Americans have an ambivalent attitude about inherited wealth. In most families, there is tension among family members about when to work together and when to be independent. We romanticize the "rags to riches" story of the independent entrepreneur as the epitome of success. Yet all people need help to achieve their goals. Arrangements of cooperation and assistance are neither signs of weakness nor indicators of excess benevolence. They are part of any negotiated long-term relationship, professional or personal. Helping each other is part of any healthy family dynamic.

With the right combination of leadership, resources, and structures, families can strengthen themselves through a focus on "cumulative advantage." A start-up company run by a G3 (generation 3) in-law can benefit from the wise counsel or networking contacts of the founder's family. A productive family network can enable the active family member to close a key business deal, secure better credit terms, or even gain competitive intelligence that provides the fledgling business enterprise with a unique marketplace advantage.

Some investment-oriented families develop sophisticated networks of advisors, industry analysts, venture capitalists, bankers, and other kinds of information brokers that give them a boost in the area of wealth management, either before or after the family sells a primary business. You can gain added investment insight, know-how, and discipline by getting plugged into the right flow of information and analysis. Doing these things enables highly motivated individuals to spot trends, identify talent, and grasp techniques to grow and transfer their wealth with limited risk. The larger the asset base and the longer the time horizon, the more valuable an effective network will be. Continuous improvement is what it's all about.

The Lucas family office has benefited from cumulative advantage for years. In our particular situation, family members are doing this voluntarily, which makes the process of working together particularly rewarding. We work together because we want to. It's fun, and we all see benefit in doing so.

Promoting cumulative advantage works well as a business technique only if it is coupled with a meritocratic culture. Meritocracy wards off the sclerosis that often accompanies raw nepotism. It also helps to keep in-laws that work for the family and non-family employees motivated.

Inherited wealth coupled with meritocracy and effective governance can help to reinforce positive family values and equates personal privilege with shared responsibility. In our family, public service and philanthropy are important shared values. We work across family groups and within family groups to manage foundation assets and support valued organizations that are doing good works. We work from aunt to nephew, cousin to cousin, brother to sister-in-law, husband to wife, partner to partner, and parents to children. We are weaving a web of support within our family and the broader communities in which we live.

Principle #5: Delegate, Empower, and Respect Independence

Members of a healthy family group learn how to row together and row separately. I have already touched on some of the advantages of working together, but it is also important to respect the individual ambitions and values of each family member and, over generations, each family unit. The challenge for the Wealth Strategist and for other family members is to balance the two and reinforce the strengths of each.

Supporting family members to identify and pursue challenges that they can call their own, away from the family's immediate influence, encourages self-reliance and risk taking. This is an excellent way to encourage the personal growth of young adults, who, if supported by their family in their personal interests or business pursuits, learn to embrace responsibility for their life choices and to develop a sturdy sense of self-confidence. Supporting the exploration of passions by one's children (whether as young people or as adults) is more than sharing in successes. It is important that support strategies should leave room for failure; it is through failure that a person develops resilience and often learns the most. Independence, resolve, periods of trial, and ultimate success within the youngest generation can be of tremendous benefit to the family later, especially if these individuals take on responsible positions of leadership within the family.

It is also important for family members to understand and experience the benefits of working and playing together to reinforce the affinities that bind the family together like the strands of a complex spider web. The Wealth Strategist must create and make the case for encouraging other family members to regularly come together. Ideally, especially in families that manage wealth across generations, all family members can be involved to one degree or another, including in-laws. Sometimes involvement means a day-to-day commitment to the family business. But this is clearly not the correct recipe for every family member. For many, the responsibility is to remain informed, to respond promptly to administrative requirements, and to participate constructively in family discussions and meetings. As the arbiter and facilitator of family discussions about wealth, the Wealth Strategist must listen, broker, offer incentives, and encourage family members to collaborate on common goals.

The principle of "Delegate, Empower, and Respect Independence" applies not only to family members, but also to members of your wealth management advisory team and your business executives. After you establish clear performance expectations for your team and an accountability system that aligns their interests with your own, it's important to step back and delegate many functions to these competent professionals. Doing so creates highly productive client-advisor or shareholder-manager relationships because your professional teams are now empowered to act on your behalf!

Principle #6: Diversify but Focus

Diversification and focus combine the best of both worlds. With diversification, you achieve risk mitigation, and with focus comes the laser intensity that most people need in order to succeed in life. Diversifying your investments is fundamental to prudent risk control. Why, you ask? Interestingly, wealth is created most quickly and most often through success in a single business. (If you can do it, birthright, marriage, and adoption are even quicker!) However, wealth is also most quickly lost by concentrating it on only one investment or a few investments. So, in order to protect your wealth, it's best to diversify it. Later in this book, I describe the Lucas family office's approach to wealth management, which includes diversification in a wide range of areas, including real estate, emerging markets, oil and gas, bonds/mortgages, private equity, and other alternative investments.

The principle of diversification applies in other ways as well. Most individuals have both taxable and tax-deferred (retirement and deferred compensation plans) investment portfolios. Some have life insurance savings plans that are tax-exempt to the beneficiary. A few people also control corporations. Each of these entity types receives different tax treatment. Because tax rates don't all rise and fall at the same time, it makes sense to diversify the tax treatment of your assets.

You can also think about diversification in terms of your human resources strategy. Periodically ask yourself, "What would happen if key partners on my wealth management team left unexpectedly?" Would you be able to replace their talent and specific knowledge readily? If possible, have a backup plan in place for all your key people, including yourself.

Although asset diversification is prudent, my experience is that my family and I reap the most benefits—success, personal satisfaction, competitive advantage, and, in business, outsized financial returns—when we struggle over specific challenges with a great deal of focused energy.

Focus and energy are integral to the pursuit of investment management, and they "enliven the pursuit of the game." Successful business is all about focus. The same can be said about being a successful investor. In this country, and increasingly around the world, achieving competitive advantage[3] in the deployment of capital—a critical component to growing diversified wealth—is very difficult. Without the focus to develop investment skills that are superior to those of most professionals, you won't add value to your investment portfolio.

Focus and experience improve judgment. Although you should make important decisions based on fact, there are also times when you have to go with your gut (when you are adept at wealth management) and go with your values because you rarely have all the facts you need at your disposal. To this end, Wealth Strategists should always be on the lookout for ways to stimulate and pursue their own focused interests and those of their children so that they learn to trust their gut when they need to rely on it.

The Nobel laureates who developed the capital markets theory of diversification did not fully account for the real world. Some businesses are built for the ages. They can withstand volatility and are well diversified. Carnation was one of those businesses. As these businesses grow, they build up a deferred tax liability that has some enormously beneficial characteristics, which are discussed in greater depth in Chapter 8, "Taxes Can Be Your Ally!" Many also pay a growing dividend, which can be used to diversify without having to sell stock. Diversification is good, and it is a profitable mantra for financial advisors, but selling your business isn't always the answer.

Principle #7: Err on the Side of Simplicity When Possible

Inevitably, advisors will present you with many fancy options for doing great things with your money. Some of these are terrific ideas, but I recommend to most people that they stick to simple wealth management strategies and products. Even if you're wealthy, it might be best for you to peg most of your investments to financial indices or to other simple, low-cost, and proven wealth management products.

Before choosing complex solutions to wealth management issues, evaluate the simple ones. Simple solutions (such as indexing) might offer you most of the benefits of more complicated plans, a higher degree of certainty, easier implementation, and greater flexibility in the face of changing personal or financial circumstances. If you evaluate the simple solutions first, at the very least you can quantify the relative benefit and costs associated with more complex approaches.

In my professional opinion, you should view complex wealth management strategies with a skeptical eye. These schemes, often highly remunerative for advisors at the time of sale, can subject clients to long-term risks. For example, recommendations that solve short-term problems or show lots of promise might not pan out as expected months or years in the future. Execution or assumptions might be faulty. Or solutions might work well under certain conditions, but unravel if market conditions change unexpectedly. The more complex the wealth management strategy, the more variables you have to worry about managing, and the more difficult it is to reverse course. Don't buy into complex wealth management schemes because they seem sophisticated. Instead, question why an advisor is proposing a particular course of action and why it is sufficiently better than simpler alternatives. Because many complex strategies are quite remunerative to advisors, be sure you understand how such complex strategies will also be remunerative to you!

There are occasions when a simple approach to wealth management isn't appropriate. Some families actively manage complexity to gain competitive advantage, which I will discuss in greater depth in later chapters. In such cases, a "keep it simple" philosophy doesn't make sense. I suggest a corollary in these instances: Err on the side of transparency. Because wealth management discussions are likely to be both complex and lengthy, not every family member will need or want to be involved in every conversation. However, you'll still need to communicate regularly with everyone about what is happening and gather input and ideas from people as appropriate.

Above all, avoid secrecy! Keeping secrets from responsible family members, advisors, or the government has a propensity to backfire. I've made my biggest mistakes in the past ten years by trying to keep secrets from family members. I did so in an attempt to avoid disagreements that I thought might ensue among family members. Inevitably, the secret leaked, and the problems ended up being much bigger than if I had just faced up to them in the first place. Secrecy is just one more variable you need to manage, and it flies in the face of healthy family culture.

Principle #8: Develop Future Family Leaders with Strong Wealth Management Skills

As a prerequisite to successfully building wealth over multiple generations, Wealth Strategists must develop future family leaders. Every family has a potential reservoir of talent, energy, contacts, and business experience that can be tapped into to lay the groundwork for the future. For example, Wealth Strategists can nurture individuals within the family who demonstrate specific interests and aptitudes. When they relate to the family enterprise, there arises the opportunity to give them progressively more responsible positions of leadership. Identifying talents who might lead the family in the future is important. But remember that everyone impacts the family and its culture. All family members, regardless of their interests, have a responsibility to educate themselves about the challenges of wealth. Everyone should be exposed to substantive family discussions of wealth-building goals and strategies, as well as to the corrosive power (and hollow rewards) of excessive spending. It's not taboo to talk about this stuff if it's done in a responsible manner and in a spirit of good will. If the adults are committed, it helps to instill values of accountability and stewardship in young family members, instead of attitudes of arrogance or entitlement. Young people can become involved in such discussions at a relatively early age, providing a powerful learning ground for becoming responsible for ongoing wealth stewardship. It affords them the opportunity to see the wealth management process upfront, to become comfortable and conversant with wealth management issues, and to observe how family members, family business executives, and wealth management professionals should interact with one another to achieve specific goals. Young people are observant. How you treat family and wealth models behavior for your children, so build your family culture deliberately.

It's my strong personal belief that no person in the next generation should become a full-time employee of the family business without spending at least a decade succeeding elsewhere, and preferably in a related field. When the time comes to return to the family business, that person will have so much more to offer than if he or she hadn't had the outside experience. In addition, they will have developed the confidence that comes from knowing that their successes were a function of competence, not last name. Of course, this approach will lead the next generation to challenge and possibly threaten existing management practices and even the authority of the senior generation. But wouldn't you rather have the family benefit from innovative, accountable leadership through the inevitable generational transitions? Also, if you are trying to send a message that you want to encourage excellence in your business, shouldn't it start at home?

In my particular case, my father encouraged me to go into the investment business rather than the food business after I graduated from college in 1981. The nearly 15 years that I spent working away from the family business taught me so much that I was later able to usefully employ on the family's behalf, thanks in no small part to my father's willingness to let me do so. My brother, William, also spent a number of years in the aerospace industry and then at an investment bank before joining the family office. He used his experience to build our investment reporting, tax, legal, and communications capabilities. It was particularly fortuitous that he married Melissa, my sister-in-law, who had many years of investment experience at The Capital Group Companies as an investment analyst and portfolio manager, before sharing the investment responsibilities for the Lucas family with me. As investors, we both relish the give-and-take of constructive debate. Now, our generation is beginning to search for the interest and talent in the next generation.

How to Use the Eight Principles in the Strategic Wealth Management Framework

Wealth Strategists are responsible for governing their family enterprise, setting direction for and reinforcing family purpose, the economic engine, and leakage management. They work with family members to build a virtuous circle of policies and practices to strengthen the connections across the key value drivers and among family members. They make the Eight Principles of Strategic Wealth Management come to life. To this end, they must play a number of complex roles simultaneously and well.

Articulate Specific Financial Goals

Along with facilitating discussion of values and family resources, Wealth Strategists need to lead discussions of financial objectives and strategy with your family and your advisors. They need to ask questions, such as the following:

- How much money can my spouse and I spend in retirement while still leaving a legacy for those we love?

- How can I help my child without spoiling him or her?

- How can my family establish shared wealth management goals across a spectrum of individual (and sometimes competing) interests?

- How can we develop a fair process for supporting, financing, and monitoring the business or service pursuits of various family members?

- How do I develop confidence that my advisors are working in my best interest, rather than the other way around? How do I prevent them from working at cross-purposes?

Wealth Strategists are responsible for making sure that financial objectives are prudent. From a broad perspective, they must understand the context of investment markets, the tax code, and the financial services industry as components of prudent asset management. At a granular level, Wealth Strategists should understand the basic tradeoffs among investment risk, return potential, taxes, and spending to formulate investment policy and a system of accountability. They should also look for way to make the case for and exploit the family's scale of wealth to realize greater opportunities for capital—financial, business, social, and, most importantly, human.

Oversee Wealth Management Infrastructure and Administration

Aligning the interests of family members with the expertise of advisors requires an integrated approach to wealth management. To this end, one of the most critical initial tasks the Wealth Strategist must undertake is to hire a Financial Administrator, or FA. In business terms, the FA is the Chief Operating Officer, overseeing the day-to-day administration and execution of the wealth management vision that you, as Wealth Strategist, establish. Typically, the Wealth Strategist and the FA work together to manage other key advisors including lawyers, accountants, investment managers, bankers, and insurance agents. The FA can also support family leaders to govern and hold accountable the family business's executive management team. For most people, the FA is an employee of a financial institution, but in larger, complex family enterprises he or she might be an employee of a dedicated family office. Chapter 6, "Picking Your Investment Strategy," and Chapter 7, "Making Your Most Important Hire," are devoted to a discussion of how to identify and manage your FA and other key advisors.

Mitigate Risk

Risk mitigation is another challenge of integration for Wealth Strategists to manage. Without appropriate oversight, unintended connections and correlations can go unnoticed until they are triggered by some unexpected event that causes a wealth management strategy to collapse. For example, excessive debt, combined with lower than expected profitability and sudden illiquidity, can trigger a vicious spiral that ends in collapse. If you follow Principles 6 and 7, you are much less likely to suffer such a calamity, especially if you apply leverage conservatively.

Risk mitigation also applies to operational aspects of wealth management, which need to be monitored carefully and consistently. For example, Wealth Strategists should be constantly on the lookout for the following:

- Eroding personal relationships among family members
- Inadequate insurance
- Overconfidence in one's wealth management abilities
- Modestly (or badly) underperforming assets
- Excessive leakages

All of these can contribute to missed financial goals, unexploited opportunities, and steady wealth erosion. Like the drip, drip, drip of a leaky faucet, these problems can be particularly insidious. No single problem might be significant alone, but multiple or chronic problems in one area can, over time, lead to steady and inexorable declines in asset performance and overall financial health.

Conclusion

The job of the Wealth Strategist is clearly an important one, and a separate one from running a family business. Any challenges to the job are far outweighed by the benefits—personal, familial, financial, and societal—that can result from effective and sustained wealth management. The Eight Principles I've outlined in this chapter are important guideposts that the Wealth Strategist can use to stay focused. They can be used to weigh each substantive decision in working though the Strategic Wealth Management Framework, whether it involves a family matter, a financial matter, or an issue of integration. They keep the pressure on advisors and family members, and they encourage productivity—not only in the current generation, but potentially in future generations. Quickly, the Eight Principles will become second nature. In a complex and constantly changing environment, they are evaluative guideposts that will help your family enterprise maintain a steady course. They work for my family and me. I know they will also help you meet your wealth management goals and objectives.

Chapter 2: Issues to Discuss with Your Family

1. Are you the most likely person in your family to be the Wealth Strategist, or are there others, alone or with partners, who are better positioned to take on this role?

2. What are the critical family issues that you need to keep in mind as you develop strategic wealth management goals and plans? How will you address differences of opinion, especially when there are strongly held opposing views?

3. What are the critical business and financial issues that you need to keep in mind as you develop strategic wealth management plans and goals?

4. What are the most significant integration issues that you will face as you develop your strategic wealth management plans and goals? How do you build a virtuous circle?

5. Have you aligned family, business, and career interests around wealth-building goals and strategies? If not yet, what remains to be done?

6. What accountability measures have you put in place to measure the performance of the Wealth Strategist and his or her professional advisors on a regular basis?

7. What options are open to you and your family when it comes to exploiting financial scale and the power of your family brand and network? Be specific.

8. What are you doing to delegate, empower, and encourage independence among family members and advisors?

9. How effectively have you diversified your family's economic engine? What remains to be done? In what ways can you focus the family's resources to achieve your goals?

10. What are you doing to develop future family leaders to act as stewards of the family's wealth?

Endnotes

1. The SEC has created two classes of private investor such that financial products sold exclusively to these classes are subject to substantially less regulatory oversight than products sold to the general marketplace. The first qualification is "Accredited Investor"; the second is "Qualified Purchaser." Each qualification has various hurdles to meet; but if investors have at least $1 million in financial assets, they meet the first criteria, and $5 million meets the second. Most hedge funds and private equity funds can make their products available only to investors who qualify for one or both classes.

2. A common pooling structure for this purpose is a general partnership. Another is an LLC (limited liability company). Our clients have used both to invest in a single company and in diversified portfolios of assets. The number of partners or members has ranged from 4 to more than 60 but could be more or fewer.

3. Popularized by Michael Porter, the author of *Competitive Strategy* (Free Press, 1980), this term was developed to help businesses think more clearly about how to compete effectively and to build on their inherent competitive strengths. I have found this concept to be equally valuable when applied to investing and the deployment of capital. Being smart and disciplined are necessary but insufficient characteristics of superior investors. The best are often aided by lower cost of capital, superior networks, proprietary know-how, or other lasting competitive advantages. Investors that actually have competitive advantages rarely draw attention to them, so they are tough to identify.

3

Start with Your Family Purpose

"I believe that every right implies a responsibility; every opportunity, an obligation; every possession, a duty.... I believe in the sacredness of a promise, that a man's word should be as good as his bond; that character— not wealth or power or position—is of supreme worth."

—John D. Rockefeller, Jr.; excerpts from a quotation inscribed in granite in front of Rockefeller Center

Have you and your family taken time to discuss what, specifically, you want to do with your lives and your wealth? Have you talked about how you want your values to shape your future and that of your loved ones? Are you even able to discuss issues of money with other members of your family?

For most of us, discussing money and wealth is difficult to do—especially in a family context. Yet having these discussions is critical for purposes of wealth management planning and choosing the appropriate investment approaches, vehicles, and timeframes to meet your needs. This chapter is intended to help you crystallize your family purpose within the Strategic Wealth Management Framework. Here are ten questions to get started.

Question #1: What Do You Want to Accomplish with Your Wealth?

Some people want to use their wealth to build new companies or pursue philanthropic interests. Others want to circle the earth in a space capsule, explore the Patagonian wilderness, climb Tibetan peaks, or move to warmer climes and a simpler life. Still others (myself included) love investing. My wife and I also enjoy the great challenge of helping our children, our (hopefully one day) grandchildren, and our nieces and nephews to flourish, and trying to pass to them a financial legacy that they will use wisely.

But my goals aren't necessarily everyone's goals. As I see it, there are seven major options for employing your wealth, none of which is mutually exclusive and all of which can benefit your descendents. You can do the following:

1. Maximize your financial security in retirement.

2. Channel your assets into additional wealth-building pursuits.

3. Spend your money.

4. Create a special place to bring family together.

5. Become a collector.

6. Donate money and/or time to worthy causes.

7. Give money and companionship to people you care about.

Maximize Your Financial Security in Retirement

Being able to retire knowing that you have enough assets to last your lifetime is a goal that often proves elusive, even for people with millions of dollars in assets. Poor investing and careless overspending can erode even significant wealth faster than you think. Also, a lot of retirees don't relish the idea of actively managing their wealth. They want to shed business and financial responsibilities, not take on new ones. So their assets suffer from chronic inattention and the insidious long-term effects of taxes, wealth management fees, and inflation.

If you fall into this camp, I have bad news and good news. The bad news is that you must take charge of managing your wealth if you want to live well throughout your lifetime and pass wealth on to future generations of your family. The good news is that there are ways to take charge of managing your financial security in retirement without taking on a huge burden.

Channel Your Assets into Additional Wealth-Building Pursuits

Continuing to grow your family business serves customers, employees, family, and nonfamily shareholders. But selling is eventually the path for most people. Although many U.S. families use a liquidity event to switch from being a business-owning family to a financial family, attitudes around the world vary considerably about what to do when you've sold your business. Other options that I frequently see include the following:

- Start or buy a new business.

- Invest in a friend's business.

- Invest in the financial markets.

- Explore funding a new and promising technology.

- Fund proprietary research that might someday lead to a medical breakthrough.

- Become an angel investor to an existing, cash-starved business that excites you or that makes a really good pitch for your financial backing.

Maybe it's obvious, but I will very bluntly state two things about allocating your capital:

First, don't—I repeat, don't—allocate all your capital to one venture. Always, always diversify your investments to mitigate the risk of large-scale market or business losses. If you want to invest in a business, fine. After you have done thorough due diligence on the venture, allocate 10% or 20% of your assets to that business and see whether you can make it grow. If you plan to continue your career, think of it as a financial asset, too.

Second, diversify the rest of your assets across a range of investments that have little in common with your career or your speculative business venture. That way, if either the business venture or the career path doesn't perform as expected, you still have a nest egg to fall back on. Better to get richer slowly than to lose it all quickly, especially if you are nearing retirement.

If you're unsure of what to do, do nothing for a while until you have time to study your situation and determine the best ways to allocate your wealth and your time. In my experience, poor capital-allocation decisions are the most common and devastating destroyer of wealth—especially new wealth. I'll have much more to say about this in later chapters.

Spend Your Money

When you have a lot of money at your disposal (especially in the aftermath of a liquidity event, such as the sale of a business), the impulse to spend lavishly, and even recklessly, can be hard to resist—especially if you've worked hard for many years and deferred a lot of personal gratification to maintain your focus on wealth creation.

But every luxury has hidden costs. Spending $60,000 for a new sports car today at age 45 means forgoing $232,000 in retirement funds that would accrue by age 65 if that $60,000 were reallocated to investments returning 7% per annum.

Spending is a fun short-term fix, but I have seen far too many people regret big spending splurges only a few years later. It's hard to be a big spender and simultaneously preserve your wealth. Moreover, if you want to teach your children prudence with money, a free-spending family culture gets in the way and is hard to reverse.

Create a Special Place to Bring Family Together

For many people, a vacation place is more than just a second home. It becomes an emotional homestead, a place where you go on special occasions—holidays and the summertime—to nurture family bonds, enjoy a sense of community with those you love, and create a retreat from the pressures, cares, and concerns of everyday life.

I fondly recall the summers my family and I used to spend on Cape Cod when I was a kid. There, in a home beside the ocean, we always took time to swim, play games, talk, and simply hang out together. It is a place to which I still return today, along with my parents, my siblings, our spouses, and our children. In this house, and on the land that surrounds it, we find sanctuary from the hustle and bustle of our daily lives for a few brief weeks each year. And it is this special house, with its well-worn memories, where we come each year to renew ourselves and rediscover a sense of tranquility and peace.

During our summer forays, my wife, Susan, and I try to slow down the pace of our lives a bit and eliminate (or reduce) some of the influences of the outside world. We have to walk up to the Inn to get the newspaper. The television is switched on only during stormy days. There are board games, books, jigsaw puzzles, and conversations aplenty, the kinds of activities that encourage human interaction. Just steps from our front porch there are a big yard, a pebbly beach, the cool sparkling ocean, nearby tennis courts, and miles of biking. In the evenings, dinner usually consists of fresh vegetables, fresh fish, and at least 10 to 15 people around the table representing three generations. Every evening, the sunset is more spectacular than the last.

Having a physical place to go to (a family summerhouse, cottage, cabin, or campground) can do wonders for any family, wealthy or not. It can be a place to spend time with loved ones, have fun, renew memories of the past, enjoy the company of others, and celebrate relationships.

Become a Collector

There must be something deep in the psyche of human beings that drives their interest in collecting. In part, it is an intellectual challenge. Some people enjoy competing for rare objects because of the sport and social standing that goes with acquiring them.

The walls of the Art Institute of Chicago, the Metropolitan Museum in New York City, and the J. Paul Getty Museum, for example, are covered with fabulous art. When I've visited the museums' collections, it has occurred to me that this art, like so many other great public collections, was assembled by private individuals with the foresight to see and acquire what others would—only decades later—hold in high esteem.

Collecting art or other objects can serve many purposes. It should be fun, of course. But for some people, it can also be a way to build wealth. If you have an eye for quality, vision, and discipline, and if you conserve your collection appropriately, the investment you make can grow considerably in value over time. A few of the highest-quality private collections attract the attention of public institutions, and in those instances people might find it advantageous to bequeath their personal collections, either during their lifetimes or after they die. There are often significant tax incentives for doing so. The result is not only a generous gift to the public, but also the establishment of a family's legacy in its community.

Donate Money and/or Time to Worthy Causes

Most people who are fortunate enough to build or inherit significant wealth (and many people who aren't) regularly look for ways to "give back." By giving back, we strengthen the communities to which we are bound and make them more effective for the generations that follow us. Civic leadership is an important tradition in this country, more firmly established here than in many other parts of the world. It is one of the things that make our country strong. The involvement of wealthy individuals and families in communities has many benefits to all parties. A devoted benefactor can serve as a catalyst to sustain the needy, promote urban renewal, or spark cultural revivals.

Effective philanthropy is often an excellent way to focus the energies and talents of wealthy individuals and their families on new goals following liquidity events. It can help reinforce family values, such as community service, education, kinship, and adherence to religious traditions. It can also provide meaningful leadership opportunities for individuals who, freed from the day-to-day obligations of making a living or running a business, can focus their time, talents, and energies on serving their communities or helping the less fortunate. Just look at what families such as the Fords, Rockefellers, Pritzkers, and Rothschilds have done with their millions over the past several generations. Their civic contributions include everything from the establishment of foundations and universities to patronage of the arts and preservation efforts on behalf of the environment.

I'll have a lot more to say about how to incorporate philanthropy into your wealth management strategy in Chapter 10, "Making Philanthropy Part of Your Strategic Wealth Program."

Give Money and Companionship to People You Care About

Giving gifts of one's wealth and time to future generations can be enormously gratifying. Financial gifts (be they cash, property, valuable objects, or family heirlooms) mean so much more when they celebrate the special relationships between benefactors and beneficiaries that come about only through shared experience. The benefactor often gives a gift in recognition of experiences shared or milestones achieved by the parties involved.

In their wills, many people leave gifts to friends and family. These gifts often have enormous emotional meaning. They are a way of saying, "Remember me or our shared experiences." Or they might simply convey the message, "You're great. I love you, and thanks for being you." Many times, thoughtful bequests from parents to children or from friends to friends give the beneficiaries life options they might not otherwise have. Thus, such gifts can be truly empowering.

If you're contemplating the future of your wealth beyond your own death, I strongly encourage you to think about the distinctions between leaving money to the next generation and the more ambitious goal of managing wealth across generations. Managing wealth across multiple generations goes far beyond making gifts and bequests that minimize the government's tax bite. It is about sharing your good fortune in ways that reinforce a sense of family purpose and that empower future generations to flourish in their own right. It involves an explicit attempt to prepare those future generations, imbuing them with skills, sensible values, and an appropriate culture as you convey upon them the opportunity to responsibly manage wealth.

I'll have much more to say about these subjects in Chapter 9, "Promoting Entrepreneurial Stewardship," Chapter 10, "Making Philanthropy Part of Your Strategic Wealth Program," and Chapter 11, "Putting It All Together: Multigenerational Planning and Wealth Transfer."

Question #2: What Is the Role of Family Business in Your Family Enterprise?

The lifeblood of every successful business is satisfied customers. Growing a successful business might make you rich, and it defers payment of taxes on the growth of your capital for decades and sometimes centuries. Business ownership also creates jobs and career paths for family members and nonfamily members alike. It also embodies values of service, hard work, integrity, and entrepreneurship.

Entrepreneurship as a core value, whether expressed in business, in the arts or sciences, in public service, or in other walks of life, is a guard against the complacency of wealth. Business ownership is closely aligned with, and is a great expression of, this core value.

If you sell your business and become a financial family, you switch from worrying about serving your customer to always being the customer. To get you to buy their products, salesmen regularly tell you how smart, witty, or handsome you are; they let you win at golf; or they regularly invite you to exclusive events. Everything comes easy. It's no wonder that you can begin to feel self-important and entitled simply because you are rich. Pretty soon the culture can become pervasive.

Many successful entrepreneurs worry that this type of environment will cause their wealthy children to be rudderless or self-indulgent. As financial families, how can we reinstate the importance of having customers in the lives our children?

Work is a good start. The discipline of regularly scheduled employment—doing what you're told and doing it proficiently even if you don't like it, dealing with the occasional unreasonable customer, or really delivering above and beyond the call of duty and receiving the satisfaction from a job well done—are all elements of living a productive life. Work is a great laboratory for dealing with failure, stress, ethical challenges, marketing yourself, winning, and serving others. Work prepares people to be entrepreneurs and, in some cases, to build the next iteration of successful family business, and its leadership.

Question #3: When It Comes to Investing, Would You Rather "Eat Well" or "Sleep Well"?

When I ask people this question, what I'm really asking is how much risk are they willing to take with their wealth and how much are they willing to sacrifice to ensure that their wealth continues to grow.

A person's financial risk tolerance—as measured by the ability to cope emotionally with the volatility of their financial worth—is something that often becomes apparent only after a liquidity event, and then with the fullness of time. After a liquidity event, assets that were frozen for years in illiquid stock or controlled by someone else suddenly are converted to cash or liquid securities and become the wealth owner's responsibility. Those assets also become subject to the daily vicissitudes of the financial markets, going up and down with the markets.

For the newly wealthy person, the combination of volatility, liquidity, and changing net worth can create a roller coaster of emotional ups and downs. A person can be euphoric one day and depressed the next, but in my experience it's the relentless assault of price trends, both upward and downward, that can grab hold of the psyches of even seasoned investors. I've observed amateurs and professionals alike who love risk in a bull market and hate it in a bear market.

All of this makes the challenge of finding investments with limited risk and strong potential much tougher and explains, in part, why so many private investors get into markets near their tops and get out near their bottoms.

Most truly skilled investors have the opposite reaction to marketplace volatility. They know that a bear market creates the opportunity to make money. Conversely, a bull market, though desirable, doesn't last forever, so there comes a time to take profits and move on.

If you feel unnerved by seeing your net worth bounce up and down in value, how can you remedy this situation? As a wealth advisor, I tell my clients that there are really two potential ways for them to handle market volatility: "You can sleep well at night by paring back your risk so that the volatility of your overall investment portfolio is reduced. Or you can opt for a strategy that enables you to 'eat well,' embrace investment risk, viewing volatility as opportunity rather than risk, and potentially put more 'food on your table'"—in other words, increase your net worth.

Applying the "eat well/sleep well" analogy to multigenerational wealth management becomes a little more complex. To successfully manage and grow your wealth across generations, it's not enough to opt for either the "eat well" strategy or the "sleep well" strategy. You need to follow a third path—one that combines aggressive investment with a willingness to live below your means. These are values that you must embrace consistently to convey them effectively to future generations of your family.

Question #4: What Talents Within Your Family Can You Tap Into to Further Expand Your Family's Productivity and Wealth?

Capitalizing on what you're good at is always a good start for getting what you want. For that reason, when setting a wealth management strategy, consider how you and other members of your family can leverage your contacts, experience, business skills, and political and community influence not just to launch new business ventures or make new investments, but also to make your mark in other areas of society—for example, in politics, civic life, education, sports, entertainment, or the arts. Money is a commodity, but talent is a specialized resource!

The decision to cultivate talent within your family starts as a question of values, specifically, the values you stress and impart to your children and grandchildren. In my own family, my wife and I strive to build a culture of meritocracy. We try to stress the importance of accountability, achievement, excellence, diligence, and ambition. We believe that our children need to embrace such values if they are to be successful in their own right.

Establishing meritocratic values within your family—emphasizing values of accountability, achievement, excellence, and ambition to your children, in whatever they do—helps to perpetuate a family culture that seeks and nurtures competitive advantage. It is an excellent way to ensure that the next generation of wealth owners in your family grows up with a strong sense of civic responsibility and wealth stewardship, not of arrogance or entitlement.

This does not mean, of course, that everyone in a wealthy family needs or should try to be in the business of wealth creation.

I once asked one of Jacob Rothschild's advisors to tell me the secret behind the Rothschild family's success in private banking for over two centuries. To my surprise, he didn't talk about competitive advantage in banking or about the fact that Nathan Rothschild made a fortune on the London Stock Exchange in 1815 in the aftermath of England's stunning victory in the Battle of Waterloo. Instead, he told me that one of the bedrock values of the Rothschild family has always been that each family member is expected and encouraged to be the best they can be in whatever walk of life they choose—be it banking, arts and culture, education, wine making, or anything else. It just so happens that since Mayer Amschel Rothschild began the Rothschild dynasty in the late 18th century, there has been at least one terrific banker in every generation. Today, Mayer Rothschild's descendents remain overseers of several leading European private banks. In addition, they are accomplished players in numerous other fields.

There are many ways you might be able to leverage your family's competitive advantage to expand your wealth or to create new professional opportunities for yourself. For example, if your family still controls a business, that business has competitive advantages you can leverage to create new business enterprises, "spinoff" ventures, or new product lines. You might also be able to use your professional success (and social profile) in one business arena to launch an entirely new business venture or career in some other area. Merv Griffin, for example, leveraged his success as an entertainer into becoming a real estate mogul. If business is not your focus, your professional stature and business contacts can potentially position you to accomplish goals in other spheres of activity—perhaps as a political leader, community activist, or philanthropist.

Also, your spouse, siblings, children, or grandchildren might have great talents for making money, organizing people, playing music, promoting worthwhile causes, or managing businesses. Consider the talents that reside within your family and how you might want to nurture these talents for public service, to build future wealth, to improve the quality of life in your community, or to ensure your family's legacy in other ways. I hope my own children find the personal fulfillment that comes from this kind of service—be it professional, artistic, or philanthropic. I hope yours do, too.

As part of executing our family's wealth management strategy, for example, our family has found unique ways to capitalize on the varied strengths of my father, brother, sister-in-law, and me. Our family is unusual in that so many family members are involved in our business operations on a day-to-day basis. This, I believe, gives us a key competitive advantage. All of us have different personalities and different talents. But through common vision, hard work, compromise, and experience, we have built competitive advantage over a period of 20-plus years. Thanks to my brother, William, we're fortunate to have built a family office with excellent management reporting and communications systems. Through our business, my sister-in-law and I are Chief Investment Officers for our family and for a select number of other wealthy families. We oversee the investment management program defined for each client. Using third-party investment managers, we build investment portfolios that express investment themes based on client objectives and our own fundamental research.

Question #5: Are You Committed to Creating a Culture of Accountability in Your Family and with Your Wealth Advisors?

Here are five common reasons I find that people don't exhibit much accountability with wealth management activities:

1. Some people believe that because they are rich they don't have to be constrained by a budget. For them, part of the fun of being wealthy is the freedom to be opportunistic, spontaneous, and even frivolous. Tensions can arise when a "free spending" person is asked to be accountable to a spouse, a parent, or other family members. When this happens, often the best way forward is to position a strong and diplomatic financial advisor as an impartial and prudent mediator (or disciplinarian) among the parties.

2. Some people have good intentions but don't have the time or infrastructure to keep good personal financial records. Simple wealth management strategies equate with simple record-keeping responsibilities. Alternatively, complex strategies can overwhelm all but the most sophisticated accounting and performance measurement systems!

3. Many people don't know how to evaluate the performance of wealth advisors. Although most advisors you hire will provide performance data on your individual investments, many don't provide performance information on your total portfolio, especially if your portfolio includes alternative investments like real estate and private equity. In addition, most advisors measure performance in percentage terms. Although this unit of measure is important, it can be misleading. I recommend keeping track of long-term performance not only in percentages but also in dollars, just as you see in the annual reports of public companies. After all, you can't spend percents—you can only spend after-tax dollars.

4. People get intimidated by advisors. Understanding the performance of a wealth advisor can be a daunting task—one that you might not feel competent to do. The wealth industry is filled with numbers and jargon that easily overwhelm even the most attentive client. It's no wonder that clients often defer to a "knowledgeable" wealth advisor for simple definitions, clear explanations, and black-and-white recommendations about investments—whether the answers are complete or not!

5. There is no standard way for individuals to objectively measure the effectiveness of wealth advisors' decisions or recommendations, especially net of taxes.[1] Institutional investors regularly compare their aggregate performance with one another. Medium-sized pension plans can easily learn how they rank compared to similar institutions. Large endowments all compare themselves against Harvard and Yale as well as the averages. No such comparisons are produced for private investors, so you can't meaningfully compare your performance against other wealthy investors. Furthermore, very few wealth management

firms produce composite performance data for their private client portfolios, so you can't measure one advisor's value added relative to another. Financial advisors will show you lots of good-looking numbers from each investment manager they recommend. But when you ask to see the long-term aggregate performance of each of your financial advisor's private clients' portfolios against an appropriate unmanaged benchmark (the truest measure of an advisor's financial advice), the data doesn't exist.

To counter all this, you will very likely need to establish performance standards by which you, other members of your family, and your wealth advisors are judged. The more complicated the wealth management strategy you apply, the more difficult it is to develop performance standards to hold people accountable and the greater the risk that your strategy can go awry without your knowledge.

Having a good system of accountability in place creates peace of mind when things are going well for you, early warning signs if things are not, and information that helps identify the source of problems when things are going badly. When the system of accountability gives you important feedback, it is also critical to know when, and under what circumstances, to take action—and what action to take. These are the judgments that come with skill and experience.

Accountability systems can reinforce key family wealth management goals and priorities. They can serve as a kind of "score card" for assessing the performance of all parties involved in the wealth management process, including the Wealth Strategist. Accountability systems should be composed of specific metrics developed by both you and your advisors and should be in alignment with stated investment goals and wealth management strategies.

As generations multiply and an ever-widening circle of people owns family assets, it becomes increasingly difficult either to gain consensus on or to mandate the discipline of good accountability. Under these circumstances, it is advantageous to have a culture of management and stewardship already established. A good system of accountability fosters open communication and education, especially in a multigenerational context. When assets are owned jointly by numerous adult family members (like a family business), learning how to communicate constructively about performance, and how to educate the next generation on its importance, are critical to long-term success.

Question # 6: Are You Bullish or Bearish on the Global Economy, Business, and Investing?

Today, even in the wake of the U.S. financial crisis and the unfolding Eurozone mess, most U.S. investment firms are bullish on America and on the world's future economic and political health. Their analyses suggest that political instability, world war, deflation or runaway inflation, economically effective terrorism, and economic isolationism are, at most, modest threats. Further, they observe that the United States is the lone superpower and our country has not experienced a conventional war on U.S. soil since the Civil War. Democracy is taking hold in more and more countries, and with democracy comes economic vitality and a greater desire for peace. Finally, they argue, the world today is so interconnected that a massive breakdown in America's way of life is highly unlikely.

I agree with all the foregoing—with a few caveats. First, throughout history, strong, powerful, and seemingly stable cultures have fallen victim to unseen political, economic, or military threats. It happened to the Roman Empire, the Ottoman Empire, the British Empire, the Soviet Union, and now maybe the European Union.

Second, if major economies, currency systems, or political systems were to unravel, it's unlikely that your financial advisors would see the threats soon enough to avoid a large drop in your asset values. Political coups, currency breaks, market corrections, natural disasters, and strategic inflection points in the worlds of business, commerce, and technology are impossible to consistently forecast accurately.

Third, it's best to acknowledge that you don't know what the future will bring and to be skeptical of those who profess to know it. That's what great investors like Warren Buffett, John Neff, Peter Lynch, Howard Marks, and Seth Klarman do. Why shouldn't you? Instead, seek opportunity, be value-conscious, hedge your bets, and diversify your assets. The strategies for doing so are outlined in the chapters ahead.

Fourth, seek to understand how your portfolio could be affected by major economic downturns, political developments, technological advances, or the emergence of new economic players or factors in the global economy. And while you ponder the nature of change in today's world, recognize that change can be both continuous (incremental) and discontinuous in nature. Examples of discontinuous events include the Asian financial crisis of 1998, 9/11, and the collapse of Bear Stearns, Lehman Brothers, AIG, and Fannie Mae all within a few months.

The message here is to avoid extreme market optimism or pessimism. Long-term wealth management is in part a game of survival and opportunism at points of maximum stress and maximum exuberance. I try to keep a global perspective that helps me to identify inflection points, keep them in perspective, see opportunity when things look bleak, and see risk where others see only opportunity.

Question #7: To What Extent Are Your Assets Under Threat?

Your assets can be threatened by various people and events: a divorce, a house fire, a disgruntled trust beneficiary, employees, neighbors, or the driver of an automobile with whom you happen to collide. Others who might try to take your assets include lenders, the IRS, or anyone with whom you have a contract, written or implied. And, of course, your assets can be threatened by large-scale political or economic events.

There are two basic methods for protecting your assets: acquiring insurance and safeguarding your assets from creditors. Both of these methods require different approaches after people become wealthy.

With regard to insurance, typically people carry health, property, casualty, and life insurance with the intent of helping them to maintain stable cash flow through life's disruptions and their aftermath. They insure against even small losses, like minor medical bills and fender benders that have a high probability of occurring. In fact, insurance is almost a misnomer. It's more like a subscription service. People who buy insurance are really just prepaying for things (plus a commission) that are going to happen anyway for the benefit of smoothing their ongoing cash flow.

In contrast, wealthy people should be less concerned about protecting monthly cash flow and more concerned about protecting the bigger picture—their assets. This means that if you become wealthy, you need to reorient your perspective on what insurance is meant to do. Start by opting for higher amounts on your deductibles wherever possible because you'll save lots of money, and you can afford to self-insure for small mishaps. More important, the money you save by raising your deductibles can be used instead to acquire insurance that protects you against infrequent, but catastrophic, loss. To supplement your basic insurance, invest in an umbrella liability policy to cover major losses that your basic insurance doesn't cover. Because claims against these policies are low among the total population, the cost is low and the true insurance value is great.

With regard to protecting assets from creditors, you should immediately investigate these commonly practiced options to see whether any can help you:

- The creation of a limited liability company, a limited liability partnership, or a trust—all of which are common ways to limit personal liability.

- The signing of a prenuptial agreement (especially in the case of a second marriage) that spells out the disposition of assets in case of divorce. It's not a romantic thing to do, but it's very practical.

- Ways to protect your home. In some states, for example, you can own your home as "tenants by the entirety," which has the effect of helping to protect your home from creditors. If one owner is successfully sued, the house is protected because the courts consider the other owner to own the whole house for the purposes of establishing ability to pay a claim.

The cost of establishing and maintaining these asset protection vehicles varies widely. The ones I've mentioned can have little setup and administrative cost. Basic trusts and limited liability corporations, for example, cost only a few thousand dollars to set up. You might also want to investigate more aggressive options for protecting your assets, though I personally do not advocate such moves, given their legally tenuous status in some cases and the dislocations they can cause. These more tenuous moves include the following:

- Moving to another state, such as Florida, to gain an advantageous position in bankruptcy, or Nevada, to eliminate state income tax

- Setting up blind offshore trusts in such infamous havens as the Cayman Islands, Bermuda, or the Bahamas

- Becoming a tax exile and moving to another country to escape revenue agents

Obviously, if you're contemplating any of these moves—the more common or the more exotic—get good, practical legal advice. You will incur some costs for periodic reviews of your asset protection plans, and though you might never change anything as a result of these reviews, your piece of mind will be well worth the cost for periodic reassessment of these plans by a lawyer.

Act now, if you're contemplating taking extraordinary measures to protect your assets—perhaps because of a high-risk lifestyle or because you want to keep assets shielded from a potential legal dispute. Hastily arranged asset protection plans amid pending legal proceedings will afford you little protection against adverse legal rulings. U.S. courts generally have the authority to undo protections you might have devised in anticipation of loss.

Question #8: How Should My Family Communicate About Its Wealth?

A couple of years ago, we were at Thanksgiving dinner going around the table and, one by one, speaking about what we were grateful for. When it was my wife's turn, she said, "I'm grateful for the presumption of goodwill within this family." Over the years, our family has overcome its inherent tendency to sublimate differences of opinion and has gotten much better at airing challenging issues so that we can address them thoughtfully. In so doing, we have actually been able to retain, even strengthen, the presumption of goodwill that is associated with each difficult discussion. There are few things about our family culture that I am prouder of. It hasn't come easy and it's fragile, yet we all believe that it is the foundation of effective family communication.

As your family's Wealth Strategist, you should conduct your communications with family members with two objectives in mind. First, it's important within the wealth management process to nurture a spirit of kinship among family members by identifying and reinforcing common family interests and wealth management objectives. This is something you can do on a regular basis through meetings, annual family reunions, and other means. Make the wealth management and investment execution process transparent to all family members who are likely to benefit from it. Allow everyone in that group who wants a voice in wealth management decision-making to be heard. In the long run, the combination of communication and listening does strengthen family solidarity around the pursuit of collective wealth management goals and maintaining the presumption of goodwill.

At the same time, as Wealth Strategist, you'll find that it's important to celebrate the merits and individuality of each family member and, by so doing, look for ways to support individuals in their various personal and professional pursuits. You will have to devise parameters and expectations here—of how wealth is to be used, how and when one will have access to it, what responsibilities young owners of wealth will have (if any) in being given access to family assets, and so forth.

To this end, there is a fine line between empowerment and entitlement. The privileges of wealth come with responsibilities, so you will need to decide how to hold the next generation of family members responsible, not only for ensuring the family's memory and legacy, but also for managing the gift of wealth that is given personally to them. As Wealth Strategist, you are in a unique position to convey family values to succeeding generations of your family. In so doing, you're poised to shape the lives and characters of family members, not just in your lifetime, but, in some cases, for multiple generations.

Question #9: Do You Plan to Build Family Leadership to Grow Your Wealth over Multiple Generations?

All successful wealth management starts with the Wealth Strategist defining a wealth management time horizon—single-generation or multi-generation. From there, you must determine how you want your family purpose and culture to affect future generations.

The values you emphasize during your lifetime will have an impact on your children and grandchildren even if your financial assets don't. Establishing a "family culture" based on the ideas of hard work, education, ambition, attentive parenting, and thrift can last for generations. Look at the legacies of some of our country's greatest leaders—Washington, Franklin, Jefferson, Lincoln, the Roosevelts (Theodore, Eleanor, and Franklin), and Ronald Reagan. The values that these individuals embody (and that they picked up from their own parents) affect millions of Americans to this day, whereas the modest wealth that they created had no long-term impact.

The values you articulate in this generation could have a similar impact on future generations of your own family—whether you pass on a great deal of wealth to future generations or not. At the other extreme, a culture of conspicuous consumption will last only as long as the money does. This is why, throughout this book, you'll see me emphasize the importance of family purpose and of using values and family culture to prioritize your financial goals and to shape your choice of wealth management strategies.

Families must recognize that the family members most likely to have the talent and skills to preserve or grow the family's wealth are also the individuals with the most options to build lucrative business careers outside the family. It's a healthy sign when it takes a competitive process to entice these individuals to commit themselves to the family. Managing the family's wealth can provide many professional challenges for the appropriate person or persons. The selection of the right family member(s) to be Wealth Strategist, for example, can strengthen family identity and energize the family to meet its wealth management goals.[2]

It is uncomfortable to talk about who in the family has the greatest potential and ability to preserve and grow its wealth. However, you must address this matter head-on. To make this process as objective as possible, here are questions to ask within the family to assess the viability of your in-house talent as business leader, investor, or Wealth Strategist, with the understanding that going outside of the family to fulfill the first two roles is also viable:

> Who in the family has demonstrated a strong interest/competency in allocating capital and has a track record of doing so successfully?

> Who in the family is clearly in sync with the family purpose, culture, and value system and is generally sensitive and able to hear the voices of others in family discussions?

> Who in the family displays the skills and temperament to be a good moderator and mediator of conflicts, if and when they arise?

> Who is willing to hold himself accountable?

> Who in the family displays strong business instincts and acumen and has options to build a lucrative business career away from the family?

> Who exhibits entrepreneurial traits or is superb at executing the vision of others?

> Who is healthy enough to manage the physical and emotional rigors of managing the family's wealth?

I'm confident that, in most cases, the selection of appropriate individuals to play various leadership roles within the family enterprise will emerge by consensus, based on answering the questions I've cited here.

That said, there might be cases in which you need to go outside the family for qualified leadership, although this isn't an ideal option. Choosing a wealthy family's future leaders can be designated as a responsibility of the family office's or company's Board of Directors. If you don't have a board that includes nonfamily members, you might want to hire the services of a leadership consultant or even an executive search firm to evaluate the position and prospective candidates.

Remember, leadership can come from within the family or from outside. Explicitly describing the required qualifications and objectively matching them with the candidate gives the new leader, whether a family member or not, added credibility to withstand friction within the family and to build a stable power base.

Question #10: How Important Is It to You to Maximize Tax Efficiency? Will It Change in Future Generations?

Tax efficiency is a major variable in the strategic wealth management process because it affects both the way you manage your assets and how you distribute them in your estate plan. For most people, taxes are either the largest or the second-largest controllable drain on wealth.

In an effort to maximize tax efficiency, some people manage their taxes as aggressively as they manage their investments. They work closely with lawyers and accountants to design sophisticated strategies to save every possible penny of taxes, and they are willing to be confrontational with the IRS if they are challenged. They also are prepared to manage complex administrative tasks to bolster the validity of their tax position. Some people change their city, state, or even country of residency in order to reduce taxes. Although in some cases this is easy enough to do, in other instances it can have a negative effect on children and family life that ultimately undercuts the wisdom of the decision.

For years, some accounting firms, lawyers, and banks promoted elaborate legal structures involving any number of offshore trusts, derivative securities, complex partnerships, or life insurance to help solve client tax problems. Some schemes converted short-term gains to long-term gains. In other cases, the value proposition was to avoid paying taxes altogether. Sometimes people wanted to raise the value of an asset to give it away and take a tax deduction. Other times they wanted to lower an asset's value for estate or gift tax purposes. These structures can be enormously complex to set up and administer, and they can be expensive. But the tax savings can sometimes more than justify the expense if the scheme is legal.

Many of these schemes have been attacked successfully by the IRS. With the huge deficits our government is piling up, the IRS is aggressively hunting for revenue raisers. When they see abusive shelters being promoted (and they have the means to turn most of them up), they evaluate the revenue-producing potential that might be gained from challenging them. In the past several years, they have moved aggressively against many promoters, including even well-reputed accounting and legal firms, as well as their clients. Governments are much more sophisticated today about sharing information with each other to stamp out tax fraud and extract major fines from tax evaders and the firms that help them.

Some people take a simpler approach to tax efficiency. They like to buy and hold assets for a long time, allowing the assets to increase in value, tax free, until they are sold. People who manage in this way might be more interested in other things, such as growing value within a company, pursuing their career, or fishing. Sometimes tax efficiency is a fortunate byproduct of having interests in other areas. In other cases, it is a conscious decision.

Many people actually feel quite proud to be able to pay their taxes. They see it as a sign of success and an opportunity to give back to their country in appreciation for that success. Where do your interests lie?

The extent to which you value tax efficiency can have broad implications when you are planning and executing tax strategies across generations. It can also influence family dynamics among siblings, in-laws, or children. In many wealthy families, for example, a small group of people makes decisions that affect the entire family. In this environment, the style of investing, the foresightedness of estate planning, or the decision to be adversarial in the payment of taxes can have repercussions for the whole family enterprise. On the last point in particular, the tone set by the family leaders might cause anxiety and disruption for family members who don't cope well with this approach. For these reasons, it's important that the Wealth Strategist and her fellow wealth managers within the family consider issues of taxes in their full family context. In many families, this causes later generations to be more conservative than the wealth creator, and rightly so.

Choosing how efficiently to manage your taxes is a personal issue. Each person must make this decision for himself. However, if you are the

Wealth Strategist, I strongly encourage you to make decisions about taxes based not only on their financial impact but also on how your tax strategy can reinforce other aspects of your Strategic Wealth Management Framework. Remember also that there are usually simple alternatives to complex strategies that can result in modestly higher tax payments but lower costs, less stress, and greater flexibility. I have more to say about taxes and how to make them your ally in the wealth management process. See Chapter 8, "Taxes Can Be Your Ally!" for details.

Pulling the Ten Questions Together: Translating Your Family Purpose into Financial Goals

After reviewing the ten questions in this chapter, let's pull this exploration of your family purpose all together so that you can begin to construct congruent financial goals.

It's important that your financial goals speak to and reinforce your values and your family purpose. You are more likely to achieve your goals—and, more important, to gain true satisfaction—if your financial goals and your values are aligned. Look at Figure 3.1. At the top of the table, a continuum of financial goals from distribution-oriented to growth-oriented is represented by a two-headed arrow. Below "Financial Goal" is a series of issues that are discussed in this chapter and a range of possible responses, again represented by the arrows. All the issues are values-based, but some, like asset threats and tax efficiency, have an operational tone.

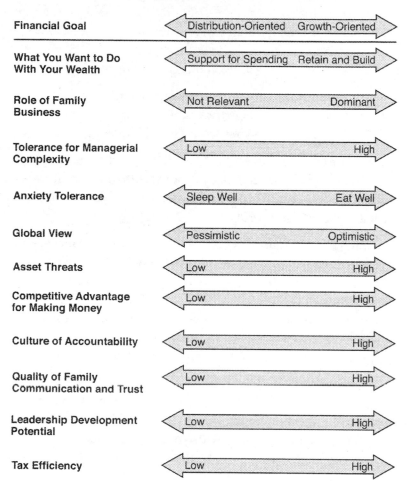

Financial Goal	Distribution-Oriented — Growth-Oriented
What You Want to Do With Your Wealth	Support for Spending — Retain and Build
Role of Family Business	Not Relevant — Dominant
Tolerance for Managerial Complexity	Low — High
Anxiety Tolerance	Sleep Well — Eat Well
Global View	Pessimistic — Optimistic
Asset Threats	Low — High
Competitive Advantage for Making Money	Low — High
Culture of Accountability	Low — High
Quality of Family Communication and Trust	Low — High
Leadership Development Potential	Low — High
Tax Efficiency	Low — High

Figure 3.1 For each issue listed below the line under "Financial Goal," mark where in the continuum you stand. Are your values and family purpose generally consistent with your financial goal?

Go through the table, and mark an "x" where you stand for each issue. There are no right or wrong answers here. By selecting answers to the ten questions that express your values and your family purpose, you can identify the financial goal that is right for you.

When you are finished, if your marks are weighted to the left, you are more likely to align with distribution-oriented financial goals. If they are weighted to the right, you are more likely to align with growth-oriented financial goals. This analysis is not scientific. It is meant to be an indicator, not an absolute. As you move through subsequent chapters and become more familiar with the wealth management process, you might want to revisit where you belong on this chart and why.

If you see yourself in the "distribution-oriented" category, it means that your financial goal is to slowly extract capital to pay for your retirement without concern for leaving your wealth to subsequent generations.

If you see yourself in the "growth-oriented" category, it means your goal is to maintain or grow the real value of your wealth for yourself and possibly future generations, while enjoying the fruits of your good fortune to the fullest extent that is prudent.

As you can see from Figure 3.1, each of us approaches the management of wealth with different expectations and goals. People who want to avoid managerial complexity, and who want, or need, to spend more, will land firmly in the "distribution-oriented" category. Those with a long view, a culture of thrift, good family communication, and a bigger appetite for risk, and who are willing to institute an aggressive accountability program, are clearly in the "growth-oriented" category.

Many people will also be somewhere in the middle. In the next chapter, I present some detailed options under each of these two broad categories. Before finishing the book, you will be able to find the set of financial goals that correspond with your own particular values and circumstances.

Conclusion

In this chapter, I've talked about the importance of identifying what you want to do with your wealth. Building on the previous chapters, I've emphasized how important the Wealth Strategist's role is in providing leadership and searching for consensus in the expression of family purpose and embracing the Eight Principles—whether over a single lifetime or over multiple generations. A sound base of shared family purpose, reinforced through trusting relationships, is the foundation on which successful financial and family strategies are built. Unfortunately, good values are not the only ones that can have lasting effect. Negative values, or intractable differences of opinion, can have an equally pro-found influence on families, and they can quickly lead to dysfunction and erosion of wealth. There are numerous public examples and more private ones that powerfully reinforce the point.

In the wake of a liquidity event, or at other turning points, deciding what you want to do with your wealth and building the financial and business skills to manage it will take time. Moreover, addressing the questions I've outlined in this chapter takes research, introspection, honesty on your family's part, and a willingness to have "difficult conversations" in some cases (as my own family has done). If these challenges seem daunt-ing, consider hiring a professional facilitator to help you. We have done so, and the process can be quite illuminating. A facilitator will moderate in-depth discussions about these issues, help you and your family mem-bers articulate your views more clearly, and give voice to the presump-tion of goodwill. The facilitator can also double as a scribe to record the conversations and decisions your family makes, helping everyone to be better listeners. The facilitator you hire does not necessarily need a financial background, though familiarity with business issues is helpful. However, avoid choosing someone from the financial-services industry or who has other vested interests in your family's decisions. If you are worried about confidentiality, you should ask the facilitator to sign a nondisclosure agreement.

I am biased toward a multigenerational approach to wealth manage-ment and so are most of the family groups I work with. But it is not the right approach for everyone. First, not everyone has children. And not everyone has a family identity and heritage that supports a multigenera-tional approach to wealth management planning. You might feel that it is enough to give your children a good childhood, a good education, and the security of parental love. In a strong, stable society like ours, many people believe that it is not in the interests of their children or society to transfer family wealth from one generation to the next.

I hope you'll take away from this chapter a hint of the issues that come into play whether you decide to manage your wealth for a single life-time or for multiple generations. As you clarify your values and fam-ily purpose, they will inform how you build out your Strategic Wealth Management Framework and will factor in discussions with your wealth advisors. You'll be able to inquire more astutely into the motives and skills of prospective advisors and sense more easily whether they will be useful additions to your wealth management team.

Let's go on now to Chapter 4, "Defining Your Financial Objectives," which explores more fully how you can translate your values into financial terms that your wealth advisors can understand, act on, and be held accountable for.

Endnotes

1. Mutual funds must now provide standardized after-tax performance reports. Although these statements make it easier to compare one fund with another, the taxes payable by individuals will vary considerably from the standard information provided. In addition, no other managers are required to provide the calculation, and most do not. Aggregating after-tax performance of multiple managers is beyond the scope of most performance measurement systems in the United States today.

2. Is your family, like many others, tempted to overinflate the responsibilities and/or compensation of family members who are unable or unwilling to pull their own weight within a family business? If you allow this, your family's pursuit of its wealth management goals will suffer. So too will relationships among family members, and between family and able-bodied nonfamily employees. It is particularly demotivating to nonfamily employees, who are generally pretty good at assessing family members' performance. Ultimately, the "free rider" syndrome is counterproductive for all parties involved, so avoid it if possible.

4

Defining Your Financial Objectives

"It requires a great deal of boldness and a great deal of caution to make a great fortune."

—**Nathan Mayer Rothschild**

After you articulate your family purpose, the next task is to translate that purpose into financial objectives. Based on the assessment you completed in the preceding chapter, your financial objectives will fall into one of two broad categories; either you will want to pursue a "distribution-driven" path to wealth management, or you will want to pursue a "growth-driven" path to wealth preservation and management.

Let's explore what's involved in following either of these paths so that you can decide which is better for you. Your lifestyle goals, the strength of your economic engine, your spending habits, and your tolerance for risk all play into which path is the right one for you.

The "Distribution-Driven" Category of Financial Management

If you opt to build a wealth management strategy based on distribution-driven financial goals...

- Your time horizon is typically 20 years or less.

- Most of your wealth is in relatively liquid (typically) financial assets and you don't have a family business.

- You can enjoy a relatively high level of spending because passing significant wealth to children or grandchildren, if there are any, isn't a primary goal.

- You require a lower rate of return on assets because your assets only have to last your lifetime.

- Investment, tax, and estate planning are relatively simple, and you prefer it that way.

- Philanthropic contributions are most likely current gifts directed to existing charities and nonprofit causes, not endowment assets to build long-lived private or family foundations.

If you choose the "distribution-driven" category of wealth management planning, you have two sets of financial objectives from which to choose. You can choose to maintain your purchasing power or to maintain a stable income.

Option 1: Maintain Your Purchasing Power Guidelines:

Target after-tax spending rates:	4.0% to 5.0% of financial assets in year one, but the dollars spent increase with inflation thereafter, and the spending rate increases each year
Maximum after-tax spending rate:	15% of financial assets per year
Required investment returns:	4.5% to 6.0% per year
Competitive advantage:	Low
Risk tolerance:	Sleep well, for about 15 years
Tax efficiency:	Low to medium

Maintaining your purchasing power is a good objective to embrace if your principal priority is to preserve a high standard of living over the next 15 to 20 years, or less. The investment strategy is conservative and can be very simple to execute.

Over time, inflation increases the prices of goods and services you buy. The "Maintain Your Purchasing Power" goal makes it the top priority to keep the dollars you spend growing in lock step with inflation.

If spending does not keep pace with inflation, your standard of living declines. For example, let's say you are spending $100,000 per year today (after taxes) based on financial assets of $2.2 million. In ten years, your spending rate will need to climb to $135,000, assuming a 3% inflation rate, if you are to maintain your current standard of living. (In addition, you will have taxes and wealth management fees to pay.)

Because the investment strategy is conservative, your assets will not be very volatile, but neither will they go up in value very much. In fact, because the combination of spending, taxes, and fees you pay to your financial advisors is likely to exceed the annual rate of return on your investments, your assets will decline over time. If enjoying your retirement is a higher priority than preserving your assets, you won't be concerned about a declining asset base. In fact, some people express the desire to spend their last dollar to pay for their funeral.

As your spending grows and your assets decline, your annual spending rate will increase, and within 15 years or so could equate to 15% of your financial assets each year. Fifteen percent is nowhere near a sustainable yearly level of spending because within just a few years, you will deplete your assets. You don't want to run out of money before you die.

You might have surmised by now that the biggest challenge with this strategy is estimating how long you will live. Of course, the problem is that none of us knows how long we will live. Given that the average life expectancy continues to rise, this can be a risky approach to managing your life, even though it is a conservative way to invest your assets. Therefore, if you choose this approach when your spending rate exceeds 10% of your assets on an annualized basis, I urge you to consider cutting back immediately rather than risk hitting a brick wall of financial hardship in a few years. One way to do this is by supplementing your financial assets with earned income. Alternatively, consider whether Option 2, 3, 4, or 5 is more appropriate.

Option 2: Maintain a Stable Income Guidelines:

Target after-tax spending rates:	2.6% to 4.8% of financial assets per year
Required investment returns:	4.5% to 6.8% per year, rising with spending rate

Competitive advantage:	Low to average
Risk tolerance:	Sleep well
Tax efficiency:	Medium to high

People who embrace this financial objective strive to provide themselves with a stable cash flow throughout their lifetimes. Their goal is to maintain a steady rate of spending while preserving the value of their assets. They recognize that inflation will eat away at their purchasing power over time, but they also anticipate that their spending needs will decline as they age. They might decide to eliminate expensive overseas vacations, buy a smaller home, or stop driving a car. If they are in their fifties or sixties, they might expect to inherit some assets from a parent or to make up any income shortfall with Social Security benefits or a defined benefit pension plan.

To achieve this wealth management goal, a person typically chooses a spending rate that is tied to the value of their assets (for example, 4% per year) and holds their spending to that level. Tax payments and wealth management fees, like tax preparation and estate planning, also must be covered.

Many people fall into the "maintaining stable income" category, either through careful planning or by default. The good news here is that if people manage their assets prudently and control spending carefully (no more than 4% to 4.5% of assets per year), they might be able to transfer assets at the end of their lives to others—family members, civic institutions, nonprofit organizations, or other beneficiaries. They can also preserve their nominal assets and spending budget indefinitely—barring some unforeseen need to shift to the "Maintain Purchasing Power" approach.

Shifting from Option 2 Back to Option 1

There are some major challenges for individuals who want to maintain a stable income throughout their lives. Over time, inflation will erode the purchasing power of that income to the point that it impinges on their lifestyle. In some cases, this can create real hardships for long-time retirees, many of whom are living today well into their eighties and nineties.

In addition, sudden large, unexpected costs such as major uninsured medical bills can add to financial stress.

One way to deal with spiraling expenses late in life is for an individual to switch from a "Maintain Stable Income" wealth management goal to a "Maintain Purchasing Power" goal. Better to deplete assets than to cause unnecessary hardship. After all, that's why you worked so hard to create and steward your nest egg in the first place.

Still, for most people, the pursuit of a "Maintain Stable Income" approach to wealth management can, if embraced early, protect one's wealth for many years and thus create a substantial financial cushion for use if and when unexpected or even "catastrophic" expenses are incurred late in life.

The "Growth-Driven" Category of Financial Management

If you opt to build a wealth management strategy based on growth-driven financial goals...

- Your time horizon spans decades and is usually multigenerational.

- You need to generate above-average rates of return from your business plus investments over time. Doing this requires careful management of your assets, a willingness to tolerate volatility of investment returns, and a lower probability of achieving your desired goals.

- You must carefully control the amount of income and capital gains taxes you pay. Otherwise, you must substantially increase what are already "stretch" investment return objectives.

- You should control spending because it's the easiest wealth management factor to control—far easier, for example, than fluctuating tax rates or rates of return from investments!

- Transfer tax management, particularly in larger estates, can get quite complex and often involves a long-term philanthropic component.

If you opt for the growth-driven category of wealth management, there are three additional options you can choose from:

- Conserve the real value of your wealth and your purchasing power.

- Retain real per capita wealth across generations.

- Keep growing your wealth.

All three choices require that you have a strong economic engine. All three also require that you cap your spending at a maximum of 3.2% of assets per year (and preferably lower). To calculate the spending rate, the numerator should be the amount you spend or give away each year, after tax. The denominator should be the combination of your financial and business assets that are or can distribute excess cash flow for you. Do not include things like personal assets, such as a home or art collection, in the denominator.

Now, let's briefly discuss each of these three additional options.

Option 3: Conserve Real Wealth and Your Purchasing Power
Guidelines:

Target after-tax spending rates:	0.0% to 3.2% of financial assets and/or dividend rate
Required investment returns:	5.2% to 10.0% per year, rising with spending rate
Competitive advantage:	Average to high
Risk tolerance:	Eat well (medium to high)
Tax efficiency:	Medium to high

When you successfully pursue this approach, you will be able to protect your income from the ravages of inflation over many decades. But you must lower your spending rate and take on more investment risk to do so. A benefit of tightening your belt and sleeping less well at night is that you might maintain the real value of your wealth.

If you take early retirement in your fifties or sixties, pursuing a strategy to conserve real wealth and purchasing power makes a great deal of sense, regardless of whether you want to leave a financial legacy. You (and/or your spouse) could easily live another 30 or 40 years. During this time frame, inflation will eat away more than half of the purchasing power of a "Maintain Stable Income" goal (Option 2), and following Option 1 could destroy your asset base long before you die.

The math is pretty straightforward. The more you want to spend, the more you have to make, especially if you want to conserve real wealth and purchasing power. At the top end of the "0% to 3.2% after-tax spending rate" range, you need investment returns exceeding 10% per year. The investment returns have to account for not only spending, but also inflation, taxes, and wealth management fees. To generate such returns, you will need above-average skill or above-average luck (and preferably both, although luck rarely lasts for decades). If wealth management is not your strong suit, you should keep your spending at 1.5% per year or lower to increase the odds of achieving this goal.

My great-aunt Ethel and her husband, Oscar, who was president of a family-owned building products company, are a good example of a couple who embraced this wealth management approach successfully during their lifetimes. They earned modest incomes but were good savers, diligent investors, and thrifty spenders. They were also lucky.

Aunt Ethel managed a community center financed by Standard Oil Company of New Jersey. As part of her compensation, she received shares of Standard Oil stock, which later became Exxon. She never sold this stock. Instead, she used the dividends to buy other blue-chip stocks, building her stock portfolio over a period of many years.

Aunt Ethel and Uncle Oscar did not have any competitive advantage when it came to investing, so they thought their investment returns would be in the lower half of the required investment return range. To conserve real wealth and purchasing power, they knew that their spending had to be held in check.

Over the decades, their stock portfolio in general (and Exxon in particular) grew in value. Because she never sold her oil stock, Aunt Ethel never paid any capital gains taxes on it—even though it appreciated many times in value. Over time, Exxon proved to be a terrific long-term performer in the stock market. It constituted more than half of Aunt Ethel's portfolio at the time of her death. (She outlived Uncle Oscar by more than 20 years.) Consequently, because of her steady, unwavering (relatively undiversified) investing, her financial legacy turned out stronger than she expected.

Aunt Ethel was also frugal. She had lovely taste but her own needs were simple. She had many friends and valued friendship much more than material goods. She remained in generally good health into her nineties. She eventually died in bed in the house that she and Oscar were given as a wedding present. She had married him at age 19.

Aunt Ethel achieved her goal to be a millionaire before she died. If times had been different or she hadn't been paid in Standard Oil stock, she might not have achieved that goal. But because of the way she lived her life, she would have had financial security in any case. That's the beauty of living below your means.

Option 4: Retain Real Per Capita Wealth Across Generations
Guidelines:

Target after-tax spending rates:	0.0% to 2.0% of financial assets and/or dividend rate
Required investment returns:	8.8% to 11.0% per year, rising with spending rate
Competitive advantage:	High
Risk tolerance:	Eat well (high)
Tax efficiency:	Medium to high

In some cases, families take a very long-term approach to building their economic engine, sometimes using a time horizon of three, four, or even five generations. Succeeding at this goal enables each family member in future generations to maintain the real income levels from financial assets and family business dividends (adjusted for inflation and other factors) that members of the current generation enjoy.

This is the goal that my generation of the Lucas family has set for itself. And while at first blush it doesn't look like a terribly aggressive strategy to pursue, consider this: Over time, families inevitably grow in size! My parents have nine grandchildren. This means we need to grow our assets by a factor of nine over about 70 years—about 3.1% per annum—after taking inflation into account.[1] At the same time, we need to combat the erosion of our wealth due to what I call "leakages." Leakages include spending, taxes, wealth management fees, charitable giving, inflation, losses due to successful claims made against you, and uninsured theft or casualty.

In total, leakages have cost us 7.6% per year over the past decade, and we manage pretty tightly! If you add the cost of "leakages" to the 3.1% per annum growth rate that I mentioned a moment ago, it means that, to reach our goal, we must exceed an annual rate of return on our investments of 10.7% per year.[2] We've set the wealth management bar quite high in our family, with a series of stretch goals designed to help us reach our objectives. I'll have more to say on our approach to investment management in future chapters.

Option 5: Keep Growing Your Wealth Guidelines:

Target after-tax spending rates:	Less than 2.0% of financial assets and/or dividend rate
Required investment returns:	More than 8.8% per year, rising with spending rate
Competitive advantage:	High
Risk tolerance:	Eat well (high)
Tax efficiency:	Medium to high

This is still another growth-driven wealth management approach that some Wealth Strategists will want to consider. Successful entrepreneurs, for example, sometimes want to keep building their wealth by owning and managing businesses while maintaining enough liquid assets for prudent diversification in other areas. For such individuals, staying involved in a business they started or pursuing a second career after a liquidity event provides an engine for wealth preservation and further wealth creation.

Different Plans—Different End Results

I have just described five approaches to wealth management planning, any one of which might be appropriate for you to consider in your role as your family's Wealth Strategist. To give you a side-by-side comparison of how each of these five plans generates different financial results, see Figure 4.1.

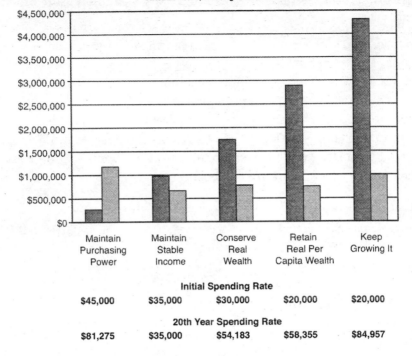

Comparison of Financial Objectives
After 20 Years, Starting with $1 Million Each

	Maintain Purchasing Power	Maintain Stable Income	Conserve Real Wealth	Retain Real Per Capita Wealth	Keep Growing It
Initial Spending Rate	$45,000	$35,000	$30,000	$20,000	$20,000
20th Year Spending Rate	$81,275	$35,000	$54,183	$58,355	$84,957

■ Assets After 20 Years
▨ Cumulative Spending

Figure 4.1 There is no free lunch. Options 3, 4, and 5 can actually maintain or grow both the real value of your wealth and your purchasing power, but they involve considerable risk and uncertainty. Options 1 and 2 involve less investment risk, but inflation degrades their viability past 15 to 20 years.

In each case, the wealth owner begins with $1 million in assets and pursues his or her financial objective successfully for 20 years. The initial annual spending rate varies for each objective, with the highest starting annual spending rate of $45,000 for the "Maintain Purchasing Power" objective (Option 1) scaling down to an annual spending rate of $20,000 for Options 4 and 5. The bar chart shows the results for each strategy in two ways. First, the black bars show how much the original $1 million is worth after 20 years. Second, the shaded bars show the cumulative dollars spent over the 20-year period. One of the things you immediately notice is that despite the wide differences in initial annual spending rates and the huge variations in the ending assets, the cumulative dollars spent vary surprisingly little from strategy to strategy. However, if you look at the numbers at the bottom of Figure 4.1, you'll notice that the final year spending rates vary even more than the first-year spending rate. This is most pronounced in the case of the wealth owner who pursued the "Keep Growing It" objective. This individual initially had the lowest annual spending rate of all the investors but ended up spending more dollars each year than all the others. By deferring spending and effectively managing his assets, this individual ultimately wound up with much more money to spend. You could do the same thing. And if you do so successfully, you'll also have a much larger financial legacy to share with others.

Two Market Forces That Affect Any Wealth Management Approach

Although each of the five wealth management approaches has specific benefits, two factors—leakages and growth—can dramatically affect the outcome.

Leakages

I've already talked briefly about leakages that erode your wealth. The most obvious of these is spending. Leakages also include the taxes, fees, and expenses associated with wealth management. Any net loss of assets due to litigation, fraud, theft, divorce settlements, and other successful third-party claims on your assets are leakages. (Unfortunately, these events often generate emotional losses as well.) Gifts made directly to charity are another leakage. (But not to a family foundation. Because family foundation assets are still under your control, this analysis does not count them as leakage until they are distributed.) In an intergenerational context, there is arguably another leakage: the division of assets among your children. Although your family's total assets might not decline, the assets available to each of your children—if you have more than one—decline by at least 50% relative to the assets you and your spouse share.

To a large extent, you have some control over all the leakages I've just outlined. One final leakage over which you have no control is inflation.

Inflation slowly but powerfully depletes the value of one's wealth. Just ask any retiree who has had to live on a fixed income for a decade or more!

Growth

Just as leakages decrease your wealth, cash additions to your assets enhance your net worth. Stimulating asset growth is a function of four factors:

1. Income and capital gains you earn from a business, family or otherwise, or career.

2. Broad and efficient asset deployment that mimics the average performance of financial markets. Another term for this is passive management or Index Investing.

3. The ability to generate above-average returns by investing in specific assets or asset classes, relative to the amount of risk incurred in doing so, through active management or what I call Active Alpha Investing.

4. Financial windfalls that occur as the result of inheritance, marriage (divorce), and adoption.

Growth Factor #1: Income and capital gains you earn from a business or career. Many wealthy people continue to work even when it's no longer necessary to maintain their desired lifestyles. Motivated by personal drive or professional ambition, they continue to build their businesses, embark on second careers after selling a business, or start new businesses—enabling them to continue to grow their wealth for years and even decades.

Sidebar 4.1: Have You Factored the Future Financial Worth of Your Career into Wealth Management Planning?

If you have a successful liquidity event and the circumstances that created your wealth are unlikely to repeat themselves, it makes sense for you to manage your wealth conservatively. Athletes, actors, and rock stars might make lots of money for a time, but their careers tend to be fickle. An entrepreneur, inventor, oil wildcatter, or lottery winner may hit a "bonanza" once, but what is the likelihood of doing it again? Building a nest egg when the getting is good can stave off hardship when the opportunity passes.

Similarly, if the same factors that created your wealth also affect broad financial markets, it makes sense for you to invest your financial assets in places that are relatively immune to the markets. In the 1990s, for example, investment bankers and dot.com entrepreneurs should have diversified their financial assets away from high-risk stocks, precisely at the moment the market was booming, even though their careers depended on them. Residential mortgage brokers in the mid-2000s would have found that shifting some of their earnings in those bubble years into the corporate bond market, or even into higher-dividend-paying stocks, would have made sense as a wealth diversification tactic. This would have put their career and financial risk in better balance.

Some people who have inherited or expect to inherit substantial wealth might not be tied to an existing career. There's both good news and bad news here. With wealth comes the opportunity for individuals to take risks with their careers while still providing financial security for their families. However, developing a new career can be risky. All too often, wealthy people compound such risks by committing a large portion of their existing wealth to the success of a new career. This action—often personified by successful business executives who finance their own entrepreneurial efforts, buy sports teams, or become angel investors—is extremely risky and often ends in disappointment.

There are usually ways you can mitigate the risks of such activities, garner valuable business experience, and reap financial rewards from your business ventures without exposing large amounts of your personal capital to such activities. This is a critical area of discussion for you to cover with your wealth management advisor.

Growth Factor #2: Broad and efficient asset deployment that mimics the average performance of financial markets (Index Investing). Since the Italian Renaissance, the economic, social, and political evolution of Western culture has generally followed a positive trajectory, significant disruptions notwithstanding. Furthermore, Western culture seems more stable and our economies more manageable and less volatile than they were 100 and even 50 years ago, despite the current economic and political tremors coming from the European Union and Congress. Since World War II, many economies and countries around the world have followed similar trends. Mature countries like the United States, England, and Germany continue to grow fairly slowly and steadily, while other countries like China, India, Brazil, Poland, Turkey, and Indonesia—often referred to as emerging markets—are today growing with greater speed and volatility.

If you use an Index Investing strategy (see Chapter 6, "Picking Your Investment Strategy") to participate broadly in financial markets through stocks, bonds, commodities, and real estate, you're likely to benefit financially in ways that mirror the economic growth in the countries I've just mentioned. With indexing, an investor buys individual securities or index funds in an effort to match the performance of a broad-based index, such as the S&P 500, the Russell 3000, or the MSCI All-Country World Index. The investor's goal is to design an asset allocation that includes a range of indices that collectively behave in a manner consistent with whichever of the five financial objectives was chosen. This is called strategic asset allocation. An investor then chooses low-cost, tax-efficient financial instruments that match the indices' performance and diversifies his or her assets across them.

Growth Factor #3: The ability to generate above-average returns in specific assets or asset classes (Active Alpha Investing). Most successful people convince themselves that they have special insights that have directly led to their professional success. These feelings often carry over when they decide to invest in financial markets. Feelings of investment prowess are reinforced by many investment advisors who feel that they, too, have special insights that will enable them to make more money for their clients, with the same or less risk than the broad markets represented by the indices.

It is the desire to apply these insights that leads so many people to try to "beat the market" or "add value" to investments whether or not they have the true talent to do it. Some succeed. Most don't. (This is in marked contrast to indexing [or passive investing], in which everyone is equally successful by design.) This activity is referred to as active investing, and the measure of value added is called "alpha."

What is alpha? Simply put, alpha is the difference in performance between an investment portfolio and a financial market index that exhibits similar risk characteristics. An investment portfolio creates positive alpha when it outperforms the financial market index and negative alpha when it underperforms the financial market.

The behavior of a financial market, as expressed in an index, is the sum of the activities of all the different investment portfolios in that market, many of which are actively managed and seeking positive alpha. However, alpha is a "zero-sum" game. For every investor who actually generates positive alpha, another investor must, by definition, generate negative alpha. When you add together all the alphas, positive and negative, in theory they add up to zero. In fact, because of "friction costs" that include brokerage transactions and management fees, alpha is less than a zero-sum game in the real world. This means that, on average, investors underperform their relevant indices. Because 90% of the markets' activities are driven by highly sophisticated, well-trained, institutional investors, competition for alpha is very tough. So if you are going to engage in Active Alpha Investing, you must think about how you and your advisors are going to be in the minority, taking alpha rather than giving it away.

Many people confuse good performance relative to an index with alpha. This usually happens when the risk of an actively managed portfolio is significantly higher than that of the broad index against which it is being compared, and the index is performing well. Most of us are familiar with a painful consequence of misattributed alpha. In the late 1990s, growth stocks went wild and value stocks were complete duds. Any manager who owned a lot of growth stocks but compared his performance against broad stock market indices like the S&P 500 had great-looking performance from 1995 to 1999 and, to many investors and their advisors alike, appeared to generate lots of alpha. When the market reversed between 2000 and 2002, what appeared to be positive alpha to the undiscerning investor turned out to be volatility. The volatility that worked in the investors' favor when markets were going up obliterated their portfolios when reversals came. During the growth stock collapse, the portfolios of most true value managers—previously the "duds"—actually increased in value.

Financial leverage in a portfolio, like borrowing on margin or speculating in derivative securities, also increases volatility. It helps performance when asset prices are going up and hurts performance when they are going down. But leverage, in general, does not add alpha. It just looks that way in rising markets.

Growth Factor #4: Financial windfalls through inheritance, marriage (divorce), and adoption. It never hurts to have a windfall to stimulate your asset growth, and inheritance is an increasingly common way in which many people are adding to their wealth today. The wealth that this country has generated in the past 30 years alone has been colossal, and in the next few decades, trillions of dollars will be transferred to baby boomers by their elderly parents.

My own family has benefited from inheritance and adoption. My mother was adopted by E. H. Stuart, the son of Carnation's founder, who then bequeathed wealth to her and to other family members. More recently, one of my brothers adopted one of his children, which means this child will likely benefit from an eventual inheritance.

Wealthy families sometimes worry when a family member marries someone who "doesn't come from money." A prospective spouse is sometimes perceived as more of a gold digger than a committed partner. On the other hand, my wife's family feared that my family's wealth might somehow make her own family seem less important to her. Sometimes it is a parent who worries about his or her child's choice of a spouse. Sometimes it's the adult child who worries about the financial implications of a parent's remarriage. With all this said, money "issues" sometimes provide a smoke screen for avoiding discussion of other issues (real or imagined) that sometimes arise in families around marriage, divorce, adoption, and other life-altering family events.

The Interplay Between Growth and Leakages

Pay careful attention to the interplay of growth factors and potential leakages when you set your financial goals. If you focus on only one factor, it's like trying to clap with one hand. It doesn't work. If you make spending plans that are incongruous with your economic engine, you won't be successful. If you think diligently about how to create alpha but don't consider the impact of your strategy on your tax efficiency or expenses, you'll end up with a lot less in your pockets than you expect. The longer your time horizon, the more tightly you must manage your wealth and the more disciplined you must be about both growth and leakages.

Specifically, if your wealth management time horizon is multigenerational, you need to "live below your means" to pass wealth on to future generations. You've already seen that if you can live below your means in the short term, it can actually net you more income and more assets in the long run.

Everybody's personal and family situations are different, and there are no right or wrong goals here. Still, it's important to understand the trade-offs among various objectives and to match your skills with your objectives.

Putting Numbers to the Different Approaches

Effective and integrated wealth management is a complex, coordinated effort. To help you better understand the subtle interplays between growth and leakages, look at Figure 4.2. The horizontal axis of this graph represents annual after-tax spending rates, and the vertical axis represents the required annual gross rate of return to support them. Behind the scenes, the graphs account for additional leakages, including fees, taxes, and inflation. Within the graph are four lines rising from left to right that represent all five financial objectives discussed earlier in the chapter except "Keep Growing It." The fifth objective, "Keep Growing It," occurs at any point on the graph that is above and to the left of the "Retain Real Per Capita Wealth" line.

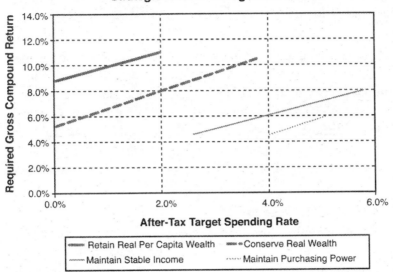

Figure 4.2 Spending more gives you less latitude to increase your investment returns and maintain your wealth.

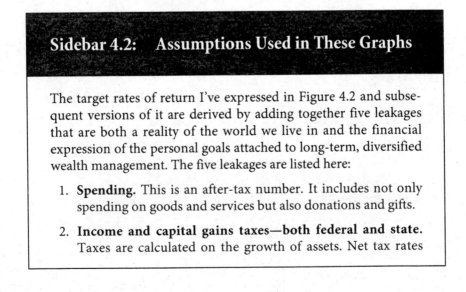

Sidebar 4.2: Assumptions Used in These Graphs

The target rates of return I've expressed in Figure 4.2 and subsequent versions of it are derived by adding together five leakages that are both a reality of the world we live in and the financial expression of the personal goals attached to long-term, diversified wealth management. The five leakages are listed here:

1. **Spending.** This is an after-tax number. It includes not only spending on goods and services but also donations and gifts.

2. **Income and capital gains taxes—both federal and state.** Taxes are calculated on the growth of assets. Net tax rates

range between 20% and 30% based on the strategy, assuming a federal long-term capital gains tax rate of 15% and income tax of 35%. Portfolios with low target returns are assumed to be fairly tax efficient, but income is a larger percentage of total return. Portfolios with required gross returns above 7.5% have tax rates of 24% to 25%. Although there is less income in the portfolios, they are more actively managed and hold more hedge funds and other assets that are less tax efficient. Higher federal tax rates or residency in a high-tax state would require a higher tax rate assumption. This would have the effect of shifting the four lines in the graph up and to the left.

3. **Fees, including asset oversight, legal, accounting, consulting, and administrative fees.** These can range widely. The fees are graduated, with the most conservative portfolios charged 0.5% and the most aggressive charged 1.3%. Direct investment management fees are subtracted before the gross investment return is calculated and are not included in these figures. Many wealth management-related fees have limits on tax deductibility that are not factored in.

4. **Inflation, as measured by the Consumer Price Index (CPI).** Over the past 50 years, inflation has averaged 4.1%. I use 3.0%. I don't have much confidence in this 3% figure. Future inflation outcomes are tough to predict and could vary significantly because of the current fiscal and monetary imbalances in our economy.

5. **A multigenerational growth factor.** The typical wealthy family in America grows in numbers over time. Even if the wealth creator has only two children, these children typically marry and, on average, their spouses bring less potential for inherited wealth to the marriage. Then each couple in the second generation has two children, who also marry. In this example, if the third generation wants to have the same per capita wealth as the first, and the time between each generation is 30 years, then the family's wealth must quadruple over 60 years. This equates to 2.3% growth per annum. If there are three children in each generation, the figure rises to 3.7%. In this model, I use 2.5%, which assumes some combination of wealthy spouses and average growth in numbers across generations among wealthy families.

Figure 4.2 assumes that within the parameters set for each goal, the required return and the spending rate rise or fall in tandem. For example, if you want to maintain real per capita wealth, an 11% target return is compatible with a 1.5% after-tax spending rate, but not with a 2% or 3% rate. To achieve the goal with a 2.0% after-tax spending rate, you need to achieve an 11.5% gross compound rate of return. If, on the other hand, there is adequate earned income to live on without spending a portion of investable assets, the required return will decline to 8.8%.

I have not factored transfer taxes (including estate tax) into the required return calculations. But if I did, the required return in Figure 4.2 would rise for really wealthy people. There is an alphabet soup of techniques (most are referred to by acronyms such as GRAT, ILET, or CRT) available today that lowers these taxes, but the larger the estate, the more likely that significant taxes will become due. I have not added transfer tax to the analysis because the estate tax is so highly variable in how it is applied and is so uncertain today.

Litigation costs, uninsured theft, divorce settlements, alimony, and other non-investment leakages that we all hope are zero, but which do arise with frequency, are also not included in the analysis.

For each objective, you can see that as your desired level of annual spending increases, the required annual rate of return to meet that objective increases.

As you move from less-aggressive objectives (i.e., "Maintain Purchasing Power" in the lower right) to more aggressive goals (i.e., "Retain Real Per Capita Wealth" in the upper left) on the graph, I've lowered the maximum annual spending rate to account for the added risk of more aggressive objectives, more speculative (and volatile) investments, and the erosion to asset values that occurs with spending, especially in declining markets. Conversely, you'll notice that, as wealth management objectives become less aggressive (moving upper left to lower right), the required annual gross return on investments drops, and your ability to spend more increases.

Now look at Figure 4.3. I've now eliminated the gridlines from Figure 4.2 and added two horizontal lines that represent the range of performance that many experts suggest is "reasonable to expect" for long-term returns from diversified stock and bond portfolios. The placement of these horizontal lines assumes that the long-term average annual return is 8.0% from equities and 2.5% for bonds. Some people believe that these figures are low, and hopefully they will be. But with current inflation ranging between 2% and 3% annually, the real, inflation-adjusted returns in this model are only slightly below the historic long-term averages, even though they are well below the returns experienced in the great bull markets of the 1980s and 1990s in stocks and bonds. A conservative expected return is also consistent with moderating growth of earnings and dividends in corporate America. The 2.5% annual rate of return on bonds is approximately the yield on high-grade, long-term bonds at the time of writing.

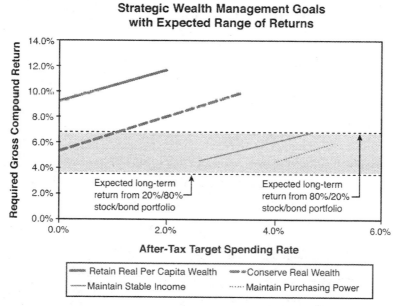

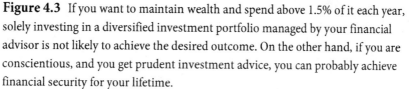

Figure 4.3 If you want to maintain wealth and spend above 1.5% of it each year, solely investing in a diversified investment portfolio managed by your financial advisor is not likely to achieve the desired outcome. On the other hand, if you are conscientious, and you get prudent investment advice, you can probably achieve financial security for your lifetime.

The top horizontal line represents the annualized average rate of return that one can reasonably expect from a typical aggressive portfolio that is 80% stocks and 20% bonds using the rates of return presented in the preceding paragraph. The bottom horizontal line represents the annualized return from a typical conservative portfolio that is 80% bonds and 20% stocks. I think that having a portfolio that is more than 80% in one asset class gives you inadequate diversification. Most standard investment portfolios should fall in the zone between these two horizontal lines.

Managing wealth within this 3.6% to 6.9% zone of annualized pretax performance is the province of most wealth management firms and is what you can reasonably expect from them if they manage your wealth efficiently over the next several decades. But most investors and their advisors should not expect a lot more.

Finding the Right Financial Objective for the Lucas Family

Now that you've learned about the different wealth management strategies, I'd like to share with you the experience of my own family in the hopes that this will bring to life the concepts that I've been describing throughout this chapter.

Take a look at Figure 4.4. In the early 1990s, members of my family were spending annually (on average) about 2% of their financial assets, after taxes, and we were invested in a 60%/40% stock/bond portfolio.

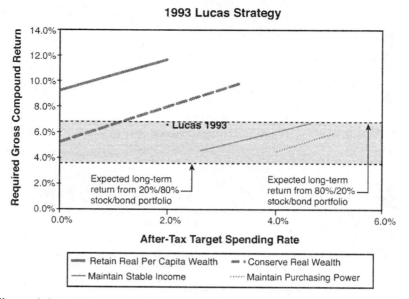

Figure 4.4 In 1993, our spending was constrained, but our wealth was still likely to erode over time.

At the time, the majority of institutionally managed trust portfolios with stated growth objectives were managed this way. We were at the point just above the midpoint of the two horizontal lines that is marked "Lucas 1993." Figure 4.4 shows that our strategy more than maintained the nominal value of our wealth but over time would lead to a loss of real asset value and real distributable income.

In the year or so before I joined the family office full time, some members of the family expressed interest in raising their annual distributions from 2% to close to 3%. In response, our corporate trustee changed the asset mix from 60%/40% (stocks/bonds) to 50%/50%. Because bonds produce more income than stocks, this shift allowed the trustee to distribute more money to the beneficiaries. At the time, this significantly raised people's income, but in the long term, it threatened to accelerate the decline of our real net worth. Figure 4.5 shows how our wealth management strategy shifted its focus away from a position closer to "Conserve Real Wealth" toward one of "Maintain Stable Income."

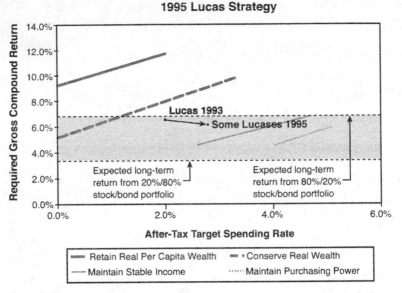

Figure 4.5 Changes in strategy threatened to accelerate wealth erosion, and we didn't realize what was happening.

Although this move increased people's income initially, over 20 years it was destined to reduce their inflation-adjusted spending power. The decision by some family members (designated as "Some Lucases 1995") to move in this direction also fractured what had been a unified family investment strategy, splitting resources and diluting our investment focus. These were not pleasant developments!

By early 1995, I was working full time to manage the family's assets. At that time, we held family discussions to highlight the changing situation and to discuss our future path. I encouraged the family to think carefully about the long-term asset-depleting implications of the decisions people had made. After much thought and conversation, we came to a consensus that our current course was a mistake. Instead, we agreed on three goals that could be shared by everyone going forward:

1. We would try to maintain our real per capita wealth across generations. (This would require moving to the left and up on the graph.)

2. We would constrain our spending to a rate that was consistent with long-term, growth-oriented trusts invested for total return.

3. We would take calculated investment risks (and risk a little lost sleep) in hopes of reaping far larger returns from our investments in the long run.

By agreeing on these objectives, we gambled that we actually had the skills, resources, contacts, and judgment to achieve a well-above-average return on investments over an extended period. These goals reversed the 1995 split and pushed the whole family to the same position, which is marked "Lucas 1997" in Figure 4.6.

Our decision to pursue more aggressive goals meant that we were aiming well above the higher of the two horizontal lines that indicate the range of performance expectations one normally has for a portfolio of stocks and bonds, even an aggressive one. Also, it meant that we began to manage our wealth very differently than we had in the previous ten years.

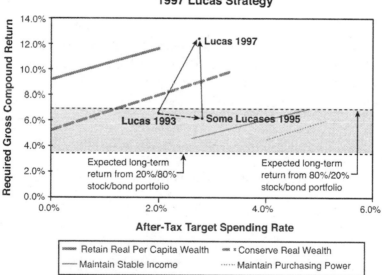

Figure 4.6 Rethinking our strategy based on the Strategic Wealth Management Framework brought us to a sustainable strategy...if we can execute effectively.

During the lengthy process of studying and eventually understanding the strategic trade-offs available to us, we learned two important lessons that most financial planners don't discuss openly with clients:

1. If you want to maintain or grow your wealth while spending more than 1.5% of it each year net of taxes, the investment strategies most financial institutions promote and execute are likely to disappoint you.

2. You are not likely to be able to spend more than 3% of your financial assets per year and have a financially secure retirement.

In the past six or seven years, given what has been going on in the U.S. and global economy, we have increasingly felt that our spending rate was too high, as was our target return given the level of risk we are comfortable with. So we have methodically decreased the spending rate to about 2.25% after tax and the target return to 11%. Our goals are still shared and still aggressive, but they are tempered by prudence and reality.

Benefits of a Unified Wealth Management Approach

I'm very proud that the Lucas family decided back in the mid-1990s to establish a unified strategy because it has enabled us to leverage competitive and cumulative advantage. It is a decision that has registered multimillion-dollar benefits for us. More important, we communicate better today than we ever have. We're able to air problems when they arise, discuss them openly, and work through them to collective resolution. This isn't to say we don't ever have issues with one another. However, we have processes and infrastructure in place that enables us to balance collective wealth management goals with individual interests, passions, and pursuits.

Each member of our family has individual goals that are not always consistent with the collective goals of the Lucas family. For example, my sister has no children, so she has less interest in multigenerational strategies. But we have built enough flexibility into our structure to accommodate her individuality to a degree that is acceptable to all. At the same time, we have built a collective set of values and family purpose around managing our wealth that we all enjoy and find to be beneficial.

Although developing a unified wealth management strategy has worked well for my family, not every wealthy family will want to adopt this approach. You'll need to appraise your situation honestly. The family dynamics have to be healthy and functional, and people have to be willing to compromise on their goals, communicate regularly, work together and be held accountable, all in a spirit of good will. If the basic ingredients are in place, the potential is there for a family's collective assets to perform considerably better than if assets are distributed and invested separately among various, independent family groups.

Adjusting for Tax-Deferred Assets

Most investors have assets in retirement plans, annuities, life insurance, or deferred compensation plans that give them some control over how the assets are invested and spent. Since the assets in these plans do not pay taxes as they grow, they will grow faster than those in your taxable accounts, all other things being equal, if you are not withdrawing any spending. However, when it comes time to withdraw assets for spending purposes, to achieve spending parity, you will probably have to withdraw more pretax dollars from a tax-deferred account than you will from a well-managed taxable account. This is true because the tax rate on distributions from tax-deferred accounts is likely to be higher than it is on distributions from taxable accounts.

If tax-deferred assets make up a substantial portion of your net worth, it might be modestly easier to achieve your financial objectives than suggested by Figures 4.2 to 4.6, but only modestly. The ultimate outcome will be determined by a number of factors, many of which are difficult to control or predict. I will discuss retirement plans, annuities, life insurance, and other forms of deferred compensation some more in Chapter 8, "Taxes Can Be Your Ally!"

Growing Wealth While Spending It Is Hard to Do

Growing real wealth is so difficult because an investor has to achieve growth factors that outweigh periodic bear markets and the drip, drip, drip of wealth erosion caused by the various leakages I described earlier. Consider this fact about the U.S. stock market. From 1900 to 2011, the

U.S. stock market has earned an average annual return of 9.2%, 6.2% after inflation, and under 5% after inflation and taxes.[3] In addition, high return periods tend to come in bunches, with long dry spells between.

In Figure 4.7, I track rolling 20-year annualized returns of the U.S. stock market from 1926 to 2011, adjusted for inflation. After adjusting for inflation, I also show in the shaded section the range of required returns you need today to reach the goal "retain real per capita wealth," as depicted in Figure 4.2. The difference between the low end of the range and the high end is accounted for primarily by the difference in annual spending rate. For the low end, I have chosen a spending rate of 1.0% per annum, and at the high end, it is 2.0% per annum. I've shown the average real return for the entire 111-year period using the appropriately labeled dashed line.

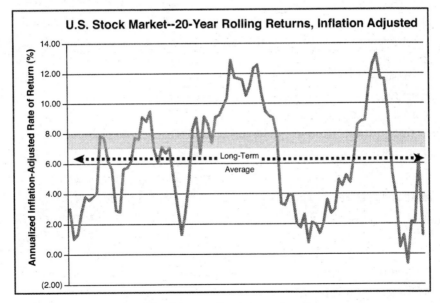

Figure 4.7 Growing wealth while spending it is tough to do.

What conclusions can you draw from this chart?

- In nearly 70% of the 20-year periods shown, stock market performance would not have enabled you to retain real per capita wealth—even if you kept your annual spending to just 2.0% of assets and had a portfolio of all equities.

- Even if you had lowered spending to a miserly 1% of assets/year, you still would not have achieved a growth-driven objective in 57% of the 20-year periods if you invested entirely in U.S. stocks.

- The average real return over the century was barely adequate to retain real per capita wealth at a 1% spending rate, even if you invested 100% in equities.

In reality, growing real wealth through the use of traditional stock market vehicles (i.e., mutual funds or traditional stock/bond portfolios) is even harder than Figure 4.7 suggests, for the following reasons:

- First, most people can't withstand the extremes of a highly volatile 100% equity portfolio, nor do I recommend this for most people. To put things in perspective, the precipitous stock market crash from October 1929 to June 1932 would have left an equity investor with ten cents for each dollar invested right before the crash! Subsequent vicious bear markets, including 1973–1974, 2000–2002, and 2008–2009, though not quite as volatile, left most committed equity investors severely bloodied. In some cases, having a more diversified portfolio actually increases the odds of achieving your objectives with lower volatility.

- Second, I calculated the range of required returns to maintain the per capita wealth shown in Figure 4.7 using current tax rates, which are at historic lows. Since the George W. Bush administration through the end of 2012, capital gains tax rates have never been lower since they were enacted in 1929, and income tax rates have been at the low end of the historic range. Higher tax rates in 2013 and beyond would raise that range and lower your odds of winning.

- Third, I base the data in this graph on a broad index of U.S. stock market performance, and most managers underperform the index over long periods.

- Fourth, this analysis considers average results but does not analyze interim circumstances. The real world is less forgiving than averages. The stock market doesn't bang out the same positive return every year—far from it. There's a high probability that during each of these 20-year periods, you will experience a bear market. You also pay taxes and fees and distribute income. In a bear market, the combined effect of all these factors can erode your wealth so much that you will never recover sufficiently to participate profitably in upward markets again.

Pulling It All Together

So what's the bottom line? You have a very good chance of achieving distribution-driven goals for your wealth as long as the following factors hold true:

- Your time horizon is less than 20 years.

- Your investment portfolio is tax and fee efficient.

- Tax rates remain reasonable.

- Distribution levels are kept in check.

- You diversify your assets and don't reach for excessive risk in hopes of making a little more money.

You can achieve these goals with limited risk using a simple and straight-forward approach, leaving you with lots of time and energy to pursue your passions.

But if you want to achieve growth-driven goals while spending above 1% to 2% per year, it's a major undertaking. You must achieve at least two out of three of the following:

- Be very disciplined about managing leakages.

- Develop and maintain a competitive advantage in your family business, investing, or career management that few other people have (including the large majority of wealth advisors).

- Be prepared to coordinate a complicated and sophisticated set of business, financial, legal, and managerial resources.

To achieve a growth-driven goal with long-term gross compound returns above 6.9% per annum (a reasonable return from a well-managed portfolio of 80% stocks and 20% bonds), it becomes exponentially more complicated, and increasingly uncertain, to achieve each additional percentage point of return.

Managing Leakages and Growth Factors

Take a look at Figure 4.8. I list each of the five financial objectives and the associated leakages and growth factors to be managed as part of pursuing each objective. As target annual returns grow, so do the number of management challenges associated with realizing them. And the dynamics of family values and culture have a profound influence on pursuing any of the five financial goals.

Critical Wealth Management Issues

	Maintain Purchasing Power	Maintain Stable Income	Conserve Real Wealth and Purchasing Power	Retain Real Per Capita Wealth	Keep Growing It
Leakages					
Spending	√	√	√	√	√
Taxes	√	√	√	√	√
Fees	√	√	√	√	√
Non-Investment Risk Mitigation	√	√	√	√	√
Inflation			√	√	√
Multi-Generational Factors			?	√	?
Growth Factors					
Manager Alpha			?	√	√
Tactical Asset Allocation			?	√	√
Leverage Management			?	√	√
Market Participation	√	√	√	√	√
Strategic Asset Allocation	√	√	√	√	√

Figure 4.8 As your financial objectives get more ambitious, your management challenges increase.

Many people believe that wealth management is largely a function of asset management—a growth factor. But, as you can see from this matrix, there is at least as much complexity in managing leakages.

Moreover, the more aggressive your wealth management goal becomes, the greater the managerial complexity associated with each relevant leakage and growth factor. Managing increasing complexity is also a factor when it comes to molding and nurturing family purpose, values, governance, and the family's human capital over extended periods.

The Advantages of Scale

If your goals are multigenerational, involve spending rates much above 1%, and are growth-driven, scale can work to your advantage. Consider the example of two wealthy individuals and their families represented in Figure 4.9. Both have assets of $15 million following a liquidity event. Client 1's assets are in a single pool of cash and publicly traded securities. Client 2's assets are divided into a variety of legal and administrative entities.

Comparative Scale Analysis

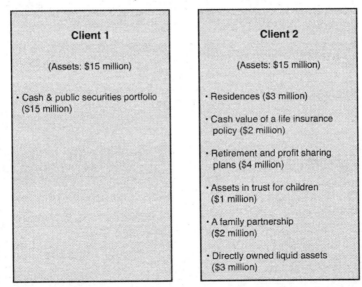

Client 1	Client 2
(Assets: $15 million)	(Assets: $15 million)
• Cash & public securities portfolio ($15 million)	• Residences ($3 million)
	• Cash value of a life insurance policy ($2 million)
	• Retirement and profit sharing plans ($4 million)
	• Assets in trust for children ($1 million)
	• A family partnership ($2 million)
	• Directly owned liquid assets ($3 million)

Figure 4.9 In wealth management, scale is a big advantage if you can achieve it.

Client 1 has far more investment options and better focus than Client 2. Client 1 has a greater scale of wealth (at $15 million) in one place, and he can focus all of his attention there. Client 2's largest single entity (his retirement and profit-sharing plans) is worth a much smaller $4 million,

and he must divide his attention and administrative resources across six different entities. As you'll see, there are both practical and legal benefits to "scale" of wealth.

The practical benefits to scale include greater access to unique investments and reduced costs. Although it is possible for investors to access most of the thousands of mutual funds that are listed daily in the *Wall Street Journal* with no more than $10,000, some outstanding money managers around the country won't work for individual investors unless they bring at least $1 million, $5 million, or even $25 million to the table. Occasionally, these highly exclusive managers commingle the assets of their investors into a single pool. In other cases, they manage each client's assets as a separate account.

Here are some ways that scale of wealth can help you:

Large-scale wealth gives you easier entree to managers who command high entry requirements. The more sought after the manager and the more specialized his or her skill set, the higher the minimums required for investment. Put another way, the greater the perceived potential of a manager to "add value" to an investment, the more capital you need to get in the door. This is true for business reasons and, in many cases, regulatory reasons.

You enjoy lower management fees, in many cases, for being a deep-pocketed investor. Reduced cost is a benefit of scale for high-net-worth investors. Managers who oversee separate accounts of public securities usually do provide fee breaks as account sizes increase. As financial management, measurement, and tracking systems become more sophisticated, more managers are offering separate account management for amounts of $250,000 or less. However, at account sizes below several million dollars, fees for these separate accounts are significantly higher than they are for comparable mutual funds, with no indication that they improve performance.

There are also a number of fund managers who operate "institutional" mutual funds, common trust funds, limited liability partnerships, or investment trusts with minimums well above typical mutual funds but who invest primarily in public securities. These vehicles usually have lower fees than their retail equivalents.

Those investment firms that manage their clients' assets in alternative investments like hedge funds and private equity typically do not give a $10 million investor a fee break over a $5 million client, though some will afford such a benefit for a $100 million or billion-dollar check. Believe it or not, sovereign wealth funds and a few large pension funds operate with this level of throw weight.

Scale also influences sales charges. Many investment vehicles, including mutual funds, annuities, and life insurance, have "loads," or sales charges, attached to them that are triggered at time of purchase or time of sale. As a general rule, the larger the client, the smaller the percentage sales charge. Some mutual funds use another type of sales charge called a 12b-1 fee that is deducted each year you own a mutual fund, which is supposed to be allocated to funds marketing. Many mutual funds have various classes of shares with varying fee and load structures. Make sure you get the class with the lowest possible sales charges given your asset size. In some cases, you can negotiate the fund you can access based on the size of your total investment in the fund, not just at each account's level of investment. If you add to a mutual fund position, you might also be able to get lower rates for the total investment.

One way you can sidestep the issue of sales charges is simply to avoid "load" funds or funds that charge 12b-1 fees altogether. Unless you plan to hold the investment for a very long time, the cost of such funds is rarely recouped relative to other similar funds that have no loads. One of the beauties of establishing this little rule is that you eliminate a substantial percentage of all mutual funds from your universe of possible investments (making your life simpler) while arguably enhancing your return potential.

In some cases, scale *does not* matter. Many of the fees associated with managing each legal entity you own (i.e., a trust, partnership, or limited liability company) are the same whether the assets total a few hundred thousand dollars or ten million dollars. Each entity also has standard overhead costs associated with maintaining and managing individual tax identification numbers, tax returns, bank accounts, and governance documents that you must periodically review and revise. Do you really need all the entities and investments that you have?

Regulatory Issues with Scale

The Securities and Exchange Commission (SEC) has created several classifications of investor, based on scale, and has put in place regulatory safeguards for some but not others. Investment firms that operate hedge funds or private equity operate with less regulation than mutual funds. To protect investors, the SEC restricts investment firms from accepting investors below certain size criteria in these funds. The SEC presumes that investors who meet the size criteria have specialized knowledge of investments and are conversant with the risks and reward potential of these investment opportunities.

A minimum of $1 million in net worth qualifies you to be an "accredited investor" or a minimum of $5 million in financial assets qualifies you to be a "qualified purchaser" for individuals, though for some legal entities the figure is higher. There is also an income test that individuals can use to become an accredited investor. Some portfolio managers require investors to meet both tests, whereas others are content if investors meet the lower standards. It's hard to participate effectively in alternative investing unless you have $5 million in a single entity today. But I would generally stay away from alternatives unless you have 20 times this scale, or $100 million in assets. The "retailization" of alternatives comes with very high fees and often poor tax efficiency.

Size also matters when it comes to retirement and estate planning. The larger your assets, the more planning that's required to manage wealth in retirement and to efficiently pass your wealth on to the next generation. Estate taxes get particularly complicated and potentially onerous when it comes to multimillion-dollar estates. So too does managing the alternative minimum income tax and the other income tax implications of retirement plans, insurance policies, and deferred compensation plans. You'll find more about these topics in Chapter 8, "Taxes Can Be Your Ally!" and Chapter 11, "Putting It All Together: Multigenerational Planning and Wealth Transfer."

Where the Rubber Meets the Road—Making Your Financial Objectives Work for Your Family

Deciding on a specific financial objective for your family isn't easy because each family member has different views of money, is at a different stage of life, and might have plans for the future that don't align with those of other family members. Don't be alarmed—these challenges are typical in most families. This is to be expected, and as Wealth Strategist, you must deal with these issues in a forthright way.

Typically, family members in or near retirement are relatively risk-averse and need to generate higher levels of income from their investments. In contrast, younger, more risk-tolerant family members in the prime of their careers don't need unearned income because they are working. In still other cases, young people might be trust beneficiaries, but not for several decades. In these instances, the trusts can grow aggressively because they don't have to make distributions in the interim.

In many wealthy families, there are individuals who are dependent on their wealth for income. These include the physically or mentally handicapped and those who have chosen careers where pay is not commensurate with their contribution to society, like preschool teachers, poets, artists, and administrators of community service organizations.

What Do You Do?

How do you juggle numerous financial objectives simultaneously? And how do you optimize your total family's wealth management strategy?

If you set your gross investment return requirements (highlighted in Figure 4.3) within the 3.6% to 6.9% annual range, you can use readily available retail investment products to meet your financial goals. By keeping your investment strategy and accountability procedures simple, you should be able to keep track of various portfolios and their investment strategies without problems.

If, however, your wealth management goals are multigenerational, your gross investment return goal exceeds 6.9%, you have a family business, or you crave simplicity in your family's financial affairs, you should consider developing a unified family strategy for wealth management.

By developing a unified family strategy around asset growth and leakages, you can reinforce common bonds and values between and across generations while preserving room for the needs and interests of individual family members. Developing a unified family wealth management strategy also rewards the good intrafamily communication necessary to refine and perpetuate your family purpose over time. It can also help bring important dimensions of control and scale to the long-term growth and preservation of your wealth.

Conclusion

In this chapter, I've explained the two paths you can take with wealth management activities. You can opt for a distribution-driven approach to wealth management, which typically has a timeframe of your lifetime. Or you can adopt a growth-driven approach to wealth management, the timeframe for which is often multigenerational. Indexing and the use of traditional investment vehicles, such as mutual funds, should enable you, in most cases, to achieve distribution-driven financial goals and some growth-driven goals. Pursuing growth-driven financial goals that incorporate significant spending involves a far higher order of family governance, investment sophistication, business management skill, financial markets knowledge, and tolerance for risk taking, which we will explore in more detail in later chapters.

You, as Wealth Strategist, will need to decide which of the two paths to wealth management planning makes the most sense for you, your family, and your financial circumstances. There are no right or wrong choices here. There are clearly trade-offs associated with each approach, and understanding these is critical in order to achieve your wealth management goals.

If you opt for a distribution-driven approach to wealth management, you can, in many cases, enjoy a relatively high annual spending rate because your assets don't need to last beyond your lifetime. However, if you opt for a growth-driven wealth management approach, especially one with a time horizon of multiple generations, you must pay close attention to "leakages" and other factors that can erode your wealth. You must make a concerted effort to live below your means, especially if you want to preserve or increase real per capita wealth in subsequent generations. And you must take a proactive approach to wealth building.

To help you become an effective Wealth Strategist, this chapter has acquainted you with some fundamental dynamics of financial management as you prepare to work closely with professional wealth advisors in the areas of investing, asset allocation, estate planning, tax law, and accounting.

Before you begin working with a professional team of advisors, however, it's important that you understand more about the professional wealth industry today—how wealth advisors work, how they make their living, and what motivates them to work on your behalf. That's the focus of Chapter 5, "The Enchanted Forest, the Secret Society, and the Capital Kibbutz."

Chapter 4: Issues to Discuss with Your Family

1. What do you see as your most likely wealth management planning timeframe? Is it your lifetime or multigenerational?

2. What are your specific financial objectives? Do you want to base your financial future on a distribution-driven approach to wealth management or a growth-driven approach?

3. If you chose a distribution-driven approach to wealth management, are you more inclined to maintain purchasing power of your spending or to strive to retain nominal wealth over your lifetime even if it means reducing your purchasing power over time?

4. If you choose a growth-driven approach to wealth management, which approach most closely matches your needs?

   a. Retain real wealth
   b. Retain real per capita wealth
   c. Keep growing your wealth

5. What is your attitude toward spending? Are you by nature a big spender or are you frugal? Do you see your own spending activities as either a threat to or a critical component of effective wealth management?

6. How strong is your economic engine today? How confident are you in the governance and management of your family business? How skilled are you at wealth management? What are your specific wealth management skills, if any? If you have invested well in the past, were you smart or lucky? In what areas will you need to identify and recruit high-caliber professional wealth advisors—perhaps including family members—to balance you out?

7. Are you happy with your current rates of return on investments? If so, what do you base this assessment on? If not, what do you think you need to do differently to generate better and more consistent rates of return?

8. What are the key "leakages" impacting your wealth? Which of these do you see yourself able readily to control? Which are likely to be more difficult to control? Based on Figure 4.8, prioritize the

top three leakages that threaten the long-term preservation and growth of your wealth.

9. What can you do, based on reading this chapter, to bring more financial discipline to your spending and your wealth management activities?

10. What systems, if any, do you have in place to measure and manage both growth factors and leakages?

11. To what extent do you enjoy "scale" of wealth? Write down on a piece of paper your key assets by entity size. Also, list and identify any liabilities.

12. Are you currently able to leverage the scale of your wealth in your financial and wealth management endeavors with advisors?

13. How happy are you with the level of service you currently are receiving from wealth advisors?

14. Are you conversant with the various factors, including the long-term effects of leakages and advisors fees, which currently affect the bottom-line value of your assets?

15. Do different members of your family have different wealth management goals and priorities? Describe these. If you don't know family members' wealth management goals and priorities, how easily can you discuss these? What, if anything, stands in the way of such discussion?

16. Do you currently have in place a unified family strategy for wealth management? If so, how well is it working? Are you pleased with it, or does the plan or your approach need to be modified to be more efficient and to more directly serve collective and individual family interests?

17. How well are you able to facilitate family conversations about wealth management goals? How frequently do you review goals and results with family members? How frequent are your communications with various family members regarding family wealth management matters?

Endnotes

1. In Figure 4.2, I present a more general model for maintaining real per capita wealth across generations. In that model, I use a factor of 2.5% instead of 3.1% because our family is somewhat more prolific than average and it is also possible for children or grandchildren to marry and then inherit assets from their spouse's family, lowering the required rate of return to maintain the objective.

2. In fact, the gross rate of return needs to be somewhat higher because we can't generate a return on the 8.5% in leakages each year.

3. Sources for market and inflation data: Cambridge Associates, LLC, and Ibbotson Associates. After-inflation-and-tax numbers are the author's estimates.

5

The Enchanted Forest, the Secret Society, and the Capital Kibbutz

"Those that have wealth must be watchful and wary..."

—Thomas Haynes Bayly

Now that we've discussed your values regarding wealth (Chapter 3, "Start with Your Family Purpose") and the various options you have when it comes to wealth management goals (Chapter 4, "Defining Your Financial Objectives"), it's time to talk about the wealth management industry—into whose hands you might ultimately place your wealth for investment. It's a mysterious industry that you must learn to navigate, but for which no easy-to-follow road map exists.

Within the industry, I will introduce you to three different worlds: "the Capital Kibbutz," "the Secret Society," and "the Enchanted Forest." Stepping into any of these worlds is like stepping off a plane in a faraway country where you don't know the language or customs. As you might expect, an eager horde of people await your arrival, jostling for position to serve as your guide to each of these strange and exotic lands. Whom should you choose?

It's essential that you learn how to navigate the wealth industry well so that you can be an effective Wealth Strategist. It's also important to understand how the wealth management industry works so that you can pick appropriate investment strategies to support your overall wealth management goals.

The good news is that I've been a part of the wealth management industry for many years and have a strong granular knowledge of how the industry actually operates. The bad news is that the industry is in the throes of a complex evolution in which issues of ethics, competition, market self-regulation, and federal law can sometimes play out at an investor's expense.

As your guide to the wealth management industry, I hope that you'll become much more familiar with what you need to do to be a successful investor and what to do when it comes to working with industry professionals.

What precisely do you need to know about the wealth management industry today in order to navigate it well and avoid investor pitfalls? The first rule of working with wealth management firms today is "buyer beware." I say this because you must—as with any industry—steer clear of working with unscrupulous advisors. I also say this because you must be an educated consumer, even when working with ethical advisors and wealth management firms with sterling reputations. For example:

- You must understand how advisors and firms are compensated and how they measure their own success.

- You must know what your own objectives are and be able to evaluate and differentiate the value propositions of different wealth management firms and advisors.

- Finally, you must know something about the world of investing and, even more important, know what you don't know.

In the wealth management industry today, having a little bit of knowledge can be a dangerous thing. That's because you, as an individual investor, are really a "free agent" investor. Like free agent athletes, you're in charge of your destiny, whether you realize it or not. In most cases, you are best off assuming that there's no one there to protect your interests from others or against your own ignorance. Even though U.S. regulators do more than those in any other country to protect the interests of individuals, education and engagement are still the best protections.

Regulation

Even before the financial crisis of 2008, the financial-services industry was one of the most heavily regulated on the planet, in large part because the government wants people to have confidence in the markets. There is even more regulation today, though I think it has done little to make individual investors feel that their interests are better protected. My advice is that you should act as if the industry is not regulated, and to be well enough informed to protect your own interests.

In 1974, a landmark piece of legislation was passed by Congress that injected the financial markets with unprecedented creativity and entre-preneurialism and at the same time made them a more dangerous place for the individual investor. This legislation was called the Employee Retirement Income Security Act, or ERISA. (See Sidebar 5.1.)

Sidebar 5.1: ERISA and the Prudent Investor Rule

Before ERISA, pension plans and other kinds of institutional investments were governed by something called the "Prudent Man Rule." The Prudent Man Rule dictated that every investment that pension plan administrators made had to be of high quality and safety. If a pension-plan portfolio consisted of 60 stocks and 20 bonds, for example, each security in this portfolio was individually analyzed to see whether it was a prudent and reasonable invest-ment. It was common practice for pension plans, endowments, and other institutional investors to hire one diversified financial service firm to manage their assets (or, at most, a few firms). The service provider managed all the assets in-house and did most of the administration as well. The industry was highly regulated and safe, and conservative portfolios were pretty much the norm from one firm to the next. There were relatively few competitors, and they each built long-term, stable, and relatively price-insensitive client relationships.

Under ERISA, the "Prudent Investor Rule" replaced the "Prudent Man Rule" as the guiding principle for designing investment port-folios. The Prudent Investor Rule takes into account the benefits of diversification. It recognizes that a well-constructed collection of individually risky assets can collectively have significantly less risk. In other words, it has "risk-defraying" characteristics.

This subtle change completely transformed how institutional portfolios are invested today. For one thing, it introduced the notion of "risk" into investment planning and selection as never before. It created legal protections for institutions so they could gain exposure to small-capitalization companies, venture capital, opportunistic real estate, and many other "risky" investments. It also created the flexibility for them to hire smaller, specialized investment managers, opening the market to new and dynamic competitors. This change of thinking in how portfolios should be managed opened the door for boutique investment firms with focused expertise to take hold, adding new competition and creativity to the markets. It also led to institutional investors wanting to invest with the best possible investors in each asset class, regardless of the firm they worked for. Many more investment options and many more managers led institutions to develop "open architecture."

The enactment of ERISA into law proved a major boon for institutional investors. Although the legislation was directed principally at pension funds, it changed the thinking of many other institutional investors, such as endowments and foundations, and eventually the market for wealth management services. After ERISA became law, institutional investors diversified their investments out of hidebound large cap stock and bond portfolios, managed by banks and traditional investment houses, and began to invest with specialized boutique money managers and investment firms. "Open architecture" was born, and with it came the opportunity for institutional investors to take advantage of a wide range of proprietary and highly innovative products offered by organizations of widely different structures and sizes. Open architecture offered institutional investors the opportunity for much greater returns on their investments than had been possible in the pre-ERISA environment.

The Four A's

The more forward-thinking institutions realized that the opportunity for greater returns equated with a greater need to analyze risk correctly. They saw that managing effectively in this new environment demanded that they develop strong in-house competencies to manage their investments. In the mid-1980s, David Swensen, Chief Investment Officer of the Yale University Endowment, and Jack Meyer, the then Chief Executive Officer of Harvard University's endowment, became innovative Active Alpha investors, aggressively investing in real estate, private equity, venture capital, risk arbitrage, distressed debt, and emerging markets. As the investment portfolios got more complicated, Meyer, Swensen, and others focused on building strong in-house competencies in four key investment areas. I refer to these as "the Four A's":

1. **Acumen.** Large institutional investors recognized that the most important success factor in investing was the accurate identification of investment opportunity. So, they developed strong expertise in the areas of investment research and professional oversight. These resources are expensive and are best amortized over a substantial asset base. Only billion dollar plus institutional investors can really afford this, and those who have made the commitment have gotten higher returns as a result.

2. **Access.** Scale, sophistication, and long time horizons are all attributes that help investors gain access to the most attractive investment opportunities. Large institutional investors recognized this and began leveraging the scale of their assets to achieve access to the best opportunities and the finest talent in traditional and alternative investments.

3. **Alignment of Interests.** Client/advisor alignment was pioneered by large institutions in order to protect their long-term investment interests. The belief was that investment managers entrusted with managing money should share appropriately in both success and failure, and conflicts of interest should be avoided or, at the very least, managed with the clients' interests put first.

4. **Accountability.** Large institutional investors pioneered the use of strong administrative and accountability systems to measure fund/advisor/manager performance. Such systems are critical in giving pension plan managers, endowment directors, and investment committees the management information they need to act with confidence. Accountability in its broadest sense involves

tracking asset allocation and aggregate results, measuring/monitoring manager performance, and flagging problems if and when they arise.

Leading institutional investors like Harvard and Yale attracted experienced professionals to construct and manage their portfolios. They did detailed research on portfolio construction, the behavior of asset classes, and the skills and ethics of managers. They hired staffs to assemble and aggregate, often by hand, the performance information they compiled from managers. They researched the amount of risk individual managers took to achieve particular returns. The same staff also double-checked the bookkeeping of their investment advisors in the same way that you and I might balance our checkbooks.

To assist such institutions with investment planning, a whole consulting industry blossomed in the wake of ERISA and is still a leading force in the investment world today. Institutional consultants, such as Mercer, Cambridge Associates, Monticello, and Hewitt EnnisKnupp, typically charge institutional investors anywhere from $250,000 to $1 million per year—or more—for the advice and support they provide.

The Mutual Funds Industry: Open Architecture Comes to Private Investors

With the success of open architecture in the institutional world came increasing interest in similar access and choice by private investors. Mutual fund companies were the first of the private wealth management firms to respond to this market demand. Taking a page from the marketing playbook of consumer companies like Coke, which in the '70s, '80s, and '90s pursued product differentiation with a vengeance (adding Diet Coke, Cherry Coke, Classic Coke, Vanilla Coke, Caffeine Free Coke, and so on to its product line), mutual fund companies soon began to offer a wide array of products via open architecture to retail investors. And the industry grew rapidly.

In 1970, there were 355 equity mutual funds, most of them broadly diversified. Today, 42 years later, more than 160 times as much money is invested in mutual funds as there was in 1970. And there are roughly 8,700 mutual funds from which an investor can choose. Less than 10%

of these funds are broadly diversified mutual funds, and the rest are equity mutual funds narrowly focused on specific industries, size of companies, international markets, investment styles, and so on.[1]

The product differentiation strategy that mutual fund companies have embraced over the past 40 years has proved a financial bonanza for these firms. According to Morningstar data, the top three mutual fund families (Vanguard, Fidelity, and Capital Guardian) have more assets under management than the next 40 combined. When Jack Bogle started Vanguard, he had only a handful of mutual funds under management. In 2011, Vanguard had 148 distinct retail funds. Fidelity had 315. Franklin/Templeton, #4, but with a third of Vanguard's assets, had 122. Interestingly, Capital Guardian's American Funds (#3) had only 42 funds.[2]

Mutual fund firms have discovered that giving investors a lot of fund choice is good for business. Although broadly diversified mutual funds today might charge investors only modest investment management fees of 0.7% or less, specialized portfolios such as a small-capitalization fund or international fund can potentially charge much higher management fees—sometimes more than double the diversified mutual fund fees cited previously, or 1.5%.

So if a mutual fund salesperson today can convince a client to transfer a percentage of their assets from lower-fee diversified portfolios into higher-fee specialized portfolios, that salesperson can potentially increase his or her fee income from that client a great deal—even if the client doesn't invest any more money.

Firms also discovered that if they have lots of products for sale, there are always some funds in their stable that are performing really well. The funds that do well become the focus of marketing efforts, they get good ratings from Morningstar (a leading provider of independent investment research), and they become the best vehicles for bringing in new assets. In fact, over 80% of the money that gets invested in mutual funds today goes into funds that get four or five stars (on a one-to-five-point scale) from Morningstar.

Unfortunately, the link between a fund earning four or five stars from Morningstar for good past performance and that fund's ability to continue outperforming the market is quite weak. Morningstar discloses this concern regularly, and they've spent considerable effort trying to improve their system. In addition, almost every time you receive performance information from an investment manager, it says in the fine print that "past performance is not an indicator of future results." Academic research findings regularly support the fine print.

One-Stop Shopping for Mutual Funds— Open Architecture Widens

As mutual funds proliferated in the '80s and '90s and firms recognized the benefits of diversifying their product lines, Charles Schwab, founder and Chairman of Charles Schwab, Inc., came up with a new business model for personal investing that forever changed the mutual funds industry. In 1992, he created Schwab OneSource, which enabled individual investors to buy mutual funds from a number of different companies through a single point of contact at Schwab. This one-stop shopping format made it easier for investors to keep track of their mutual funds and made fund administration for wealth advisors using the Schwab system far easier. Schwab OneSource didn't bring open architecture to mutual funds, but it certainly accelerated its widespread adoption. It has been hugely successful. Fidelity followed Schwab's lead a year later in 1993 by offering its own version of one-stop fund shopping, FundsNetwork. By 2000, FundsNetwork was offering 3,400 funds for sale. Many other mutual fund firms have followed suit.

What Has ERISA Done for Individual Investors? Not Much!

Although the introduction of open architecture proved beneficial to large institutional investors that could afford to develop deep in-house competencies to manage their accounts, it has not proven beneficial to individual (retail) investors.

First, open architecture left individuals on their own when it came to developing the investment skills and business acumen to manage their investments through supermarket fund shopping. And results show that individual investors (often guided by professional advisors) haven't fared well when put in charge of selecting their investment vehicles. From 1992 to 2011, for example, the stock market (S&P 500) earned an annual rate of return of 7.8%. This is a so-so return, somewhat below the long-term average, adjusted for inflation. However, the ordinary equity mutual fund investor did considerably worse on average. Because most people tend to buy investments that have done well in the past rather than those that might do well in the future, the average dollar invested in equity mutual funds returned only 3.5% during the period from 1992 to 2011, an underperformance of 4.3%.[3] This might not sound like a big difference, but consider this: Had you invested $10,000 in the stock market in 1992, you would have had $44,913 in 2011 (excluding taxes). Had you invested the same amount like the ordinary mutual fund equity investor, you would have realized only $19,859!

Second, ERISA deals with the tax-exempt world, but individual investors pay taxes. In Spring 1993, two researchers—Robert H. Jeffrey and Robert D. Arnott—released a groundbreaking study titled "Is Your Alpha Big Enough to Cover Your Taxes?" in the *Journal of Portfolio Management*. They took a top-down approach that studied the actual long-term performance of actively managed equity mutual funds. The study showed unequivocally that in most cases the answer to their question was a resounding "No!" Their conclusion raised a lot of controversy in the trade press among active managers, but their research and conclusions were sound. In 2000, in the same well-respected journal, Arnott and two other researchers published a reexamination of their original work, with even more data and better analysis. In response to this updated work, Robert H. Jeffrey had the following to say in an article he wrote several months later in the *Journal of Wealth Management*:[4]

> This newer, broader, and deeper study shows once again that "the vast majority of alphas are not big enough to cover their taxes." But the icing on Arnott's empirical cake is the observation that while 14% of the funds over a 20-year period outperformed the Vanguard 500 on an after-tax basis by 1.3% per year, the 86% that underperformed did so by 3.2%. My math is pretty simplistic, but I'm not thrilled with the odds of a bet on which I have a 14% chance of picking up 130 basis points of return, and an 86% chance of losing 320.

Over the years, others have tested long-term investment performance of active managers—of mutual funds and separate accounts alike—on both a pretax and an after-tax basis. Most of them come up with similar results. Because the majority of active managers don't outperform the index, it should come as no surprise that even fewer managers do so when measured on an after-tax basis.

Third, ERISA doesn't help individual investors from the standpoint of fees. For example, there's a cost problem with mutual funds. Repeated studies by academics and industry practitioners confirm that mutual fund management fees, administrative fees, marketing fees, and transaction costs are all a drag on the performance of actively managed mutual funds and give them an overall lower rate of return than low-cost index-linked investments. The same cost trends prove true when comparing bond mutual fund performance against the bond market itself.

Fourth, and the biggest problem of all, ERISA and open architecture have spawned an environment in which individuals sell and buy investments with greater frequency than in the past. Before open architecture, most owners of mutual funds invested for the long term. But today, people read in the newspaper about funds that are outperforming the market. Or they hear some stock market forecaster rhapsodize about a hot new stock on *The Today Show.* Or they watch Jim Cramer shout, "Buy!!" and, "Sell!!" to his viewers on the appropriately named *Mad Money* program. All this makes it hard for the ordinary investor to resist the impulse to buy or sell stocks and mutual funds when he or she is hearing the message almost daily: "Act now!"

In short, although open architecture has been great for institutional investors and the mutual fund industry, it hasn't worked out as well for private investors. Instead, private investors have become caught up in the excitement and complexity of open architecture without having the investment acumen and access to investment options that institutional investors have. Private investors also have much more difficulty aligning their interests with advisors or holding their advisors accountable for results than large-scale institutional investors.

Mutual funds are only one place where individual investors can get lost in the fog of the rapidly changing wealth management industry. There are other places as well.

Should I Use a Retail Brokerage?

It is a badge of honor and a sign of success for private clients to be advised by blue-blooded firms, such as Goldman Sachs, or Morgan Stanley. Both are outstanding firms that have built great businesses. Major banks, such as UBS, Bank of America, and JP Morgan, also have huge brokerage operations. They all possess the Four A's, and so do many others. The leading brokerage firms and their affiliated investment banking activities are at the epicenter of the financial-services world today. They see trends early and have both muscle and smarts to assess and take advantage of opportunity. Their forte is trading assets and selling ideas. They make money by completing transactions, whether they are distributing mutual funds, trading blocks of IBM stock, or floating an IPO. These transactions make money for the firm, whether or not the deals subsequently make money for clients. If clients of these firms simply bought and held their investments, the brokerage business would not be very profitable. But clients don't. Encouraged by their investment advisors, clients periodically sell some funds and purchase others, always generating fees for their advisors when they do.

Brokerage firms have tremendous expertise, but because of their transaction-oriented cultures and because they often sell both internally manufactured products and third-party products, they have conflicts of interest that you, the Wealth Strategist, must manage.

Trust Bank Services

Banks have historically been major players in the private wealth business. Although the Glass-Steagall Act of 1933 prevented them from engaging in the brokerage business and interstate banking restrictions limited their distribution reach, for over a century firms such as Northern Trust, JP Morgan, and U.S. Trust built substantial businesses to set up and manage trusts for their private clients. Trusts have several functions. One of them is asset management. Many private clients who lack investment acumen, scale of wealth, and the infrastructure to manage their investments delegate these responsibilities to trust banks in hopes of better results and less complexity in their own lives.

Unlike mutual fund companies, trust businesses have been slower to embrace open architecture. Part of the reason is trust law, which is governed at the state level, not the federal level. Changing trust law to ensure easier use of open architecture by trust businesses is logistically more complex and takes greater time to accomplish due to the lack of uniformity of trust laws across the U.S.

For almost 20 years after ERISA became law, most state trust laws were still mired in the "Prudent Man Rule" (see Sidebar 5.1). Finally, in 1992, a national body called The American Law Institute, trying to encourage states to adopt the "Prudent Investor" concept for trusts, created a document called the Restatement (Third) of Trusts. This document updated the legal principles of trust investing to reconcile with emerging best practices in the wealth management industry.

After the Restatement (Third) was completed, states began to change their trust laws in earnest. But more than ten years later, only two-thirds of states had adopted most of the updated principles. For the laggards, there is too much legal risk for trusts to embrace open architecture.

Trust companies that act as trustee have a high standard of fiduciary responsibility that they must follow. This means they have a legal duty to safeguard their clients' interests. These organizations tend to have conservative cultures and less cutting-edge investment expertise. They are more concerned about protecting their clients' assets than about helping clients maximize their returns. Employee compensation structures are often lower and less incentive-driven than in brokerages or mutual fund firms. But their interests are more closely aligned with clients than in many other financial firms.

Trust companies and their more conservative approach to wealth management occupy an important niche in the wealth management industry. As trillions of dollars are passed from one generation to the next over the next 50 years, I predict that trust companies will eventually capture a significant share of these assets.

The Gap in the Individual Investment Process

With open architecture, the total shape of your investment program is even more important than the individual mutual funds, stocks, hedge funds, or other products in your portfolio. According to a long-term study done by DALBAR, Inc., from 1992 to 2011, the S&P 500 generated a return of 7.8% but the ordinary equity mutual fund investor earned on average only 3.5%. That 4.3% difference, each year over 20 years, has a huge adverse impact on the ordinary investor's wealth. With all the upheaval (mergers, deregulation, and reregulation) that's taking place in the private client business, there doesn't seem to be much focus on helping individual investors acquire the Four A's of investing. Advisors get paid to sell financial products, not strategy. Private clients become enamored with products and fail to perceive the need for a strategic approach to wealth management. Institutional investors like Swensen and Meyer saw the need for a strategic approach to investment management, and they filled the gap. Attempts to address the need for a strategic approach to investing in the individual investment market have largely been unsuccessful, except for a few consultants and outsourced Chief Investment Officers who work with families that have assets of $100 million or more.

If your private client portfolio is simple, you don't need to build the Four A's beyond a basic level. And you can achieve that basic level on your own. However, if you want to invest the way institutions invest, in specialized products and in such things as venture capital or hedge funds, you have to be just as skilled as they are to have a chance of winning. Just how tough is this?

How Can You Distinguish Among Wealth Advisors?

There are few businesses in which salespeople can make more money than in wealth management. As a result, the industry attracts many bright individuals. These are the folks who most individual investors hire in hopes of achieving the Four A's needed to compete using complex strategies and products. Wealth management professionals are highly competitive, have a nose for new business, and possess great powers of persuasion. They exude success and smarts, wear designer suits, carry platinum credit cards and thick pitch books, and are supported with billions in advertising dollars.

To the inexperienced person with newly liquid assets, salespeople from wealth management firms present two challenges. First, a prospective client can potentially sit through hours of PowerPoint presentations from different wealth management firms outlining their investment options without being able to truly differentiate one value proposition from another. Second, in these interactions, it can be even tougher to discern the track records of individual advisors in adding value to their clients, even when they work for firms with good reputations.

So, how do you measure one wealth advisor's knowledge of financial markets against that of another? How do you gauge a person's instinct for the market, his or her knowledge of emerging market trends, or the degree to which he or she is ethical in everyday client interactions?

Believe me, it's tough. A friend of mine, an entrepreneur, recently sold his software business. Even before sale terms were finalized, my friend was inundated by phone calls from representatives of leading wealth management firms. After listening to hours of sales presentations, he complained to me that the exercise made his head spin, and in the end he couldn't differentiate one sales pitch from the next:

> I didn't learn anything I could use from all these meetings. Whenever I told one of these sales reps that I couldn't differentiate his proposal from all the others, I was told my analysis wasn't "granular" enough. So, I went back and reviewed all the proposals again, but again came to the same conclusion: I couldn't tell one from another. Eventually, I began to worry that by the time I had gotten granular enough to distinguish the differences among the proposals, they would be inconsequential, and I wouldn't be able to see the forest for the trees in any case!

Each team of prospective advisors explained to my entrepreneur friend why its firm was the best choice to manage his money, and each brought stacks of material to back up the argument. Each firm managed billions of dollars in investments and offered him a vast array of well reasoned investment products. All the teams presented diversified investment strategies that included smatterings of hedge funds and private equity offerings. In every case, they offered up mountains of financial data along with colorful pie chart diagrams.

No team, however, tried to educate my friend about how to distinguish among wealth management proposals. And although each team espoused the virtues of its firm and the services it offered, none could demonstrate a track record of adding long-term value to investors' aggregate portfolios, other than by offering reference checks with their satisfied clients.

My friend's dilemma is typical of that faced by anyone trying to choose among financial advisors today. Not only do many firms' investment models look alike, but even within the same firm there can be vast differences in the quality of investment execution among advisors, and even from client to client using the same advisor.

In the end, five different firms presented equally impressive wealth management models to my friend. But because he couldn't differentiate among their value propositions, he ended up choosing three of them and splitting his assets among them, hoping that in a few years he will have better information with which to make future investment decisions.

A year or two from now, it's my guess that one of these teams whose performance appears to be falling behind will be tempted to play catch up by recommending riskier investments to my friend. If he accepts their recommendations and the investments do well, that firm will keep his business and might get more. If the recommended investments decline in value, that firm was probably going to lose his business in any case. In this kind of head-to-head competitive arrangement with wealth management firms, the investor rarely emerges the victor. The odds are stacked in favor of the advisor in a "heads I win, tails you lose" way because the advisor makes money whether or not the client does.

Meanwhile, my friend will be very busy overseeing three teams of advisors and trying to juggle their investment advice—a tough challenge indeed. A long-standing industry manager, commenting on the manner in which some clients "manage" their investment advisors, puts the challenge this way: "Wealth advisors are much better salesmen than their clients are wealth managers."

In many cases, people are ambitious for their wealth to grow quickly, but don't have the skills and resources to make it happen. When confronted with decisions, they might get overly aggressive, make rash decisions, err by employing the wrong advisors, fund ill-considered projects, or quickly spend a fortune that might have taken generations to build. If such individuals are lucky, they stumble early on and only in a modest way. This allows them time to scale back ambitions and risk taking to more appropriate levels. But in some cases, people with a lot of money don't learn about the perils of wealth management until it's too late.

The bull market of the 1990s made it easy for many people to overestimate their own investment skills. Almost everyone—from day traders to dot.com millionaires—was rapidly rewarded for taking risks because of the general rise in stock prices. Indeed, as people put more and more capital into the stock market, the rewards got better and better. However, instead of being emboldened by the rising stock market, wealth advisors should have prompted their clients to take money out of the market to keep their assets in balance—and clients should have listened to them when they did. But many investors and their advisors became greedy. They exercised imprudent aggression and a lack of discipline during this period, and they were overly exposed to the brunt of the bear as soon as the markets cracked.

Today, we have almost the opposite situation. The Federal Reserve, by driving interest rates close to zero, is encouraging investors to take more risk. But after a decade of two major financial scares, first the dot-com bust and then the financial and housing crisis, many investors are scared. And that's before considering the Euro-crisis that is unfolding before our eyes. Yet "low-risk" investments such as high-quality municipal bonds and U.S. Treasury securities have yields that are below the rate of inflation today. In other words, you are guaranteed to lose money if things go well. And if inflation and interest rates rise, the outcomes will be worse. As I write this, the dividend yield on the S&P 500 is higher than the yield on the ten-year Treasury. Maybe it's time to take more risk, not less.

Successful salespeople identify attractive prospects quickly; then they foster empathetic relationships that result in the sale of services. Beyond meeting minimum client expectations, they must effectively manage the dynamic tension between the quality of advice they offer to clients and the revenue they generate for their firm.

Today, some advisors have a strict fiduciary duty to put their clients' interests first, as defined by the Securities and Exchange Commission (SEC). Investment advisory firms and their representatives have this duty. On the other hand, broker dealers and their registered representatives operate under a different set of guidelines, defined by the Financial Industry Regulatory Authority (FINRA). They do not have to uphold a fiduciary standard. Neither do many salespeople of life insurance or annuities. In the wake of the 2008–2009 financial crisis, Congress has made some noises about trying to reconcile these two standards, but intense lobbying and politics have delayed a resolution indefinitely, just exacerbating an already confusing situation for the public that Congress and the SEC are supposed to be trying to protect. As you can see, it can be very confusing (even for sophisticated clients) to determine whether a salesperson is giving quality advice. So, how does one effectively navigate the wealth management industry today? It isn't easy but you can do it. I like to think of the industry today as being divided into three unique worlds. I describe these three worlds as "the Enchanted Forest," "the Secret Society," and "the Capital Kibbutz."

Each world is inhabited by financial professionals ready to assist visitors with asset management. Each has a distinct culture and value proposition. These worlds aren't constrained by the lines that once separated brokerage firms from mutual funds from trust banking; each world may contain all three. The only thing that you, the private investor, must do is decide which of the three "worlds" is the best destination for you. Let's look at each of them in turn.

The Enchanted Forest

I refer to the first world as "the Enchanted Forest." It is an investment land populated by ambitious clients and equally ambitious wealth advisors, both looking for the secret formula to investment success.

On its face, the Enchanted Forest is a beautiful and alluring place—its people energetic, entrepreneurial, and gregarious. The wealth advisors who live in the Enchanted Forest, for example, are compelling salespeople who regale prospective investors with stories of their investment prowess and client success. "Come with me, and I'll show you how to make money," they note to prospective investors in their face-to-face client meetings, in marketing brochures, in their expensively produced TV ads, and on their high octane, interactive websites. They offer to act as financial guides to neophyte investors who can't understand the markets and who don't really want to understand the vagaries and complexities of investment, asset allocation, stock diversification, and wealth management goal setting. They add to the allure of their promises with slick advertising, enthusiastic market predictions, and expert commentary on the ever-changing nature of investing.

For their part, the clients you find in the Enchanted Forest are usually in search of easy keys to prosperity and financial success. In many cases, wealthy people who are open to suggestion and vulnerable to persuasion can become easy prey for advisors who overwhelm them with financial jargon and promises of quick market success.

As a result, marriages of convenience often take place in the Enchanted Forest—between ambitious wealth industry people on the one hand and eager and impressionable investors on the other. When private clients sign on with an investment "guide," their guide entertains them, dazzles them with investment savvy, helps them choose investments, and collects his or her fees. Some of these investments do well, and when an investor scores success, his or her investment guide trumpets that news to the Forest's treetops, hoping to entice other would-be investors to sign on as well. Meanwhile, other investments languish, and are quietly sold off and soon forgotten—by client and advisor alike.

Many of the investment "guides" who operate in the Enchanted Forest are hardworking professionals with winning personalities. They are usually competent and ethical, but sometimes not. Bernie Madoff was an exemplar of the latter. In any event, investors invariably marvel at their energy, creativity, and grasp of investment principles and theory. Such adoration, mixed with insecurity, keeps clients coming back to these advisors for advice time and time again, even when there's not a real track record of success to support doing so.

As its name implies, the Enchanted Forest is occupied by many clients and advisors alike who think and act as though they know what they're doing when it comes to investing, but just don't have the Four A's to compete against leading institutional investors. Remember when, in Sidebar 5.2, I said that when it comes to investing, make sure you know what you don't know? Well, there are a lot of people wandering around inside the Enchanted Forest who don't really know what they're doing, and don't know what they don't know. The stakes they face are high.

Conversely, some clients might simply play in the Enchanted Forest to have a good time, knowing full well there are better ways to generate alpha. For them, it doesn't really matter if they blow a little money; they're in the game for the thrill of the chase. A good example of the kind of fun-seeking investor you often find in the Enchanted Forest is what I refer to as "the Country Club Gambler." The Country Club Gambler is drawn to the Enchanted Forest not to generate alpha, not to preserve his or her wealth, not to ensure a secure retirement, but largely to have fun. So he or she dabbles in hedge funds, buys and sells securities or mutual funds, or invests in venture capital because doing so stimulates competitive juices and, when things go well, a sense of satisfaction—regardless of whether success is a function of skill or luck.

The Country Club Gambler is a casual investor—at least insofar as his Enchanted Forest investments are concerned. To him, investing is a high-end hobby, a kind of "brain candy" that goes hand in hand with discussions about economics, politics, and how successful companies grow. A Country Club Gambler might get into investing because he likes doing the math associated with calculating the odds of success or because he enjoys watching charts of stock prices tick up and down. Other Country Club Gamblers like the adrenaline rush of buying a stock at $10 and selling it at $20; or they are driven by greed, especially in the heat of a bull market. Still others use investing as a way to bond with their friends. They form investment groups or compare notes about their latest tips while playing poker at the club. Some of them even brag from time to time.

A common form of the Country Club Gambler is the "Angel Investor." I regularly observe people who've made some money trying their hand at providing financial support for fledgling businesses. Some are also interested in sitting on the boards of the companies they back. Angel Investing is theoretically a great way to grow your wealth on the back of other people's hard work. But it is also very risky. Angel Investing provides some really expensive education for most who are brave enough to try it. But that doesn't matter to the Angel Investor. To him or her, the heroism of embracing a compelling "vision of the future" wins out over the reality of protracted negative cash flow in the venture, and even their own wallet. At least it seems that way to me when I've heard some Angel Investors describe why they do what they do.

Sidebar 5.3:   The Perils of Angel Investing

Angel Investing is not for the faint of heart. One of the reasons that being an Angel Investor is so attractive to many wealth creators is that they correctly identify that the one resource many capital-starved companies want more than anything is money. The potential to be of help to fledging cash-starved start-up companies, especially those whose mission is close to a benefactor's heart, or that are involved in exciting research or breakthrough technologies, can be tough for a business entrepreneur to resist.

The problem is that many would-be Angel Investors are overconfident about their ability to invest in viable enterprises. So their due diligence is inadequate, or their knowledge of capital structuring doesn't adequately protect their interests, or they don't have the right industry contacts. The situation can become especially perilous if the start-up venture is in a field or industry unknown to the Angel Investor. In one case I'm familiar with, someone who had operated and then sold a successful business lost more than 25% of his net worth within two years of his liquidity event because of a misguided angel investment. All the while, several of his advisors pleaded with him to reconsider how he was investing his money. He was asked to consult with industry experts, to audit the numbers that were being given to him, and to stop putting good money in after bad. But all of this was to no avail. Unfortunately, this is an all-too-frequent occurrence.

Suffice it to say that Country Club Gambling is more a form of entertainment than a real investment strategy. And entertainment almost always comes with a cost. Based on the billions of dollars people spend every year to go to football games, attend concerts, gamble in Las Vegas, or ski in Lake Tahoe, reasonable cost doesn't get in the way of having fun, nor should it.

Whereas obviously you pay for football tickets or seats at a rock concert, most of the time there is no perceived out-of-pocket cost to Country Club Gambling, which makes it appear inexpensive—and all the more seductive. If you start investing with $100, and you finish with at least $100 in your pocket, even if you don't keep up with the market or inflation, you feel like it has cost you nothing.

If you have fun doing it, indulge your desire to be a Country Club Gambler. But as with any sport or leisure pursuit, do it in moderation, and watch out for creeping "opportunity costs" that, if unchecked, can begin to put a real crimp in your lifestyle or drag down the earnings from your "real" investments.

You might wind up being one of the few who is good enough to truly create alpha with a Country Club Gambler's strategy. But until you convince yourself that you're good enough to really become a serious investor, I encourage you to allocate only a small portion of your net worth to this strategy. By doing so, you'll get all the mental stimulation, adrenaline, and stories that go with investing, but if things go wrong, the pain you suffer isn't that severe.

Sometimes country club investments do, in fact, pay off and turn into serious alpha-generating investment strategies. This is exactly what happened to me. After nearly a decade in the investment business, I started out investing in alternative investment funds very slowly. But unlike many investors in the Enchanted Forest, I didn't sit back and wait for magic to strike. I did my homework nights and weekends. For nearly seven years, I ran a small experimental partnership before my family and I had the confidence to add alternative investments to our core strategy. Since then, we have learned a lot and been pleased with the results. We have built the Four A's, and our investment results have improved considerably, but now I am nervous all the time about what can go wrong!

The Secret Society

"The Secret Society" (not to be confused with some fraternity or elite military organization) is a domain for those who have figured out how to add value ("positive alpha") to investment assets. It is the world of hedge funds, private equity funds, concentrated actively managed mutual funds, and opportunistic real estate professionals *that outperform standard investments*. It is also the world of skilled business owners and people who leverage their careers to great business and financial advantage. E. A. Stuart and his son E. H. were bona fide members of the Secret Society, even though neither of them ever bought a stock. Finally, it is a world that is widely speculated about in the pages of business and finance magazines because most of its players like to keep low profiles and actively avoid the press. Notoriety, and the copycats that come with it, often works to their detriment. The last thing they want is more competition.

In the domain of the Secret Society, inhabitants have learned how to consistently add value through good investment performance. Their return on investments exceeds expectations relative to an index for the market. An investor is able to create this so-called "positive alpha" by identifying and extracting value from individual companies or securities, or by choosing other professionals who have this skill. This is a rare and highly refined wealth management competence. Those who do it well have highly developed instincts. They also have deep investment expertise and resources to measure investment performance.

You might think that if you could see into the Secret Society, it would be filled with euphoria and hubris. After all, these are people who have made it big with their investments, right? This isn't the case. Most of the residents of the Secret Society are on edge. They are driven investors and wealth advisors who are aggressively looking for new opportunities. At the same time, they are defensive, even a bit paranoid. Although personalities run the gamut, most residents of the Secret Society are surprisingly modest and very self-assured, a rare but useful combination.

Those who operate in the investment world of the Secret Society display other unusual investment traits. For example, they are always looking for what is wrong with their investment perspective. George Soros, one of the great hedge fund investors and manager of the Quantum Fund, puts it this way: "By and large, I found managing a hedge fund extremely painful. I could never acknowledge my success, because that might stop me from worrying, but I had no trouble recognizing my mistakes."[5] How many advisors whom you run across think like that?

Secret Society investors are also constantly on the hunt for what's wrong with other people's perspectives and for ways to take advantage of those misperceptions. Remember that alpha is a zero-sum game. To create alpha, you have to take it from someone else. No one willingly gives away alpha in a market economy.

Most of the strategies that create alpha are sophisticated and involve complex analysis and (sometimes) execution. The plans devised in the Secret Society are highly confidential, customized, and sometimes proprietary. They're hard to replicate, and they usually command high fees. Investors and advisors who operate in the Secret Society recognize that they are in privileged company and that too much public recognition of how they make money will actually make it more difficult for them to continue producing stellar investment results.

As such, there is no formal entrance to the Secret Society. Sometimes investors arrive in this investment world but don't know it. More often, people think they've arrived but really haven't. The signs of entry are elusive, subtle, and, at times, contradictory. There are a lot of imposters (both advisors and investors) who claim to have discovered a secret doorway into the Secret Society, but they're often fooling themselves and others. Most imposters take excessive risk and then are lucky for a time. They call their good performance alpha when it's not. When their luck runs out, the extra risk causes the investments to fall more violently. Therefore, the cost of thinking you're in the Secret Society when you're really not can be very high. That's why it's important for travelers looking for an entry into the Secret Society to possess highly developed wealth management skills, instincts, and resources—and to pick their advisors extremely carefully.

Most private and institutional investors who navigate the world of the Secret Society try to identify people like Soros who can create alpha for them. They look for money managers who have what it takes to add alpha to investments and who are looking for additional capital to manage. These investors ask prospective managers to discuss what they do in hopes of evaluating the depth of their investment expertise and whether they can add enough value to cover their fees and still return some of the benefit to the investor. It's a tough job, and it carries with it a lot of anxiety.

Besides shrewd investing, there are still other ways to enter the Secret Society. You can do it by leveraging your past career success and social prominence to pursue new business ventures or to start and build a new business. These aren't easy ways to gain entry to the Secret Society—and they certainly create anxiety. But some people are better suited to creating wealth in these ways than through shrewd investing. You be the judge of what might be best for you!

The Capital Kibbutz

Finally, after the Enchanted Forest and the Secret Society, there's a world of investing I call "the Capital Kibbutz."

A kibbutz is a form of communal living, practiced in Israel, in which everyone in the community shares in the risks, contributes to the resources, and shares the wealth that comes to that community. There are also kibbutz-like communities in many other parts of the world, including the U.S.

The Capital Kibbutz is an investment zone in which everyone who participates shares in the rewards and risks of investment together. It is populated by institutions and individual advisors who help clients who want to participate in the growth of the global economy but who recognize that they don't have sufficient proprietary expertise or resources to engage in Active Alpha Investing. It thus provides the perfect sanctuary for these investors.

For all practical purposes, the Capital Kibbutz is the world of indexed mutual funds, exchange traded funds, and term life insurance. It is a rather safe and tame investment world—one where the investor is taken care of but in which the investor rarely if ever gets a chance to take big risks.

To operate effectively in this world, you don't need to compete against institutions with highly developed competencies to extract alpha from the market. You don't need to think about which securities are cheap or expensive, and you don't buy or sell much. Most of the time, you sit passively and let the economy work for you. For these reasons, the costs of market participation are quite low.

In the Capital Kibbutz, clients don't have to make many decisions. There isn't much opportunity to make big mistakes, and there is little incentive to abuse the system. Therefore, clients need to exercise a lower level of vigilance to responsibly protect their own interests. Clients have time available to pursue interests other than investing and can sleep well at night. In the Capital Kibbutz, investments don't earn the kind of returns that one experiences in the Secret Society, but so long as the economy performs relatively well, the ordinary investor earns a better return than in the Enchanted Forest.

Occasionally, there's an innovation in the Capital Kibbutz that every-one can share in. The growing interest in indexing by individuals has led some firms to create new tax-managed, index-linked products that try to add a little value to indices. Whatever "value added" is realized, however, comes not from advisors being better stock pickers, but from advisors managing their clients' taxes very efficiently. They do this by selling stocks that generate losses while letting the gains of others keep growing unrealized (and untaxed).

Meanwhile, "harvested" losses can be used to offset gains and make a portfolio even more tax efficient than a standard index fund would be. The added turnover from realizing losses does cause a portfolio's perfor-mance to diverge slightly from the index, but not much. Sometimes, this divergence is slightly additive, whereas other times it detracts slightly. But with improved tax efficiency, some Capital Kibbutz firms are able to generate alpha after tax, and they can do so with reasonably high probability. I include this kind of strategy in the domain of the Capital

Kibbutz because even though it is a little more complicated than standard indexing or mutual funds, the investor's goal is still to participate broadly in financial markets.

As a wealth advisor, I encourage my friends, clients, and colleagues to thoroughly explore the world of the Capital Kibbutz because it is a relatively safe investment harbor. Even though many people have tremendous ambitions for their wealth, most affluent and wealthy individuals, families, and institutions simply don't possess enough wealth management expertise and resources to operate in the Secret Society. What's more, the Capital Kibbutz is a wonderful place to get one's feet wet, investment-wise. You can operate with a safety net so that you're never financially overleveraged or locked into a high-risk investment strategy with only slight chances of yielding big returns.

A Travelogue: Helping a Friend Get Out of the Enchanted Forest and Into the Secret Society

Some years ago, a friend who had been wandering around the Enchanted Forest—and had ended up being attacked by bandits and then a bear—came to me for help. He is a smart businessman, but like most smart businessmen, he didn't understand the financial world. He had been sold a large number of specialized high-fee products in the mid-1990s. The general rise of the financial markets had hidden the wealth transfer that was taking place from him to his advisor. But this client was diligent enough to measure what was going on and to eventually recognize that things were not going according to his plans.

When he came to me, I recognized that trying to get him into the Secret Society right away was not a wise choice. He had become disenchanted with the Enchanted Forest and wanted out fast! Before he could enter the Secret Society, I needed to help him acquire a more thorough education about wealth management, and this would require time. I also needed to earn his trust and understand his responses to the volatility of financial markets and to the inevitable periods of underperformance that even the best investors have.

What did I do? I recommended that he leave the Enchanted Forest and enter the Capital Kibbutz. This would give him time to regroup and give us time to build a strong foundation for our professional relationship. He made this move more than ten years ago by selling most of his high-fee, actively managed investment assets and moving them into index funds. We moved immediately from a largely equity portfolio to one that had a more balanced blend of global stocks, bonds, and cash. We then began an education program and built a better performance measurement system.

Within a couple of years, he was ready to consider additional asset classes and the occasional opportunity to invest with an active manager. Over time, we have supplemented his indexed portfolio with well-chosen, actively managed accounts.

My friend started, owns, and runs a business that has considerable assets in real estate and collectibles, as well as significant cash flow—three good diversifiers. We periodically discuss the risk and return profile of his entire economic engine: his career, the business, and how they complement the risk and return profile of the investment portfolio. We have integrated the three elements of his economic engine with his leakage management and family purpose, executing a holistic strategy for his entire family enterprise.

Over the course of the past 12 years, my friend has tasted the Secret Society, but he still retains a firm foothold in the Capital Kibbutz. With time, his education has improved and opportunities to create alpha have presented themselves. His confidence that he can distinguish between the Enchanted Forest and the Secret Society has grown as well, ensuring a more secure position in the Secret Society.

Mutual Fund Indexing: Why It's the Investment Path for Most Individuals

When push comes to shove, investing well is tough. For that reason, it's probably best that most investors limit their investment ambitions to the world of the Capital Kibbutz. And there's nothing wrong with that.

Of all the investment instruments available to investors in the Capital Kibbutz, there is one that is ideal for most investors to consider using. It's not a glamorous, exciting solution. It doesn't mirror the bold impetuosity of the Country Club Gambler. Nor does it embody the secrecy and mystery of the Secret Society. Even the term to define it isn't terribly compelling. But it is truly the best way for most investors to go. It's called "indexing."

Briefly stated, indexing involves investing in a statistical composite of securities that mimics the characteristics of an entire investment market or asset class, such as the S&P 500, the Russell 3000, or the MSCI All-Country World Index.

Because most index funds contain a broad and representative cross section of desirable financial markets, there's no portfolio manager trying to improve performance by buying or selling individual securities. For that reason, most of the well-designed indices create very little in the way of investment fees, brokerage commissions, or capital gains taxes—at least until the index itself is sold.

So, should you pin your wealth management strategy on the effective use of index funds? Consider this: Trillions of dollars of professionally managed retirement assets are invested in passive indexed investments, and this number has been growing quickly over the past 20 years.

Corporations know the value of indexing. In the past 20 years, most large pension plans have gone from having dozens of portfolio managers with various risk strategies to having a core stock portfolio that is indexed to a broad market benchmark.

What's more, there's broad agreement that indexing makes sense for a wide variety of investors.

"Most investors, both institutional and individual, will find that the best way to own common stocks is through an index fund that charges minimal fees. Those following this path are sure to beat the net results (after fees and expenses) delivered by the great majority of investment professionals," notes Warren Buffett, Chairman of Berkshire Hathaway, and considered by many people to be the world's most astute investor.[6]

There are a couple of things worth noting about this quote. First, Buffett talks here about most, not all, investors. He recognizes that a few investors—and he is one of them—do belong to the Secret Society. There just aren't a lot of people like him. Second, he states that both institutions and individuals will benefit from indexing, even though institutions have far greater clout in the marketplace.

Despite Buffett's advice, individual clients have been surprisingly slow to embrace indexing. It's hard to understand why. After all, most individual investors don't have the expertise to build the Four A's needed for Active Alpha Investing. What's more, the case for indexing is actually stronger for individuals than it is for institutions for two reasons:

1. Indexing is tax efficient relative to active management. This can save taxable investors a lot of money, but is of no benefit to pension plans or endowments.

2. Although most private investors can't compete with institutions for access to the best active managers, they do have access to the same indexed products as institutional investors do at almost the same cost. Indeed, for index products the fee differential between institutions and individuals is a mere .2% or less. By contrast, the fee differential (between individual investors and institutions) in actively managed products is often a half a percent per year or more.

Indexing really is the way most individual investors should go. It might not be the most exciting route to take, but it can bring with it predictable and consistent investment returns. In Chapter 6, "Picking Your Investment Strategy," I'll have recommendations for you on how to index successfully, as well as ideas you can use to explore the worlds of the Enchanted Forest and the Secret Society, if you wish.

A New Perspective on the Wealth Management Industry

The financial-services world is a world in transition. Distinct lines separating mutual fund companies, brokers, bankers, life insurers, and trust companies no longer exist. For the past 15 years or so, all of these business models have been on a path to convergence. Today, you can buy mutual funds in a trust, you can get brokerage services from the same company that manages your mutual funds, and your broker most likely has a trust company. Life insurance and annuity products look a lot like mutual funds. Banks do a lot more than lend money. Hedge funds have become regulated. Private equity has gone public. This blurring just adds to the complexity of the industry and confusion around the merits of the ever-growing array of products you can buy.

Open architecture is also here to stay. Traditional stock and bond portfolios have been sliced and diced in infinite ways. Alternative investments such as venture capital and hedge funds are becoming more elaborate and more accessible every day. The administration of wealth management businesses is also becoming more complicated, as previously distinct financial industries merge and we have to deal with the realities of terrorism and globalization.

All this change continues to complicate the work of financial advisors. Fifteen years ago, you could make a good living advising people about stocks and bonds, maybe in a mutual fund, maybe in a trust, maybe in a brokerage account. Today, financial advisors have a hard time just keeping up with all the products available to their clients. Everyone is asking about hedge funds, commodity trading, venture capital, and timber. On top of that, financial advisors now have many new regulatory requirements. The Patriot Act, passed by Congress in the wake of 9/11, mandates that financial advisors comply with numerous new "know your customer" provisions, which adds significant administrative responsibilities to an already staggering amount of mandatory paperwork. In the wake of the Financial Crisis, Congress passed the Dodd-Frank Wall Street Reform and Consumer Protection Act, which adds additional regulation to financial advisors and requires all hedge funds and even some family offices to register with the SEC. Finally, wealth advisors today face time pressures to achieve specific sales goals and have organizational obligations that further cut into their time to be active advisors to their clients.

Traveling the Investment Landscape

As an investor, you need not visit only one investment world because, depending on your investment skills and interests, you can achieve investment success in any of the places I've just described.

If you tire of the safety of the Capital Kibbutz, or the pressure of the Secret Society, or the costs associated with the fun and excitement of the Enchanted Forest, you can move around.

If you are just getting started on a journey through the financial-services world, I recommend you start by visiting the Capital Kibbutz. It is by far the easiest investment world to figure out, and it won't cost you much to learn from your mistakes. You can also establish a solid benchmark of success from which to determine the potential "value-added" profits that can come from increased complexity and fees as you navigate the other investment worlds.

You are less likely to get lost or confused in the Capital Kibbutz than in the Secret Society or the Enchanted Forest. If you establish a strong base there, you can travel to the other worlds with only a small part of your financial assets to see how much you like the experience. If you enjoy the complexity of the Secret Society and you possess the skills to navigate your way successfully there, you can shift your wealth management objectives to pursue more aggressive, growth-driven financial goals. On the other hand, if you are by nature entrepreneurial and are willing to watch your back a bit, exploring the world of the Enchanted Forest might be more to your liking and a good foray away from the safety and predictability of the Capital Kibbutz—with its focus on broad market participation and indexing. Just keep one thought in mind if you go into the forest: Keep your eye out for bulls. And beware of lions, tigers, and especially bears!

Conclusion

Now that you've learned a little bit about the three worlds described in this chapter, ask yourself: Which is the best match for me?

This chapter has focused extensively on the nature of the wealth management industry today and on the importance of matching your investment skill set (the Four A's) with an appropriate strategy. I have discussed the relative merits of open architecture and mutual funds, indexing and alternative investing, brokerage and trust companies. I've also introduced you to "the Capital Kibbutz," "the Secret Society," and "the Enchanted Forest" in hopes that you can see more clearly where you should reside.

In upcoming chapters, we'll explore specifically what you should do to develop your investment prowess so that you can truly understand your options and successfully execute your chosen wealth management strategy to meet your needs and those of your family. The course you embark on will depend, of course, on where you see yourself positioned in the wealth management industry at this particular moment.

Before we proceed to the next chapter, answer the review and discussion questions I've put at the end of this chapter, because they will help you put your thoughts in order for what's coming up next.

Chapter 5: Issues to Discuss with Your Family

1. How knowledgeable are you about investing? How hard do you want to work to become more knowledgeable?

2. Do you have that rare personality type that is suited for the Secret Society? Do you enjoy the thrill of the Enchanted Forest even if it is likely to cost you? Will you grow impatient with the Capital Kibbutz? Where are you now?

3. Does your wealth management competence match your investment strategy? If there's a mismatch, where is it?

4. To what extent do you "put yourself in the hands" of your investment advisor(s) rather than take charge of meetings with investment advisors? Do you trust your advisor because of his or her skill or because of his or her character?

5. Does your advisor's competence match the strategy he or she is recommending to you? What specifically are the value-added services that your current wealth management firm claims it provides to you? Can you describe the specific services you receive?

6. Can you measure the value of your advisor's advice?

7. What makes you think that your advisor's investment advice is significantly better than average? Are you getting that advisor's best advice? That advisor's firm's best advice?

8. Do you have enough wealth to compete effectively in the world of alternative investments?

9. Are you pleased with the rate of return you are currently realizing on your investments? Do you know what it is?

10. To what extent are you aware of the fees, taxes, and administrative expenses that you pay as a percentage of your investment profits? Do you know the dollar value of what you paid last year in fees, taxes, and expenses? Can you estimate what these expenses are?

11. Do you currently use index funds? If so, what has been your experience with them? Are you interested in combining them with other kinds of investments? If not, why not?

---

12. What has been your overall experience with investment advisors or financial consultants? Is it generally positive or not? If not, what was lacking for you in the relationship? Be specific.

13. What are your future investment and wealth management goals? Please be specific.

Endnotes

1. Bogle Financial Markets Research Center, "As the Index Fund Moves from Heresy to Dogma...What More Do We Need to Know?" Remarks by John C. Bogle, April 13, 2004, www.vanguard.com/bogle_site/sp20040413.html. *The 2004 Mutual Fund Fact Book,* published by the Investment Company Institute, and ICI's *2012 Investment Company Fact Book, 52nd Edition. Financial Analysts Journal,* January/February 2005, "The Mutual Fund Industry 60 Years Later: For Better or Worse?" by John C. Bogle.

2. *Investment News,* "The 100 Largest Mutual Fund Families," August 16, 2011.

3. DALBAR, Inc., Quantitative Analysis of Investor Behavior (QAIB) Study, 2012.

4. "Tax-Efficient Investing Is Easier Said Than Done," by Robert H. Jeffrey, *The Journal of Wealth Management,* Summer 2001.

5. The Crisis of Global Capitalism, by George Soros, Public Affairs Press, 1998, page 24.

6. Berkshire Hathaway Inc., 1996 Annual Report, Chairman's Letter to Shareholders.

6

Picking Your Investment Strategy

"To a very large extent, of course, we associate truth with convenience—with what most closely accords with self-interest and individual well-being or promises best to avoid awkward effort or unwelcome dislocation of life. We also find highly acceptable what contributes most to self-esteem."

—John Kenneth Galbraith

Picking an investment strategy and sticking with it through market ups and downs is essential to your long-term financial health. Over the past 15 years, we have had more than our fair share of ups and downs in the equities, home prices, commodities, and many other investable assets. Choosing your strategy is the single most important financial decision you will make! Like any long-term decision, it requires careful consideration. This chapter describes three options for constructing an investment strategy, each of which has specific benefits and requires specific actions on your part to implement.

Three Value-Added Financial Strategies for Managing Wealth

The investment strategy you choose will be based on how aggressively you want to grow your wealth, how much time and skill you're willing to allocate to managing your wealth, and your actual net worth. These are the value-added financial strategies for managing wealth:

- Index Investing

- Barbell Investing

- Active Alpha Investing

Strategy #1: Index Investing

I introduced indexing when I talked about the Capital Kibbutz in the preceding chapter. Indexing is the act of investing in a total financial market (i.e., the U.S. stock market, international stocks, or the U.S. bond market), rather than trying to select specific securities within that market in the hope that they will grow faster than the market as a whole.

I often recommend indexing because it is a proven method to secure a long-term annual rate of return of 4% to 7% on your financial assets, as long as you carefully control investment-related costs and manage your risk. Adopting this approach puts you squarely in the investment world of the Capital Kibbutz. The actual rate of return you achieve, whether higher or lower, depends entirely on your asset mix and on how well financial markets perform. But, regardless of the investment environment at any point in time, study after study concludes that if you index, you are likely to end up with more money in your pocket than most people who choose more aggressive and time-consuming investment strategies. This conclusion applies whether your account is taxable or is held in a tax-deferred retirement plan.

How Do You Implement an Index Investing Strategy?

Implementing an Index Investing strategy is quite simple and involves four critical success factors (CSFs) that are essential to success:

CSF #1: Strategic Asset Allocation

CSF #2: Index Selection

CSF #3: Tax Management

CSF #4: Rebalancing

The good news with indexing is that you have to deal with each of these factors only once, after which you can institute a process that puts the entire management of your assets on autopilot. I still recommend that you review your strategy once a year, but interim decisions can be formulaic. Your annual performance review is focused more on ensuring that everything is on track than on making additional strategic decisions.

Let's briefly discuss the four CSFs in the context of an indexing strategy.

CSF #1: Strategic Asset Allocation

With indexing, strategically allocating your assets to different investment funds or pools is a long-term decision—one that might last unchanged for years or decades. Allocation is driven by a desire to optimize the return you expect to achieve for the amount of volatility that you feel you can withstand in your portfolio. In any diversified investment strategy, including indexing, you must invest in a blend of asset classes, each of which responds somewhat differently to economic stimuli.

For example, stocks, bonds, real estate, and commodities all tend to react somewhat differently to combinations of real economic growth, inflation, and interest rates. Emerging market stocks respond differently from large-capitalization U.S. stocks. The stocks of energy companies respond differently from those of healthcare companies, and both respond differently to economics and demographics than automobile or paper companies do.

Optimizing a strategic asset allocation is something that wealth management firms do reasonably well. Most advisors who work for these companies have the training to help you determine the strategic asset allocation that's right for you.

It is my belief that everybody who pursues an Index Investment strategy should be well diversified. They should invest in most or all of the following asset classes: U.S. stocks, international and emerging markets stocks, commodities (especially energy-related) investments, real estate–related investments, high-quality U.S. bonds (either taxable or tax exempt), high-quality foreign bonds, and high-yield bonds. None of these asset classes should exceed 40% of your exposure. For example, someone willing to take reasonable risk might have a strategic allocation target that looks like this:

- U.S. stocks: 30%

- International/emerging stocks: 30%

- Commodities-focused: 7%

- Real estate–specific: 8%

- High-quality U.S. bonds: 15%

- High-quality foreign bonds: 5%

- High-yield bonds: 3%

- Cash: 2%

CSF #2: Index Selection

In the past five years, there has been a rapid proliferation of indexing choices. There are traditional index mutual funds and exchange traded funds (ETFs), some named after creepy animals such as SPDRs (spiders) and VIPERs, that own the underlying securities in the index. Index managers can also buy options and futures on indices that can be used to create "synthetic" index funds. Synthetic funds are index funds made up of derivative securities and cash—not actual underlying stocks and bonds. The number of traditional and synthetic index funds that mimic a wide range of indices has proliferated in the past ten years.

Given what's available in the market, what would I own? As background, remember that I have a long-term time horizon and am comfortable with volatility. I also own a business and have a career that provides additional cash flow. Here's an example of an asset allocation invested exclusively in index products that could work for someone like me:

- A total U.S. stock market index mutual fund (30%).

- An international stock market index mutual fund (including emerging markets) (30%).

- Instead of separate U.S. and international funds, you can buy one "All Country World Index" (60%).

- A total U.S. bond market index fund, including high-yield bonds (18%).[1]

- A foreign bond market index fund (5%).

- A money market fund or bank account (2%).

- A commodity ETF with an emphasis on energy (7%).

- A REIT (Real Estate Investment Trust) index fund (8%).

I buy only "no load" mutual funds and recommend that you do the same because the costs are lower. It reduces the universe of mutual funds you can buy and therefore makes choice easier.

CSF #3: Tax Management

By its nature, an Index Investment strategy is the most tax-efficient investment strategy around.

A broad U.S. equity index fund has roughly 5% turnover in a year, mostly caused by merger and acquisition activity, so that the typical stock is held within the fund for nearly 20 years! Over most 20-year periods, stocks generate a lot of gains and, as long as they aren't sold, the gains aren't taxed. This is a valuable characteristic of some, but not all, index funds. Generally speaking, the more broadly diversified the fund, the lower the turnover.

By contrast, a very low-turnover, actively managed fund buys and sells each stock in its portfolio about every four years, and the average mutual fund "turns over" once a year. Such rapid turnover means that your gains are taxed much more frequently and sometimes at higher rates. Not only does high turnover add tax cost, but it also adds transaction costs, another reason to lean toward indexing.

CSF #4: Rebalancing

I recommend you periodically rebalance your fund positions so that their weightings remain consistent with your strategic asset allocation objectives. The fund mix can get out of balance when one or more of your funds does especially well or comparatively poorly relative to the other funds. Whenever any of your funds differs from its strategic allocation target by 15% or more, it is time to rebalance. For instance, if your U.S. stock exposure rises from 30% to 35% (a 17% increase), I would rebalance the exposure at least halfway back to 30%. If your exposure to commodity-related assets drops to 5% from 7% (a 29% drop), add assets to bring it back toward 7%.

The best way to rebalance your portfolio is to use your cash flow rather than selling an investment (which incurs taxes and transaction costs). For instance, say you want to reduce your exposure to U.S. stocks. If you are adding to your investments with cash flow, buy other asset classes first to bring the overall portfolio into balance relative to your strategic asset allocation target. If you are withdrawing capital from your investments for spending or to pay taxes, draw it first from stocks. That way you don't create taxable transactions simply for the sake of rebalancing. If you need to shift assets from one fund to another to get back into balance, minimize the amount of net gains you have to realize by first selling shares in those index funds that have the highest costs associated with them. Obviously, tax-efficient rebalancing is not an issue in tax-deferred accounts, but due to potential transaction costs, you still want to make changes as efficiently as possible.

Sometimes, an index fund with an average cost that is well below the current price includes some shares that you bought above the current price. If you sell those shares and account for them correctly, you can realize a loss and use it to offset gains you have realized elsewhere. This is called tax lot accounting and is another useful, simple tool of integrated wealth management.

Part of the beauty of a well-diversified portfolio is that individual asset classes perform well (and badly) at different times. Done systematically, rebalancing forces you to trim investments that have done well and add to those that haven't done so well in the recent past. Why do this? If an investment is going up, shouldn't you keep it?

In many cases, you'll want to keep high-performing investments because they are profitable. On the other hand, investors have a tendency to fall in love with their winners (that have gotten more expensive), and very few investments remain good investments forever. Investors also get frustrated and sell the ones that have declined in value (and become cheaper). Periodically rebalancing your portfolio forces you to engage in counterintuitive behavior that is usually beneficial to investing. It also reduces potential downside risk and ensures that you don't become overly dependent on a few investments that have appreciated a lot in value. This is what happened to many investors who had great exposure to high-flying growth stocks in March of 2000 and who saw their portfolios decline a lot over the next several years. Think of rebalancing in terms of what the skipper of a sailboat does to catch the wind on the ocean. He or she periodically trims the sails to remain in the wind's favor, stay on course, and continue on a steady and smooth path toward the ultimate destination.

Final Thoughts on Indexing

By choosing an indexing strategy, you'll reap long-term results better than most investors, assuming that the global economy continues to progress, as it has over the past 100 years. And you'll pay relatively modest taxes. This approach often outperforms more complicated investment strategies, whatever the economic and market environment looks like.

So, why don't wealth advisors push this approach more with clients? There are four reasons.

First, indexing isn't very profitable for the wealth management industry. As is often the case, Vanguard's Jack Bogle[2] said it best: "The problem faced by low-cost, no-load index funds is that, as I have often observed, '(almost) all the darn money goes to the investor!'"

A typical diversified U.S. stock or bond index fund[3] has annual costs of 0.25% or less. With this fee structure, an indexed portfolio of $10 million generates less than $25,000 in annual fees and expenses. A $1,000,000 portfolio generates about $2,500 dollars in fees. A $100,000 portfolio generates just $250 in fees. Furthermore, index funds have almost no transaction costs associated with them.

By contrast, the typical equity mutual fund can have management fees and expenses ten or more times those of low-cost equity index funds. Actively managed separate account fees can approach or even exceed the fees of active mutual funds. The extra $100,000, $10,000, or $1,000 you pay for the privilege of having your fund actively managed adds a lot to your investment firm's pockets. On top of management fees, actively managed funds typically have annual transaction costs of 1% to 2%. In short, actively managed funds are much more lucrative for advisors than are index funds!

Second, wealth advisors don't push indexing because low index fund fees generate less revenue for firms to spend on marketing. Profit margins are so low on index funds, that firms that offer them have little excess cash flow to spend on marketing. Yet these same firms have built trillion-dollar businesses simply by relying on sophisticated investors who understand the benefits of indexing to seek them out.

Third, indexing isn't nearly as interesting for advisors to talk about as the other two strategies that I'll be covering shortly. After you make the decision to index and set up a structure to do so, the investment decisions move to autopilot. For people who live and breathe the markets, "being on autopilot" with your investments isn't a very exciting place to be.

Fourth, if you select an indexing strategy, it sets a higher standard for any active manager that comes across your path and promises to deliver to you an above-average rate of return on your investments. By gaining experience in indexing, you will know what "average" means and will hold active managers to a higher standard. They will know that they have to beat indexing (maybe even on an after-tax basis) to gain your trust and your business. That is a tough performance hurdle.

All that said, if you absolutely must indulge the temptation to try something more "ambitious" than indexing, I suggest you do some research and then allocate no more than 10% to 15% of your assets to more complex strategies (outlined later in this chapter), and then see how you do over a three- to five-year period. If you're successful, then and only then add another 10% to 15% for several more years. This gives you time to experience different market conditions, sharpen your skills, and test your advisors.

Strategy #2: Barbell Investing

The Barbell Investing strategy is best for anyone with an economic engine—remember that key value driver in the Strategic Wealth Management Framework—that includes an operating business, careers, and/or the management of financial assets. By looking at Figure 6.1, you can see why this strategy references the weights that many of us use to keep fit. One end of the barbell represents the management of your financial assets, probably using the Index Investing strategy. The counterweight is the energy and capital you have tied up in your career, a family business, or a new business enterprise. Holding the two weights firmly together is sound cash flow management. Many people who engage in Barbell Investing maintain a high savings rate. For periods of time, others rely on investment income to support their business when it is in a start-up phase, but then revert to a high savings rate when the business is stable.

More mature businesses throw off excess cash, which can be used to feed the growth and diversification of financial assets.

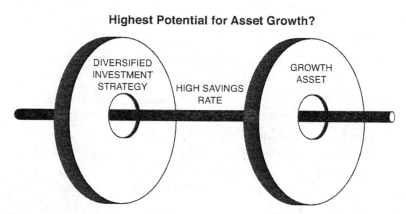

Figure 6.1 Can you handle the weight and keep the barbell balanced? If so, it's a ticket to the Secret Society.

Barbells are heavy and need to be balanced. The left-hand weight might have some or most of your assets but require only a modest amount of your time to manage. This leaves you free to focus most of your time on the right-hand weight. The right mix of time and assets on each side of the barbell keeps the weights in balance.

You will be working hard to manage the barbell. It is the most likely way for non-investment experts to gain access to the Secret Society because they leverage their skills, past business experience, and relationships to keep building wealth, yet they are also diversified in the face of an uncertain future.

The level of diversification you choose is highly subjective. A small number of family businesses are truly built for the ages. If you are fortunate to own one of these, you can be prudent in adopting a lower level of diversification than you would otherwise. This can make sense both to enhance long-term growth and to defer tax payments. Plus continued business ownership can enhance the family's sense of purpose.

Some careers are risky and volatile and others are stable. The more risk you take in your career, the less you should probably take in your investments, and vice versa. Just remember that almost no one gets rich managing a diversified portfolio. Diversification is more valuable as a safeguard of wealth than as a means for getting rich.

What Can You Expect with a Barbell Investing Strategy?

The Barbell Investing strategy represents a powerful approach to wealth preservation and wealth building because it encourages you to keep working. Because you are (probably) earning compensation while you are building your career or business, your financial assets keep growing without a drag from spending. This bolsters financial security and clears the way for you to take modestly greater risks with your investments. This, in turn, can help you earn more from those investments and enjoy more discretionary income in the future. This is a virtuous cycle if you can make it work. It means you can embrace a growth-driven financial goal instead of being forced to opt for a distribution-driven goal. As you now know, there's a quantum difference between the two! On the other hand, if you take entrepreneurial risk and the business fails (which businesses often do), you can rest assured that your financial assets will be there when you really need them.

Figure 6.2 shows the annualized rate of return you might achieve if you use a Barbell Investing strategy that invests 80% of your assets in index funds and 20% in a concentrated growth asset over a ten-year period. This might be the typical circumstance of a business owner or executive who has had a liquidity event but has gotten back in the game of business building. In this instance, there is no rebalancing between the two sides of the barbell over the entire ten-year period. The left vertical column shows various likely rates of return from the index funds; the top horizontal row shows the possible rates of return from the concentrated growth asset.

The shaded areas show those combinations of returns that will position you solidly in the Secret Society, even though most of your assets are indexed. For example, let us say that you earn 7% per year for ten years on the assets that are indexed. You also allocated 20% of your assets to a business at the beginning of the decade. The business was successful and its value grew at a rate of 20% per year for ten years. At the end of the decade, your combined assets have grown at a rate of 10.9% per annum, almost tripling in value and deferring a lot of tax.

Barbell Strategy: Annualized Rate of Return (ROR) Over Ten Years

		ROR Growth Assets (20%)				
		−100%	0%	10%	20%	30%
ROR Indexed Assets (80%)	6%	3.7%	5.0%	6.9%	10.3%	15.4%
	7%	4.6%	5.9%	7.7%	10.9%	15.8%
	8%	5.6%	6.8%	8.4%	11.5%	16.2%

ROR Blended Assets (100%)

Figure 6.2 Following the Barbell Investing strategy can achieve well-above-average rates of return while keeping your wealth prudently diversified.

Let's look at the two extreme examples of potential results that are represented within this chart.

Worst-Case: If you invest 20% of your assets in a growth asset that turns out to be a total write-off (−100%) after a decade's work and your return on indexed assets is 6% per annum over the same period, your combined assets will still have a positive return of 3.7% before leakages, if any, are taken into account. This is because you've been prudent about the amount of capital (20%) you committed to the risky venture, because you didn't dip into savings to cover your living expenses, and because the conservatively invested "indexed" portion (80%) of the barbell generated enough return to make up the loss.

Best-Case: If your indexed assets generate an 8% return per annum and your growth asset generates a 30% annualized rate of return, after ten years (before any leakages), you will have generated a 16.2% rate of return on your combined assets. What the chart doesn't show is that even with solid results from indexing, after ten years of compounding, your growth asset constitutes 57% of your total portfolio, up from 20%. You are really growing your wealth quickly and deferring a lot of tax, though you are running a larger and larger risk by owning a single concentrated asset. At this point, you should consider trimming some of your concentrated assets or declaring a dividend, and investing the proceeds on the other side of the barbell to keep things in balance. This isn't the right solution for every business, every career, or every person. But for many concentrated positions, especially those that are highly leveraged or susceptible to competitive, legislative, or technological threats, risk diversification to protect your capital makes sense.

Critical Success Factors for the Barbell Investing Strategy

To implement a Barbell Investing strategy, there are three CSFs. You must do the following:

> CSF #1: Target the right growth asset.
>
> CSF #2: Select the percentage of assets to put toward your growth asset.
>
> CSF #3: Adjust the strategic asset allocation of your diversified investments to account for your concentrated growth asset.

CSF #1: Target the Right Growth Asset

For your allocation to the "growth" side of the equation, you have to think deeply about the long-term sustainability of the business you have, or, if you've already had a liquidity event, decide what type of new business to target. You could do one of the following:

- **Start, Buy, or Control a Company**

  Some people manage to have significant liquidity events through refinancing, dividends, or partial sales, while still controlling a profitable company. This is a great opportunity for those who can pull it off. They get diversification and continue to oversee a business they know very well. They know their employees, customers, suppliers, and competitors. They know the pricing structure of the industry and understand the regulations. Their "guts" are well attuned to the issues of the business.

  Many wealthy people cannot engineer such a low-risk Barbell Investing strategy. After a liquidity event, they need to acquire or start a new business. In making new acquisitions, the further you get away from your field of expertise, the greater the risks. Most people who make the transition from one industry to another for the first time underestimate how difficult the transition is. You obviously want a business that has potential, but you also want to accurately calibrate your level of competence to evaluate and manage new ventures. It helps to stick with what you know.

One harmful pattern that I see regularly repeated is the successful business executive turned angel investor. Even business executives with substantial experience in acquisitions often discover (painfully) that their existing skill set and that of a successful financier are different. It is a much tougher transition than you expect.

■ Extend Your Career

If you have built a lucrative career, you might not have to invest any capital to build a growth asset (like a business) that substantially increases your net worth. Many people extend their careers beyond liquidity events by staying with their company after it is sold or by switching to another company. By working in a corporate environment, they earn stock options, restricted stock, and other forms of long-term compensation that defer tax and can grow significantly in value without putting up any capital at all.

Most lawyers, doctors, social workers, and teachers do great work, serve others, and never have a liquidity event. The savers among them keep putting a significant portion of their earnings aside each year, manage these savings responsibly, and watch their assets grow. The longer they stay in their career, the greater their opportunity to channel their earnings into savings and the longer those savings grow without being tapped for spending and monthly expenses.

If you love what you do, keep working into your sixties, seventies, or eighties. Do it for enjoyment and the extra income. Want more free time? Don't retire! Just scale back the hours you devote to paid work and begin to tap into your savings to make up the difference. You'll be happier, and from a financial planning standpoint, you'll be better off too.

The key to choosing the right growth asset is to take advantage of your skills, experience, judgment, personal contacts, and professional network to identify attractive opportunities to pursue. The "next act of your life" might very well focus on something that you enjoy with a passion, that you know a lot about, that leverages your expertise, that enables you to generate income, and that reduces your reliance on unearned income.

CSF #2: Select the Percentage of Assets to Put Toward Your Growth Asset

A key distinction of being wealthy is that you can afford to take bigger financial risks than most people can. A person with $100 million in assets, for example, can afford to put a larger percentage of their assets "at risk" without jeopardizing their financial security than a person who has accumulated $1 million in assets.

Still, the riskier the business venture you want to undertake, the less capital—as a percentage of your total wealth—you should put toward it regardless of the size of your assets. You might have a great idea for a new product or service, or want to launch a biotech start-up to create new drugs. But if that venture fails and you've invested all your disposable assets in that initiative, you won't be in a position to try again.

So, what should you do? If you feel comfortable allocating 20% of your wealth to the high-potential return side of your barbell, and your risky business idea has only a one in four chance of succeeding, consider allocating just 5% of your wealth to this particular venture. That way, if your venture fails, you will still have capital left over to try again—to take more "bites of the apple" through other endeavors—without depleting your total assets.

You should also consider your age when addressing this CSF. If you invest a large amount of your wealth in a new business in your late forties or older, it might be tough to recover financially if the business fails. You could find yourself living a more frugal retirement than you planned. However, the same situation in your thirties gives you several decades to rebuild your retirement nest egg.

Sidebar 6.1:   The Pros and Cons of Leverage

Almost everyone who has investable assets also has debt or some other form of financial leverage. Leverage can take the form of credit card debt and home mortgages, but it also includes taxes payable, debt in a company, margin loans, or derivative securities. When things are going well, leverage can be a wonderful thing. As the recent housing crisis painfully reminds us, during hard times leverage undermines net worth, forces untimely asset sales, and, worse, can increase the correlation between otherwise unrelated assets. A careful analysis of financial leverage on your personal balance sheet can improve returns or protect against a rapid decline in wealth caused by the spillover effects of excessive leverage.

The most dangerous form of debt you can have is "recourse debt" that can potentially lay claim to your entire estate. Recourse debt enables the lender to seize any or all of your assets if you don't meet the terms of your loan. Most personal loans, except mortgages, are recourse loans. If you get into an illiquidity crunch, you might be forced to sell your assets at distressed prices to meet payment terms. This risk is particularly acute when a family shareholder pledges stock in the company against a loan he ultimately can't repay. In so doing, he threatens family control of the business and the family's emotional fabric through his individual action. Multigenerational family businesses should write provisions into their constitutions, trusts, and other family documents that prohibit or severely limit the pledging of stock in the family business.

But even nonrecourse debt can have ripple effects. Nonrecourse debt, like first mortgages, has only specifically named collateral—like a house or a car. In a diversified investment portfolio, two asset classes—for example, private equity and real estate—can each have discreet, nonrecourse loans associated with them. Under normal circumstances, one asset class might remain steady in value when another declines. These assets are uncorrelated, an expected benefit of owning a properly diversified portfolio. However, if both are leveraged, a general move in interest rates could affect both assets similarly and simultaneously, increasing the correlation of otherwise uncorrelated asset classes.

Leverage in investment portfolios can also be hidden. If an investment manager buys stocks in highly leveraged companies, she adds leverage to a client's portfolio. But the client sees only a portfolio of stocks, not the debt and other leverage of the companies in the portfolio. If the manager is correct and the companies improve, their stocks will soar even though the combined value of the company's stock and debt (its enterprise value) increases just a little. But the reverse is true as well, adding considerable risk to the portfolio.

Modest amounts of the right kind of leverage can be attractive. Putting a million-dollar mortgage on your primary or secondary residence is very tax efficient because, at least today, you can deduct the interest expense from your taxes. Furthermore, mortgage interest rates are much more attractive than most other forms of consumer debt, and the debt is usually nonrecourse. I own a fixed-rate mortgage rather than an adjustable-rate mortgage because I want the security of knowing what my payment commitments will be.

As a general rule, I believe that the risks of leverage are substantial. Leverage can dramatically reduce your flexibility to respond, either defensively or opportunistically, to a stress environment. Excessive leverage can also set off a contagion effect that can run out of control and quickly destroy wealth that took decades to build. Periodically, hedge funds unravel because of contagion effects. But individuals can be wiped out, too. The country has suffered through a four-year housing bubble during which prices dropped by 30% or more practically everywhere, wiping out more than a trillion dollars of homeowner equity, resulting in record foreclosures and leaving many other "homeowners" (speculators or not) with mortgages exceeding the value of the home.

CSF #3: Adjust the Strategic Asset Allocation of Your Diversified Investments to Account for Your Concentrated Growth Asset

The side of your barbell that contains your strategic asset allocation is generally designed by wealth advisors with the assumption that you don't have any concentrated growth assets on the other side of your barbell. Therefore, if you still have a career or control a business, you need to adjust your asset allocation accordingly. For example, if in your business you accumulate real estate investment properties, you can use your properties to achieve your real estate asset allocation target, instead of REIT index funds. If you have a career in banking or the securities industry, you might want to consider reducing your exposure to stock market investments so that you don't experience losses in your investment portfolio at the same time your job is in jeopardy for precisely the same reasons. Finally, if you are in a job that isn't affected by economic downturns (you're an undertaker, dentist, or tax accountant, for example), your earned income stream is very stable and has "bondlike" characteristics. Consequently, you might feel comfortable with greater exposure to stocks.

Final Thoughts on Barbell Investing

Even if the scale of your wealth affords you the opportunity to devote yourself to investing full time, consider strongly whether you really want to do this. I've seen many people quit their careers to devote themselves to actively managing their portfolios only to find that they would have fared better if they had stayed focused on what they were good at and indexed the rest of their assets! Barbell Investing makes sense for people who are good at business, who have a family-controlled company, or who have successful careers in other areas.

Strategy #3: Active Alpha Investing

The words "active" (read, aggressive) and "alpha" (read, dominant) suggest a strategy that is all about Ferrari Testarossas. Active Alpha Investing involves integrating a diversified portfolio of traditional securities in relatively efficient markets like stocks and bonds with exciting, high-return potential alternative investments, such as private equity, venture capital, commodities, real estate, and hedge funds.

Most of the people who build such portfolios have bought the marketing hype and are thinking "Ferrari." Their goal is getting into the Secret Society, but they wind up instead in the Enchanted Forest. Indeed, for every 1,000 happy travelers to the Enchanted Forest, there might be just 200 people executing an Index Investing strategy in the Capital Kibbutz and only 150 people who add value through an Active Alpha Investing strategy.

Even then, the majority of Active Alpha seekers who succeed in their endeavors will beat the returns of those who employ an Index Investing strategy by only a small margin, despite enormous amounts of work.

Given these odds, Active Alpha investors have a steep hill to climb. Why then do so many make the attempt? Probably for the same reasons mountain climbers climb Mount Everest—for the challenge! Beating the odds is at the heart of the psyche of most private investors.

What Can You Expect with Active Alpha Investing?

If executed well, an Active Alpha Investment strategy has the long-term potential to generate an 8% to 12% annualized return in a variety of market and economic circumstances. The key is to achieve modestly above-average returns consistently over a long period.

The Lucas Family Uses the Active Alpha Investment Strategy

Almost 20 years ago, I convinced my family to undertake an Active Alpha Investment strategy that we still use today. It is similar to the strategy used by endowments of many leading educational institutions and a growing number of pension plans, though we have adapted it to account for our taxable status. After having extolled the virtues of an Index Investing strategy, why does my family stay dedicated to an Active Alpha Investment strategy? More than anything, it's due to these factors:

- We pursue a long-term, multigenerational wealth management approach.

- We have the financial resources to develop in-house expertise.

- We have a family culture that supports it.

- We have a talented team in place to execute it!

Our style is more like my father's 1965 Plymouth Valiant—steady, long term, and understated—rather than a Ferrari Testarossa, though both are red! We didn't exactly embrace this strategy overnight. In 1982, we started the Lucas family office with virtually no investment experience, but with two CEOs from highly respected investment firms as trusted advisors, service agreements with a blue-chip brokerage firm, and a well-respected trust bank.

Then, in 1988, after spending seven years as a financial professional investing OPM ("other people's money"), I established a partnership financed with a small amount of family money, a quarter of which was my own. Its purpose was to serve as a "laboratory" in which we could build our alternative investing competence, experiment with different asset mixes, and develop some core beliefs and best practices around successful Active Alpha Investing. The partnership performed well, and we learned a lot about alternative investments in the early years.

In 1994, I scrubbed and analyzed data on the core Lucas family asset base managed by the trust bank and found that we weren't even realizing returns achieved by the indices. At that point, with 13 years of investment experience and 6 years of experimenting with our "laboratory," I convinced the family to embrace an Active Alpha Investment strategy for managing our entire portfolio with the goal of achieving an annualized rate of return of 12.5% over a long period. After the decision was made, it took six more years to complete the big changes necessary to fully implement our new strategy.

In the past few years, our strategy has continued to evolve. There is more competition than ever in the alternatives space, and we needed more scale to effectively compete for access to managers and information. So in 2011 my firm, Wealth Strategist Partners, became a Registered Investment Advisor with the SEC and now acts as Chief Investment Officer not only to the Lucas Family but also to several other large family offices.

How to Implement Active Alpha Investing

Implementation of a successful Active Alpha Investing strategy depends on three critical success factors:

> CSF #1: Choose a strategic asset allocation based on the right mix of traditional and alternative investments.

> CSF #2: Build sustainable relationships with managers who add value net of fees and taxes.

> CSF #3: Make investment decisions based on opportunity, not process or capacity.

In addition to these CSFs, this strategy demands a foundation of family purpose to see through volatile markets throughout a multigenerational timeline, and a roof that provides effective leakage management (cost control). The schematic in Figure 6.3 represents this strategy well.

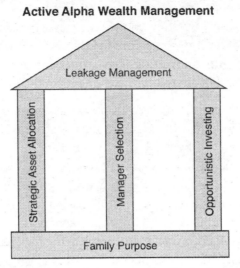

Figure 6.3 All the components need to be in place for the Active Alpha Investing strategy to work.

Assuming you have a solid roof over your head and a strong foundation on which to build your investment strategy, here are details on the three CSFs, weighted heavily toward the perspective that we continue to employ for my family and other clients at Wealth Strategist Partners.

CSF #1: Choose a Strategic Asset Allocation Based on the Right Mix of Traditional and Alternative Investments

You already know that traditional investments include stocks, bonds, and cash. But what is alternative investing?

Alternative investing is a catch-all term to describe just about every investment strategy or asset that is not a portfolio of stocks, bonds, or cash. It includes hedge funds as well as less efficient markets like private equity, venture capital, real estate, distressed debt investments, commodities, and emerging markets. Alternative investments generally provide useful diversification to stock and bond portfolios. However, performance results have been mixed.

If you ask people why they invest in alternative investments, most of them say they do it to achieve increased diversification and reduced volatility. But if you press, there's usually the expectation of generating better returns as a result of these investments. Given that these investments are usually illiquid and often entail more risk, an investor should expect additional return.

When you mix alternative and traditional asset classes, you obviously have a lot more choice than is available to indexing investors. The broad objective with Active Alpha Investing is no different than it is for an Index Investing strategy—to build a series of asset classes that, in combination, generate solid returns with acceptable volatility. For that reason, you might want to consider each of the following asset types if you are interested in embarking on an Active Alpha Investment approach.

Private Equity and Venture Capital

Private equity is, quite simply, equity capital invested in a private company. In some cases, the company can be worth billions of dollars when it is purchased. Often, these purchases are financed with a relatively small amount of equity and a large amount of debt. In other cases, private equity finances new companies or companies that are struggling to grow rapidly and are still generating losses. This type of private equity financing is called venture capital and it is usually 100% equity financed.

How wise is it for you to invest in private equity? Steven Kaplan, the Neubauer Family Distinguished Service Professor of Entrepreneurship and Finance at the University of Chicago, and two colleagues, Robert Harris from University of Virginia's Darden School and Tim Jenkinson from Oxford University, produced a paper that evaluates the performance of actual cash flows that went into private equity funds from 1984 to 2008 vintages and compared this to the performance of the same cash flows invested in the S&P 500. They concluded that private equity fund returns (net of fees) performed significantly better than the results achieved by the S&P 500 over the period of the study.[4] Right now, however, private companies are, on average, just as expensive than public ones so there is no guarantee that this average outperformance will persist.

Many people (and some statistics) suggest that private equity is a diversifying investment that lowers the risk of equity portfolios. I disagree.

Many portfolios of private equity investments have characteristics similar to public equities except that they are smaller companies, more heavily leveraged, and illiquid. These three characteristics make them riskier than public equities, more difficult to value, but not necessarily good diversifiers. Therefore, you should expect a significantly higher rate of return from private equities than from public ones, but not much diversification benefit.

Private equity managers charge high fees, usually 2% to 2.5% of committed capital per year. Plus, they take between 20% and 30% of the profits that they generate. Kaplan et al. say that the average private equity manager has added considerable performance relative to the index both before and after fees, but make no mistake that fees are hefty whether or not the fund outperforms for you. Kaplan and other academics have noticed other important characteristics of private equity performance. First, they have noted much wider dispersions of return around the averages than you might expect from a group of public equity portfolio managers. In other words, those managers in the best-performing quartile did much better than the averages, and they shared that added value with their clients. Conversely, managers in the bottom quartile did much worse, but they still got their management fees even if their clients got nothing.

In summary, the biggest risk with private equity isn't with the volatility of the asset class or its correlation to stocks. What's risky is doing a better job than most investors in choosing and being able to access the right managers!

The academics also draw another important conclusion. Their data show that, unlike in the public equity market, there is strong persistence of return in private equity investments, and returns improve with partnership experience. In other words, those managers who have performed well are likely to continue doing so in the future. This means that the small print that accompanies all advertising of the track records of traditional portfolio managers, "Past results are not an indicator of future performance," might not apply equally in the private equity world.

It's pretty tough for the private investor (and even "fund of funds" vehicles) to consistently gain access to top funds. Leading institutions have large budgets available to search out and hire attractive private equities managers, and they have many long-standing relationships with private equity and venture managers. They also talk with one another. So, if a respected chief investment officer finds an attractive first-quartile fund with available capacity, a few phone calls can quickly fill it up. This means that even if you identify top funds, you probably can't get consistent access to them unless you have a well-placed network and substantial assets to invest.

Hedge Funds

Hedge funds aren't really an asset class. They are lightly regulated pools of capital investing mostly in public securities that charge their investors a management fee plus a percentage of the profits generated by the investment strategies that they employ. Hedge funds invest in a wide array of asset classes, including but not limited to publicly traded stocks and bonds. Many hedge funds also sell assets short. Simplistically, this means they bet that such assets will decline in value. In other words, a hedge fund manager has the potential to make money on securities that are rising (longs) and on securities that are falling (shorts) at the same time. Of course, they can also lose money on both their longs and their shorts at the same time. Hedge funds have the ability to use leverage. A declining number also invest in less efficient private markets including private equity. The ones that do this have to compete against dedicated PE firms, plus it's harder for them to be nimble in changeable financial markets. Note that it will take longer for you to remove all of your capital from these types of hedge funds if you choose to withdraw.

The universe of hedge funds is reputed to include many that have "fat tails." This means that a hedge fund's strategies can work well for years, producing consistent returns with low volatility, and then suddenly unravel. Some combination of losing money on both longs and shorts at the same time coupled with illiquidity and leverage periodically causes hedge funds to "blow up." When a fund blows up, it can lose 50% of its value or more in a matter of months. Investments with "fat tails" are riskier than they appear on the surface.

Some hedge funds stick to one strategy all the time. Others shift strategies depending on where they see opportunities. Most hedge fund managers trade their portfolio aggressively, making them relatively tax inefficient. When they were first designed, the conceptual idea behind hedge funds was to use a combination of longs and shorts and varying strategies to hedge out, or reduce, the risk of investing while still participating in most of the upside. This is certainly a laudable goal, but not an easy one to execute. With the growth that has taken place in hedge fund assets over the past 15 years, it's hard to generalize anymore about their behavior. Some hedge funds have high risk but shoot for big gains; others aim for steady, stable returns. If you are going to use hedge funds, it is important to understand what you own.

I've advised my family to invest in hedge funds only sparingly, despite their popularity. The combination of high fees, low tax efficiency, and tricky risk evaluation leave me with two big concerns. First, only a few managers will generate net alpha. To overcome the drag of fees, carried interest, and tax, a manager has to generate over 500 basis points of gross alpha before the limited partner gets any benefit. The idea that markets are relatively efficient until someone comes along and charges you high fees to generate lots of alpha in those same markets defies logic. I know that a few people have done it, but the bar is very high. Second, I'm concerned that I won't be able to discriminate early enough in the funds' lives between the few superior managers and the rest, to access the good ones while they're still open to new money. Intensifying competition in the industry is only making these challenges tougher to overcome. Fifteen years ago, hedge funds were in an esoteric corner of the market. Since the first edition of *Wealth*, assets have more than doubled to more than $2 trillion under management.

It's very difficult to get valid information on the performance of hedge funds because there is no consistent measure of performance when looking at a single fund or when evaluating funds more broadly. Strategies vary among funds and can vary within the same fund as well. But one thing is clear: Hedge funds that build up high-performing track records over five or ten years are very difficult for new investors to access. Investors, institutional or individual, really like the combination of great returns and low volatility. Some think it's like having your cake and eating it, too. When hedge funds are performing as advertised they can be excellent diversifiers.

Several firms now produce composite benchmarks for hedge fund strategies that combine the performance of a broad cross section of the market. However, these composite benchmarks have serious flaws. For one, hedge fund managers do not have to participate in these composites. As you might imagine, there is little incentive for a manager who is performing poorly to continue reporting his numbers. Likewise, some managers who do really well aren't interested in attracting additional assets, so they don't report their numbers either. As a result, the composites have real sampling problems. I think that the indices probably overstate the actual performance, but a few composites might actually understate performance.

Regardless, you are unlikely to get consistent access to the good-performing managers whether or not they report their numbers. In 2004, a talented group of managers left Harvard Management Company to set up a hedge fund. They didn't crisscross the country conducting marketing meetings or talk with the consultants who are gatekeepers for wealthy individuals, foundations, and pension plans. They didn't speak at conferences about alternative investing. Harvard Management agreed to be a cornerstone investor, and before the fund opened on its first day of business, it had raised several billion dollars from a handful of sophisticated institutions. Unless you were part of the "inner circle" and could write an eight-figure check, you stood no chance of entry. This kind of thing continues to happen with some regularity. Although, in the aforementioned case performance has been excellent, other situations have not turned out so well. Even the inner circle doesn't always get it right. Investor demand is no guarantee of manager performance! Even with lots of care and due diligence we all make mistakes. The trick is to keep them to a minimum and to limit the pain when they happen.

Real Estate

Real estate takes almost as many shapes as hedge funds. Houses, hotels, rental apartments, raw land, office buildings, and industrial facilities are all real estate assets. Managers of real estate investment vehicles have diverse strategies. Some acquire and lease only very high-quality properties with very high-quality tenants. Others develop raw land into buildings, office parks, and communities. Still others redevelop properties that have not been well managed, are losing tenants, or are even vacant. Depending on your strategy, your expected return on real estate and the risk associated with achieving it will vary.

Many real estate investors finance their properties with significant amounts of leverage (borrowing). Leverage adds to the risk of a property investment and makes the asset vulnerable to changes in interest rates and the availability of credit. If interest rates rise significantly and/or credit tightens, the value of real estate might be impaired, even if the property is financed with fixed-rate debt. All other things being equal, potential buyers of the property will have a harder time attracting credit and will have to pay more for it. As a result, their net cash flow will decline, even though the performance of the property itself hasn't changed. Declining cash flow adversely affects property valuations. Obviously, this scenario can work in reverse too.

It's hard to generalize about the behavior of real estate because it's the quintessential local investment market. Any manager of real estate should have demonstrated capabilities to effectively evaluate local market conditions, to select those that are favorable, to shun those that aren't, and to effectively manage all the properties in the portfolio. "Local" in this case means evaluating traffic patterns in the community, knowing where people are shopping, and understanding what vacancy rates and lease terms exist in a local area. A real estate manager's knowledge and influence become as granular as knowing which side of a residential street has access to the good public schools, gaining the support of neighbors for redevelopment plans, and even knowing whether the property owners adjacent to you once spilled contaminants on their property that have now leached into your soil.

Including real estate in a portfolio can provide needed diversification, but because real estate is so diverse, it is important to understand the type of diversification you want. Before the financial crisis of 2008, many people liked real estate because they saw it as a safe, secure alternative to high-quality bonds, with the added bonus of inflation protection, and some tax shelter on the income they produce that comes from depreciation. Unfortunately, many also felt comfortable leveraging their real estate investments, and the results sometimes turned out to be ugly. The basic hypothesis was correct, and many high-quality properties are today selling at record low cap rates (i.e., record high-valuation multiples), but greedy investors didn't heed my lesson about how leverage changes the nature of any investment. As I said in the original *Wealth*, if you want this kind of asset, it is prudent not to use much leverage.

Other people like to buy speculative real estate with little or no use of leverage. There is a whole county in Florida (Collier County) named after a family that was smart enough to buy vast amounts of land when most people thought it was useless swampland. Now the land is covered in orange groves and vegetable farms that grow high-value crops year-round. Northward, there are a few families that for generations have owned tens of thousands of acres of rich, black farmland in the states of Illinois, Iowa, and Indiana. By renting the land to tenant corn and soybean farmers, they continue to reap the benefits of the vision shown by their forebears a century ago to acquire land that had to undergo the backbreaking work of being drained and tiled (to aid water runoff) to grow anything but cattails. In southwestern cities like Phoenix, Las Vegas, and Santa Barbara, most real estate developers in the past 25 years did extremely well if they remained value-conscious and didn't overleverage. Because the demographic trends have been so powerful, even though the housing crisis hit places like Phoenix and Las Vegas extremely hard, those who invested early, remained value-conscious, and built in a margin of safety by limiting leverage have done just fine. In the industrial northeast, some people like to buy properties in old industrial cities that can be acquired inexpensively, fixed up, leased, and sold for a tidy profit.

The characteristics of these property types and locations vary tremendously, and so do the insights necessary to turn them into profitable investments. One or all of them could be useful additions to a diversified portfolio, but each is sensitive to both general and local market conditions. The skill of people "on the ground" managing such properties is vital. Properties that require a lot of hands-on work to make them profitable add another dimension to the real estate analysis. You need to choose first-class operators because their skill is as likely to determine the success of the investment as general market conditions.

Distressed Debt

When a company starts to fall on hard times, the value of its equity usually declines because potential buyers of the stock are less willing to own it, and owners are more likely to want to sell. Prior to the 1980s, most corporate debt, especially that of small and mid-sized companies, was owned by banks that didn't have the ability to readily sell the debt they controlled if the company's fortunes were declining. However, they had the benefit of being able to seize control of the company from the equity holders if the company was not meeting its obligations. Then, they could restructure or liquidate the company to try to recover their investment, often by forcing the company into bankruptcy.

In the 1980s, the world of distressed debt changed because of Michael Milken and his firm Drexel Burnham Lambert. Almost single-handedly, Milken and his associates created what is now called the "junk" debt market. They convinced institutional investors that it was good business to provide debt financing to companies that didn't have great credit. They made it possible for investors to buy and sell the debt in public, liquid markets, just like stocks. Milken also convinced promising companies that Drexel could raise financing less expensively than if they turned to banks. When some of the companies that were financed in this way inevitably ran into difficulty, the distressed debt market was born.

Some people, especially ex-Drexel employees, became experts in evaluating these fallen darlings. Many also became experts in bankruptcy law, enabling them to figure out what to do when the sellers of distressed debt became fed up enough (with the companies they were financing) to sell their holdings at a cut rate. Then, these experts would snap up the debt at a fraction of what they expected it to be worth one day. Sometimes they would fight to take control of the company in bankruptcy. At other times, their analysis showed that the company would never enter bankruptcy and would simply continue to pay the interest on its debt and slowly recover its former strength.

This talent was well positioned in 1989, when Congress created the Resolution Trust Company to seize control of, and then sell, the loan portfolios of failing savings and loan institutions. Combined with the economic downturn in 1991, a perfect storm was created that played right into the hands of distressed debt buyers. At the time, there was an abundance of sellers of distressed debt and relatively few people who understood how to analyze these investments and consider them for purchase. Those in the know scooped up these assets at a fraction of what they believed to be their true value. When the markets recovered several years later, they were proven right with handsome returns.

In the 1990s, the distressed debt market developed further. Banks found there were willing buyers of the distressed loans they held on their books...at a price. Many felt that it made better business sense to sell these deteriorating loans than to get into the messy job of bankruptcy and restructuring. Meanwhile, the "junk" market continued to expand, creating the fuel for the next disaster in the distressed market. Sure enough, it came in 2001 and 2002, and again those with the skills and the strong stomach made out very well.

The next distressed debt crisis came in 2008, but it was a rather different animal. Corporate distressed debt collapsed in value as the financial crisis unfolded. Banks, AIG, General Motors, mortgage insurers, and others collapsed during the crisis. Many needed government bailouts and debt holders suffered severe losses. But many nonfinancial distressed situations were the outgrowth of "covenant-light" financing for LBOs in 2005–2007. Even when these companies got into trouble, lenders had little power or influence. After some nervous times, debt markets quickly recovered and many of these overleveraged companies were able to refinance without entering bankruptcy.

We all now know that the residential mortgage market was a completely different story. Some subprime securities plummeted 90% or more and many have never recovered. Numerous mortgage-backed securities (MBS) lost their AAA credit ratings and declined dramatically and permanently in value. Fannie Mae and Freddie Mac were taken over by the government because they were effectively bankrupt. The underlying collateral for this debt, housing values, has only recently begun to stabilize. Some people believe that the next major distressed debt market will be municipal bonds....

Needless to say, distressed debt is not for the faint of heart. There are times when one can make a lot of money as a buyer of distressed debt, but for a number of years from 1993 to 2001 and 2004 to 2007, the market wasn't particularly attractive. Today, the types of distressed debt and the know-how needed to evaluate them are much more widespread. Many more firms have gotten into the business, including hedge funds that invest in distressed debt when they see opportunity and get out when they see better opportunities in other asset classes. The fluidity of capital, its wide availability for this asset class, and broad access to investment know-how lead me to believe that in coming cycles many parts of this market will be more competitive than in the past. That said, distressed debt has tended to do reasonably well when the stock market has struggled, so it might continue to be a good diversifier in broadly invested portfolios.

Emerging Markets

Investing in emerging markets makes investing in distressed debt look straightforward. To be successful, you need access to all the analytical tools that a good investor in this country must have, and you must be able to adjust for variances across currencies, languages, cultures, accounting practices, legal systems, political systems, and national economies around the world.

Most investors who choose to tackle emerging markets do so with broadly diversified equity portfolios that invest across Central and Eastern Europe, the Middle East, Latin America, Asia, and Africa. Many of the emerging economies that are developed enough to have their own stock markets are growing at a faster rate than the United States and Western Europe. By investing in the public markets in these countries, people hope to capture some of that additional growth in the value of their investments. In some cases, they also hope that, as these countries' economies grow, their currencies will strengthen relative to the U.S. dollar, creating another source of return.

Emerging markets equities are volatile. A study of 13 major asset classes from 1993 to 2004 showed that emerging markets equities were in either the top two performers or the bottom two in 10 out of 12 years. Yet over the 10-year period from 1995 to 2004, they were the worst-performing asset class in the group.[5] So investors got a lot of volatility (risk) and a poor rate of return, which is hardly a compelling case for enthusiastic investing!

In the six subsequent years emerging markets were still volatile, but overall they were the best performing of the asset classes, by a significant margin. China and India have become even more important to the global economy, as have others like Brazil and Turkey. Emerging markets are here to stay, and they will present opportunities to both earn and lose large sums.

Commodities

For centuries, the prices of most commodities have fallen steadily as advances in productivity have driven down the costs of production—even in the face of ever-increasing demand. In the past few years, we have seen a reversal of this long-term trend, specifically in such areas as oil prices and the prices for industrial metals like copper and precious metals like gold. Does this speak to a fundamental change in the price of commodities, or is it a cyclical rebound that reflects general economic activity?

It wasn't that long ago that oil prices were under $10 per barrel. Now with prices around ten times that amount, the days of cheap oil are only a memory. For some years, major energy companies have found it difficult to replace their reserves with new discoveries. Yet as the global market continues to grow, and emerging economies such as China, India, Korea, and Brazil consume ever-larger amounts of oil, some people think that we are at a fundamental turning point. I don't think so.

Back in the 1970s, some experts projected that the world would run out of food. There were forecasts of famine, and in some parts of Asia and Africa, global population growth was projected to accelerate while arable land remained a finite resource. Now, agriculture is more productive than ever as new seed stock and tillage techniques have increased productivity. Distribution systems are also more efficient, getting food to where it needs to be. It's true that famine remains a problem in parts of the world today, but this is often due to issues of nationalism, ethnic conflicts, and dire poverty, rather than the inability of the world to produce enough food.

If we look more closely at the energy market, we see some parallels. New technology will eventually bring us hydrogen fuel cells, a virtually limitless source of energy, as the scientific community makes new breakthroughs. In the meantime, Canadian oil sands that are not economic at $10 per barrel very profitably produce oil at $60 per barrel. On the supply side, at some point higher prices will drive people to change their energy-consumption patterns and to purchase more efficient automobiles.

The big energy story that is becoming clear only in the past five years is shale gas. Higher commodity prices coupled with entrepreneurship mixed with technology have revolutionized the natural gas market and, by inference, electrical energy production and maybe even the economic viability of solar and wind power. The U.S. could also become the low-cost producer of plastics and other hydrocarbon products produced with "wet" gas. These are highly disruptive, but ultimately very exciting, changes. And they are a continuing reminder of why most commodity prices are likely to remain volatile, both up and down, for decades to come.

So, how do you make money in commodities? Some investors can do so by playing the cycles. Few financial investors actually ever buy and sell volumes of gold, wheat, natural gas, wool, pigs' feet, or copper. Most either buy financial futures that (poorly) mimic the spot price behavior of the underlying commodities, or own the stocks of companies that manufacture commodities. For long-term investors, this is a tough way to make money. Although the Lucas family does allocate some portion of its portfolios to commodity price risk, we also look at the major players in energy, energy distribution, and commodity markets to find ways to make good returns while limiting direct commodity exposure.

Concluding Comments About Alternative Investments

Alternative investments are like ninja swords. In experienced hands, they can be used powerfully to achieve dramatic results. But it's also easy for unskilled users to hurt themselves.

The Lucas family now allocates up to half or more of its assets to alternative investments when we think they are attractively priced. Over the past 15 years, the family's allocation to alternatives has slowly but steadily risen as we've developed the skill to wield our ninja sword. We do our own research. We develop a thorough understanding of the strategies embraced by various alternative investment managers before we hire anyone. In some cases, we monitor a manager for a period of up to a few years before hiring him or her. Over the years, we have built our knowledge and constructed a network of sources for generating ideas and cross-referencing due diligence. We take educated risks on individual funds and asset classes with the goal of constructing a total portfolio that generates consistent growth with moderate volatility. We've had one hedge fund blow up on us, and several private equity, real estate, and emerging market funds perform below our expectations. On the other hand, through our commitment to alternatives, we have generated excellent returns and achieved broader diversification. Overall, the Lucas family is willing to tolerate the illiquidity and volatility, and we are pleased with the results so far. But, we don't sleep all that well at night.

As you review various alternative investments, you may be considering fund-of-funds as investment vehicles. A fund-of-funds is a single entity that invests its assets in a range of other funds, typically with a specific focus. There are funds of hedge funds, private equity funds-of-funds, and real estate funds-of-funds. Even some mutual funds are funds-of-funds.

I don't recommend using funds-of-funds. You should either have the scale and expertise to go direct, or avoid alternative investments. First, if you invest in a fund-of-funds, you give up information and direct contact with fund managers because there is an intermediary representing you and the other investors to fund managers. You lose direct contact with people managing your assets and the flow of information that comes directly from those managers through their quarterly correspondence and annual meetings—two vital advantages to have when pursuing an Active Alpha Investment strategy. Second, fund-of-fund managers charge their own fees on top of the fees charged by underlying funds. Finally, the return data of fund-of-funds is not compelling and recent cash flows out of hedge fund-of-funds suggests that investors are not pleased with the results.

CSF #2: Build Sustainable Relationships with Managers Who Add Value Net of Fees and Taxes

Most people choose managers because they have good past performance. They don't understand the skills managers need to make that performance persist. I believe in building deep understanding of our managers and the spaces where they invest. Performance is actually one of the last things I look at. Here's why.

For traditional managers investing in public markets, the evidence indicates that past performance is not a good predictor of their future ability to add value. As a case in point, a few years ago I asked U.S. Trust Company and CTC Consulting, Inc. to do a study for me to test this thesis using data provided by Morningstar, Inc.[6] We isolated the top 25% of all equity mutual funds based on performance over the period from 1997 to 2001. I then asked them how well these top-performing managers did for the subsequent three-year period (2002 to 2004) compared to all other equity managers with a track record over the full eight years. If the performance of these top-tier managers was entirely random, you would expect that 25% of them would fall into each of the four quartiles of performance. However, Figure 6.4 shows that nearly 40% of the "Top" managers ended up in the worst-performing quartile. Over 50% were in the bottom half! If you'd wanted to pick top performers for the period 2002 to 2004 on the basis of their previous five years' experience, you'd have had a better chance if selecting from among the worst 25% of all the funds in the Morningstar database from 1997 to 2001 than from the top 25%. This type of analysis has been repeated time and again by academics with similar results.

For private equity and venture capital managers, the opposite appears to be true. There seems to be a correlation between past and future performance, but by the time a manager has a long enough track record to be meaningful, he or she usually isn't interested in adding new clients.

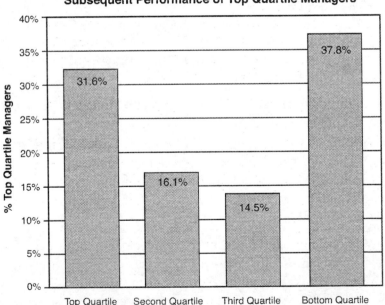

Figure 6.4 Looking at the subsequent performance in 2002–2004 of managers in the top quartile from 1997 to 2001, we see that more than half performed below average and nearly 40% were in the worst-performing quartile.

So, how do you as an investor solve this dilemma? Over several decades, and after interviewing hundreds of managers and watching them perform, here are my well-weathered recommendations for selecting a good manager:[7]

- **Can I get access?** It makes no sense to get excited about a manager if you can't do proper due diligence and you can't get into their fund. So, early in the evaluation process, I check for two critical items: minimum investment sizes that the manager will accept and whether the manager is open to new investors. These two criteria eliminate many funds that might otherwise be attractive, especially to investors who don't have $5 million, $10 million, or $25 million to allocate to that manager. What you're left with is typically smaller and newer organizations looking for new investors. (Sometimes, large managers hire marketing agents who set up sidecar funds that have additional fees and allow only very limited manager access; so you're back with several of the fund-of-funds problems.) Occasionally, a well-established investment firm will try to raise money in a tough fundraising climate by allowing access to new investors. Ironically, often the best time to invest is when it's really hard for a good manager to raise new money in an asset class that everyone is shunning.

- **Do I like the manager's approach to investing and to his business?** A prospective manager has to differentiate himself when it comes to managing risk, buying well, adding value when he owns an asset, and having a set of contacts, operational resources, or proprietary knowledge that sets him apart. That prospective manager also has to add value to my investment, net of fees and taxes. Few managers truly belong in the Secret Society. Doing the analysis takes hard work, experience, and access. Today, alternative investment fund marketing is a highly sophisticated trade. Marketers know the "hot buttons" and they know how legally to make numbers look good. They have glossy pitch books and pre-packaged DDQs (Due Diligence Questionnaires). Lawyers refine the terms of limited partner agreements to sound like the standard "2 and 20" fee structure. However, they can write in subtle but material differences that slant the economics even more heavily in the manager's favor. The manager's organizational structure and employee incentives are also important criteria for evaluation. Remember, with many funds having lockups of a decade or more, choosing an alternative manager is a long-term commitment. Organizational stability is as important as investment skill.

- How does the manager manage leverage? In tough times, managers with too much leverage implode. In good times, you are paying them a chunk of your profits just because they've put a lot of debt on your investments. This is a pretty fundamental issue, yet the details can get distractingly complex. When evaluating managers' returns, look at how much leverage they use, and how it is structured. Was their track record based on sound investments or on aggressive use of leverage? For the past 30 years, declining interest rates have been a tail wind to leveraged investments. With current rates about as low as they can go and setting the stage for a reversal, in the future investors will have to make money the old-fashioned way, by earning it.

- Is the manager in a niche (and planning to stay there) where lack of size is an advantage? Alternative investment markets are getting more efficient. So much capital is going into them that excess profits are being squeezed out. But occasionally there are niches that remain too small for large institutional investors, and therein lies potential to create alpha. Unfortunately, managers who start in small niches often outgrow them because the economics of their business often reward growth in assets under management more than good investment performance.

- Does the manager have sustainable competitive advantage? Finding an attractive investment niche is valuable only if you can capitalize on it through access to a competent manager in that niche. At the other end of the opportunity spectrum, some managers build competitive advantages that translate into sustainable top-quartile performance in large and competitive asset classes. In my mind, you need access to both. Competitive advantage is getting tougher to attain and to recognize. For example, more than a decade ago, a few private equity managers started building out internal operations capabilities. These skills enabled them to view the value and risk of potential acquisitions differently. Roll the clock forward to today and virtually every private equity firm claims to add operational value. It takes increased experience and digging to differentiate good marketing from real competitive advantage. Top managers recognize the growing competition for investments and the unpredictability of outcomes regardless of the quality of due diligence. When making an investment, the best managers think through "multiple ways to win," in advance. They ask themselves, "If my primary investment thesis turns out not to be workable, how else can I make money?" This kind of thinking lowers risk and enhances return.

- Are the manager's financial incentives aligned with the investor's? This question directly relates to Principal #2 in Chapter 2, "Eight Principles of Strategic Wealth Management." I've always believed that there are certain potential problems I prefer to avoid. If a manager's business structure invites a lot of conflicts of interest, I just say no and keep looking. Sure, I miss some good opportunities, but I also sleep better at night. I generally prefer managers who focus on doing one thing well rather than having a wide range of different investment products. For this guideline, I do make exceptions, though I have found over many years that the success rate from broadening product lines and hiring new managers to run them is pretty hit-and-miss. I do look for managers who have "skin in the game" as another measure of alignment, but it is an imperfect measure. Unfortunately, the hefty fees that many active managers earn usually outpace earnings from the returns they generate on their own investment. What might turn out as an average return for you can be a terrific return on the manager's investment after you take into account all the fees and carried interest.

- Is the manager a disciplined investor? I like to watch managers perform over a number of years or carefully study their track record, investment by investment, to answer this question. In investing, there is a delicate tension between aggressively trying to find deals and waiting for the right ones (on the right terms) to materialize. Some of the managers I use haven't made an investment for up to two years in a row because they didn't see anything they liked. I've seen others persist on a deal through busted negotiations, lawsuits, changing legislation, due diligence revelations, and changing markets, doggedly pursuing an opportunity but not closing on it until all the conditions are right. In both cases, they served my interests well.

- Who is performing due diligence on the manager? Big, sophisticated institutions do extensive due diligence. When they invest $50 million or $100 million with a manager, they can afford to do all sorts of research to protect their investment, and to some degree you or I can ride on their coattails. But it's important to note that just because large sophisticated institutional investors have hired a manager, that does not make the manager a great investor, or suitable for private, taxable clients.

Managers in small niches don't have big, sophisticated institutional investors, so there isn't someone else doing the heavy lifting when it comes to due diligence. As a result, you have to take responsibility for doing enough due diligence to gain comfort that your investment is secure. Examples of due diligence might include doing reference/background checks on the advisor, evaluating a manager's risk controls and his firm's decision-making processes, and being familiar with a firm's legal counsel, its custodian or prime broker, and its accountants. It also might make sense to make a smaller commitment until you really get to know the manager and the stability of his organization.

- Is a financial intermediary involved? There is so much capital looking for a productive home that most managers who meet the criteria I just mentioned don't have to hire an intermediary to raise money. Even so, there is a huge market of financial intermediaries who do just that. They raise money in small amounts of a few hundred thousand, or in big chunks of $5 million, $20 million, or $100 million per investor! And they charge the manager, and sometimes you, a fee for doing so. We have used intermediaries only sparingly, even though lots of institutional and individual investors justifiably rely on intermediaries for ideas and due diligence support.

CSF #3: Make Investment Decisions Based on Opportunity, Not Process or Capacity

Many wealth advisors work with you to design your "optimal" strategic asset allocation and then they move you to that target as quickly as possible. They have a process for putting money to work and they want to slot you easily into the process. The strategic asset allocation pie slices have been agreed on. The advisor's manager research group has built a stable of approved managers for each slice of the pie. The advisor simply fills each slice with capacity from the approved manager group. This might be efficient and straightforward from a typical advisor's standpoint, but it is not optimal for you.

The relative attractiveness of asset classes and the availability of superior managers aren't timed to dovetail with an advisor's process or your personal agenda. Financial markets dictate when the opportunity set of attractive investments is large, and when it is small. The opportunity set varies not only with time but also with asset class, and with top managers' fundraising cycles. You have to work with imperfect information when deciding when to invest with a particular asset class or manager. Often an asset class is most attractive when things look bad. Even though superior investors do a good job of separating out the fundamentals from the hype (or the fear), they still hedge their bets by "averaging in." Even if they thought the timing was perfect to do everything at once, they know the risk of making a huge single timing bet. Better to be 80% right on multiple smaller decisions than 100% wrong with one big one. These investors diversify their entry points, all the while being opportunistic, value-conscious, and selective.

Superior investors also want each decision to count. Sometimes I see private client portfolios with 100 or more managers. To me, this shows lack of discipline—a "spray and pray" mentality. It takes hard work to research a manager and its value proposition, and then to determine how that manager is additive to the rest of your portfolio. As a rule of thumb, I like manager selection decisions to have the potential be at least 3% of assets. It might take several years, and sometimes two or three funds from the same manager to get there, but with this level of concentration you are forced to make trade-offs between opportunity A and opportunity B, both of which appear attractive. Using critical thinking and good research to make tough choices builds a sharper, more value-added investment process.

At Wealth Strategist Partners, we estimate that it takes five to ten years to build a mature multiasset, alpha-seeking portfolio. If a client is new to investing, we prefer to start by indexing most of the client's public equities to gain the desired market exposure at very low cost. Over time, we add alternative investments to the portfolio, but only when we think the opportunities, the way in which alpha is created, and the managers are all compelling. Sometimes we fund these new investments with indexed assets; other times, with cash. What happens over time is that a portfolio matures into layers of attractive investments, some of which are mature and distributing cash, and others of which are young, are undervalued, and need cash. Mature client portfolios become diversified by asset class, sources of alpha, manager, and time. Portfolios of this type might take longer to assemble but they are less risky and generate better returns on average. Whether a client portfolio is fully mature or not, we tend to ease into a new asset class, slowly building it over six months to two years or longer, often while it is under duress. For part of this time, it almost invariably looks as though we are making a bad decision because the new asset class continues to decline in value. Usually our moves into an asset class coincide with sellers who are driven by non-economic stimuli to sell. Sometimes the stimuli are regulatory, sometimes they are structural, and sometimes they are driven by panic. Of course, in addition to identifying an attractive asset class, we also need to find a competent manager who will take our capital.

One person who understands opportunistic investing well (though he refers to it differently) is über-investor George Soros. In 1992, Soros gained global notoriety for betting against the power of European governments to maintain a managed value for the British pound. The pressure built for months due in part to Soros and others betting against the pound. The more he bet against the pound, the more the British government had to spend to hold its value steady. Finally, the government's power was simply overwhelmed by the market. When that happened, the pound's valuation collapsed in a matter of hours after pegs for the currency were abandoned.

In ensuing weeks, there was a contagion effect throughout Europe as the pegs in other currencies fell. When Soros was proven right—that markets determined to change are more powerful than governments determined to prevent change—he made over $1 billion. In targeting the British pound, Soros identified a situation in the financial market where governments were acting for non-economic reasons. They wanted fixed exchange rates for political reasons. Currency traders felt that the pound was overvalued, but government structure had not allowed the free markets to define a clearing price. As time went on, pressure built and Soros seized the opportunity to invest. When the pressure built to an unsustainable level, the governments were forced to delink the pound and Soros made a fortune! Given the mess that is European finance today, I can't help but wonder whether there is a lesson somewhere in Soros's experience. Do European central banks and political leaders really have the unilateral power to control financial markets, stabilize the Euro, and get their economies back on a growth footing? I hope so, but as a realist I am not confident.

Politics, Economics, Regulation, Structural Flaws, Panic, and Euphoria

The British pound example underscores how moneymaking opportunities can occur because prices or economic conditions move faster than regulation or market structures can adapt. In other cases, investors' perceptions regarding risk will change, causing an imbalance of supply and demand for certain financial assets.

For example, when defaults on junk bonds rose more quickly than generally expected in 2002, in part because of the unexpected collapses of Enron, Worldcom, and Adelphia, many investors started dumping junk bonds much faster than the market could absorb them. With a huge imbalance between supply and demand, prices plummeted. For those with strong stomachs and the research capabilities to sift through the bonds and determine which were worthless and which were highly undervalued, it was a once-in-a-career opportunity to make a killing. In 2007 and 2008, a similar phenomenon played out in housing. Some of our best-performing assets in those years were residential mortgage-backed securities. We identified a manager who had deep knowledge of this sector of the market and, with the market crashing on all sides, he could buy assets from forced sellers at highly attractive prices with great cash flow characteristics. In every crisis, there are forced sellers who create opportunity for a skilled few.

Sometimes opportunity is created by a combination of politics, economics, and short-time horizons. Back in 1997 when oil prices eased below $10 a barrel and natural gas was going for about $1.50 per 1,000 cubic feet (or "MCF"), a combination of near-term excess supply and constrained demand drove prices so far down that there was hardly any economic incentive for oil companies to drill for new sources of energy. At the time, the political climate in the Middle East and Latin America was also relatively benign.

Then, everything changed. Growing global demand for energy in China and India, increasing challenges in finding new supplies of hydrocarbons, political insecurity in Venezuela (a major supplier of oil to the U.S.), stagnant domestic refinery capacity, the war in Afghanistan, and the second Iraq war all conspired to quintuple the price of energy. Since 2005, the price of gas has again collapsed back to nearly the prices of 1997 because of shale gas. Will we see a similar cycle play out again? It might take a while to get back into a higher-priced equilibrium, and technology has lowered the cost of extraction, but the basic laws of supply and demand are pretty powerful.

Euphoria can be just as destabilizing as panic. The first decade of the 21st century seems to have been the bubble decade. We started with the Internet and ended with housing. The "madness of crowds" was working overtime! Twice in ten years, greed and a herd mentality drove prices up to stratospheric levels that had no basis in reality and then with equal inertia drove them down. It will happen again and again.

The oft-quoted line from Mark Twain "History doesn't repeat itself but it does rhyme" reminds us that there is no substitute for experience when it comes to opportunistic investing. Having lived through numerous cycles, I know how gut-wrenching as well as how opportunity-laden they can be. Each one shares characteristics with previous cycles, but each is also unique in certain ways. At WSP we respect Mark Twain's sentiments, but we also remember Richard Feynman's blend of intellectual curiosity and humility (see the quote at the beginning of Chapter 2).

Having the Right Stuff

Making successful investment decisions based on opportunity, not process or capacity, depends on an investor's skills in three areas:

- The ability to assess value in a different—and correct—way relative to the hordes that are driving the markets way up or way down

- Access to liquidity when competitors don't have it

- Having a mechanism to capitalize on the opportunity

Opportunities sometimes exist to make dynamic changes to asset allocation because large numbers of people have assessed risk incorrectly. Sometimes people think something isn't very risky when, in fact, it is. Think of Enron when it was flying high, Internet stocks in late 1999, or all those AAA-rated mortgage-backed securities that were money-good. Nobody thought of these as financial train wrecks just waiting to happen. Conversely, people sometimes think things will be risky but they don't turn out to be. Investing in distressed debt in the early 2000s or after Lehman Brothers collapsed in late 2008 was considered a gamble when we did it, but the gambles paid well.

To be effective at opportunistic investing, you must have strong confidence in your skills as an investor to go against the grain and seek opportunities where most people see only danger ("buy low") or to walk away from situations where others see only riches ("sell high"). Good research and courage have to be accompanied by adequate cash to invest in such situations. Often, as we saw so plainly in the financial crisis, panics are accompanied by credit squeezes and weak economic results that make it difficult to quickly execute a sale and a subsequent purchase. One of the advantages of maintaining a broadly diversified portfolio is that you're likely to have a liquid asset that you can sell quickly to take advantage of especially attractive buying opportunities.

But even if you see an opportunity and have the cash available to invest, you still need a mechanism. Wealth Strategist Partners invests through third-party money managers because we don't have the resources to develop that level of expertise in 20 or more asset classes ourselves. But we don't wait for a crisis to start looking for a manager with expertise in a potentially desirable asset class. We have built a "bench" of excellent managers who our clients haven't hired today, but who we might advise that they hire tomorrow if the right opportunity arises. Although it is frustrating at times, we always try to have significantly more good ideas than we have capacity to invest. It makes for healthy debate and better decisions.

The Lucas Family Track Record with Opportunistic Investing

So, how much success has the Lucas family had with our form of opportunistic investing? Let's put it this way: The family is very pleased with our efforts in this arena over many years, but Wealth Strategist Partners is always striving for continuous improvement. As I indicated previously, we've been successful because of our ability to assess risk well. We manage portfolios to have access to liquidity when competitors don't, we have a mechanism to capitalize on opportunity, and we've undoubtedly had some good luck.

As a family, we have made tactical commitments to emerging-markets debt, small-cap growth stocks, large-cap value stocks, distressed corporate debt, collateralized mortgage obligations, energy stocks, and Asian private equity. Some of our early successes involved investing in "distressed debt" in the late 1980s and early 1990s as the Resolution Trust Company was trying to clean up the Savings and Loan debacle here in the U.S.

In 2001 and 2002, we again bought up distressed securities and made good money through the cycle. We had liquidity to make this commitment in a bear market because we had sold many of our growth stocks in 2000 ("selling high"). We were able to repeat this with a few tweaks in 2007, 2008, and 2009. Although the value of our portfolio dropped considerably in 2008 and early 2009, the investments we owned were fundamentally solid and we were able buy additional assets at very attractive prices. We have now recaptured the paper loss, and then some.

But not all our tactical bets are successful.

After the Asian meltdown in 1998, we committed to private equity investing in that emerging-market region. We thought our timing was great and we found a superb manager, but the first fund barely broke even. We stuck with it, though, and in subsequent years have done well. Now, though, we find that capital is in excess supply, terms are not nearly as attractive, and foreign capital is less desirable. We still like Asia's long-term growth prospects, but we are now more attracted to public markets than private ones.

When oil was below $10 a barrel, we made a big investment in an energy hedge fund. We trimmed back our position a couple of years later after making excellent returns, but we did not anticipate the 2005 run-up and were underexposed, at least relative to where we had been. Then, in June 2008, in response to this run-up, we cut our position again; but in retrospect, I wish we had cut it more.

Opportunistic investing isn't for the inexperienced or faint of heart. It also doesn't make sense unless you have hundreds of millions or more to commit to the strategy, plus the energy and experience to do it well. The strategy really benefits from scale and an intense focus on the investment process for each client. That is why we built Wealth Strategist Partners in a particular way and why we focus only on investing for family offices. During each program that I teach at the University of Chicago, I quote David Swensen when speaking about Active Alpha Investing: "With a casual attempt to beat the market, you're going to fail."[8]

Sidebar 6.2: Choosing an Outsourced Chief Investment Officer ("CIO")

My family was lucky. It turns out that my sister-in-law, Melissa Lucas, and I both enjoy and have been successful at investing using the Active Alpha Investment approach that I've described. We have been co-CIOs for the Lucas family for almost 20 years and have added considerable alpha over that time.

Most wealthy families that wish to pursue an Active Alpha Investment strategy don't necessarily have the skills and the interest within the family. Or the family dynamics make it awkward to choose a family member as CIO. They look outside the family for an investment advisor. You know from Chapter 5, "The Enchanted Forest, the Secret Society, and the Capital Kibbutz," that I think few investment advisory firms are well suited to deliver on the promise of Active Alpha Investing. It's just too hard for advisors to do all the personalized client service required and develop the requisite investment expertise. Most readers of this book don't have the luxury of hiring their own full-time CIO because you really need hundreds of millions in assets to justify the cost. Even the wealthiest families must compete for investment talent with hedge funds, sovereign wealth funds, endowments, and pension plans that are measured in the billions, or tens of billions, of dollars. The worst decision you can make is hiring an unqualified CIO whom you have to supervise and whom you pay handsomely to destroy value.

More and more midsize institutions and families with hundreds of millions or even a few billion in assets have found it more efficient and effective to hire an outsourced CIO firm. They seek a partner that embodies the three Critical Success Factors, customized to the circumstances of each client. Simultaneously, the outsourced CIO firm can use the combined scale of their clients to attract top investment talent, negotiate better access and/or terms with managers, build more robust governance, and ultimately add alpha to their clients' portfolios. Each CIO in the firm is truly an investment expert and decision maker who has only a few client portfolios to manage. Some firms comingle their clients' assets. But I think this model has real rigidities that are not well suited to families, their changing dynamics, and taxes. I think it is better to manage each client separately. Outsourced CIOs are explicitly not full-service wealth management firms—they focus on investing. Wealth Strategist Partners is one such firm.

Conclusion

At the beginning of this chapter, I told you that choosing among Index Investing, Barbell Investing, and Active Alpha Investing is the single most important investment decision you will make. It is more important than asset allocation or manager selection or any of the other investment-related decisions you might consider.

If you choose the Index Investing strategy, you don't need to dedicate much time to the wealth management process or build specialized expertise. On the other hand, with a Barbell Investing strategy or an Active Alpha Investing strategy, an extraordinary commitment is required for either of these wealth management strategies to succeed.

All three investment strategies have merit. There is no right or wrong answer. You can follow other, riskier paths, but they will reduce your chances of success and potentially jeopardize the wealth you have created.

Since hiring a financial advisor is a pivotal move in helping you to identify the right financial path for you, let's move on to Chapter 7, "Making Your Most Important Hire," for information on how to proceed in finding the right fit for you.

Chapter 6: Issues to Discuss with Your Family

1. Do you enjoy investing, or do you see it as a necessary burden?

2. How would you characterize your ability to take risk? Which of the following are you?

   a. Very risk-averse

   b. Somewhat risk-averse

   c. Willing to take moderate risk, with moderate growth goals

   d. Willing to take significant risk to grow the value of your assets

3. What is your ability to assess risk accurately when it comes to allocating capital? Under what circumstances are your abilities enhanced or impaired?

4. If you are averse to indexing, why do you think you're more skilled than most other investors?

5. What special skills, insights, or resources do you and your family have that could support the concentrated growth asset in the Barbell Investing strategy?

6. Are you convinced of the merits of working into your sixties, seventies, or even eighties, as indicated in the discussion on Barbell Investing strategy? If not, what would it take to help you think more about doing this?

7. How can you gain better access to alternative investments than the average sophisticated investor? To what extent do you feel knowledgeable about alternative investments? What more would you like to know about them?

8. Do you see yourself pursuing an Active Alpha Investment strategy but feel you lack the skill set to do it? If so, what can you do to develop, attract, and manage deeper investment skills?

9. To what extent do you think your investment managers' economic interests are aligned with your own?

10. What questions do you have for your own wealth management advisor, in light of reading this chapter?

---

11. Given your answers to the preceding questions, which one of the wealth management strategies discussed in this chapter is most in line with your wealth management goals and your tolerance for risk-taking?

    a. Index Investing

    b. Barbell Investing

    c. Active Alpha Investing

Endnotes

1. Although in a normal environment I am reasonably comfortable owning fixed income index funds, today, monitoring credit quality is extremely important, even for "investment grade" bonds. Therefore, I'm actually more comfortable at the moment with low-cost, but actively managed bond funds, with no longer than an intermediate duration. You might also notice that I've modestly decreased the recommended weight for fixed income and increased the equity weight relative to the first edition of *Wealth*.

2. John C. Bogle, Remarks from the Gary M. Brinson Distinguished Lecture, "As the Index Fund Moves from Heresy to Dogma...What More Do We Need to Know," April 13, 2004, www.vanguard.com/bogle_site/sp20040413.html.

3. Some diversified, actively managed bond funds also have share classes with fees at or below this level.

4. Robert S. Harris, Tim Jenkinson, and Steven N. Kaplan, "Private Equity Performance: What Do We Know?" February 10, 2012, http://papers.ssrn.com/sol3/papers.cfm?abstract_id=1932316.

5. "Leadership of Major Asset Classes," produced by CTC Consulting, Inc.

6. ©2005 Morningstar, Inc. All Rights Reserved. The information contained herein: (1) is proprietary to Morningstar and/or its content providers; (2) may not be copied or distributed; (3) does not constitute investment advice offered by Morningstar; and (4) is not warranted to be accurate, complete, or timely. Neither

Morningstar nor its content providers are responsible for any damages or losses arising from any use of this information. Past performance is no guarantee of future results. Use of information from Morningstar does not necessarily constitute agreement by Morningstar, Inc. of any investment philosophy or strategy presented in this publication.

7. These questions are experience based, not empirically based. Asking the questions without the experience to evaluate the answers effectively is of little value. If you insist on using an Active Alpha Investment strategy, this is just one more reason why you should expose only a small portion of your financial assets to the strategy until you become an expert. Also, keep accurate and complete performance records over three to five years to demonstrate your skill!

8. *Wall Street Journal,* January 13, 2009.

7

Making Your Most Important Hire

*"Recognize the skills and traits you don't possess,
and hire people who have them."*

—Howard Schultz, Chairman, Starbucks

N ow that you've articulated your values, defined your financial objectives, and chosen a strategy to achieve them, your next step as Wealth Strategist is to make a key hire. You need to select a Financial Administrator.

A Financial Administrator (FA) is the practitioner that every Wealth Strategist should have as a partner in the integration and execution of an integrated wealth management strategy. Although the FA is an individual, he or she is usually affiliated with a financial company and, by extension, the financial industry. The company could be a small component of a large financial conglomerate with multiple sources of revenue or a fee-only boutique firm with only one or two employees. Firms come in a wide variety of shapes and sizes with widely varying fee structures. Some Wealth Strategists who employ a simple investment strategy like Index Investing opt to play the FA role themselves. Others with sizable and complex wealth establish family offices to serve this function. Some family offices do the investing in-house; others hire outside private banking firms. Some seek the expertise, focus, and alignment of interests of outsourced CIOs.

The performance of the FA will be driven by his or her own skills and experience, of course. But performance is also dependent on the structure and resources of the firm for which the individual advisor works.

Therefore, choosing an FA involves an analysis of both the individual and the firm, and both need to be first-rate to add value to the relationship. This chapter advises you on how to choose the right FA and how to do a thorough evaluation of the FA's firm.

Selecting the Right FA

An FA's job is to support and partner with you, the Wealth Strategist, to meet or exceed your financial goals using the investment strategy you have chosen. In other words, the FA's primary job is to help you execute and measure your strategy and coordinate all the players involved. The issues the FA needs to manage include the following:

- **You, the client.** To help you keep good records, manage your cash flow, and stay on target with long-term financial goals.

- **Your other advisors.** To ensure that your CIO (if you have one), investment managers, lawyers, accountants, and other advisors perform to expectations, individually and collectively.

- **The totality of your financial assets.** To measure your portfolio's performance, monitor your financial risk, and administer your wealth management activities.

It's not easy to select an outstanding FA. You have to find someone who is conscientious, who is of strong character, who is of high integrity, who is accountable to you, whose interests are aligned with yours, and who is able to strike a delicate balance between your needs and the demands of his or her employer.

With these qualifications, it's no wonder that even sophisticated Wealth Strategists struggle to select a single FA. Some Wealth Strategists give up on finding one person or team that can deliver all of these qualifications. Instead, they divide their assets among different firms with the expectation that they can set up a competitive environment that will, after a year or two, highlight a clear winner. I urge you not to do this, for a couple of reasons. It can become an unwieldy, time-consuming process, and even when you attempt to aggregate the performance of different FAs, it can be very difficult to accurately compare the performance of these individuals and their firms. Meanwhile, during the appraisal period, you're likely to take your eyes off of a big issue: your overall financial risk and performance!

Core Skills of an FA

What are the key skills that an FA must possess? Regardless of the investing strategy you choose—Indexing, Barbell, or Active Alpha—you need to find an FA with skills in several key areas.

For the purposes of all three strategies (Indexing, Barbell, and Active Alpha), you need to find an FA with in-depth experience and expertise in the following four areas:

1. Measuring financial performance

2. Managing key client financial records

3. Coordinating and recommending the work of specialists

4. Strategic asset allocation

To pursue an Active Alpha investment strategy, it's important to find support and expertise in two additional areas:

5. Selection of outstanding investment managers

6. Opportunistic Investing

Responsibility #1: The FA Should Be Able to Measure Financial Performance

First and foremost, the FA is charged with holding accountable everyone involved with managing your wealth, including you and your family. It's imperative to track your overall investment performance as well as the performance of each investment manager. The FA should also make sure that asset allocation is in line with your strategy and that leakages are under control.

Investment performance metrics can get very fancy and complicated. Typical portfolio performance metrics can include attribution measures, style analysis, risk measures, measures of diversification, and the list goes on. Some of these metrics can be useful to illuminate financial performance and risk. However, just because a performance measure is complicated doesn't make it useful. How many times have you reviewed a presentation from a financial-services company; found the statistics impenetrable, uninteresting, or off target; and ended up tossing the presentation into a file cabinet, a shoebox, or even the wastebasket?

Make sure you understand what specific performance data you need in order to gauge investment performance. To that end, there are several critical sets of data that you should ask your FA to collect and evaluate on a regular basis:

- After-fee performance of each individual fund manager, using standard industry practices[1] compared with the most appropriate index. Each fund manager can tell you the index against which you should measure performance. If the manager recommends using a compilation of other managers—such as Morningstar or Lipper—as the benchmark, also insist on using a passive index. A passive index is usually harder to beat than the Morningstar or Lipper benchmarks of other active managers and thus raises the bar of expectations for managers. In addition, comparison against a passive index is a truer measure of value-added growth.

  When Active Alpha managers are used, the most important measures are three-year or even five-year returns. Measuring the performance of a manager over shorter periods is more a measure of the vicissitudes of market behavior than of a manager's skills at generating value-added growth. Short-term performance is useful as a point of inquiry with a manager if his or her actual performance diverges from the index.

- Your aggregate portfolio's performance against an appropriate composite benchmark. A composite benchmark is a selection of indices weighted in such a way that in aggregate they are likely to have the performance and risk characteristics of your desired portfolio. A simple composite is 70% S&P 500 and 30% Barclay's Aggregate Bond Index. Your FA can help you decide on the right composite benchmark. Again, use indices, not manager compilations.

  If you're pursuing an Index Investing strategy, many firms have the necessary software to generate your aggregate performance. If you are pursuing an Active Alpha Investing strategy that includes illiquid investments such as private equity or real estate funds, there are very few wealth management firms in this country that have the capability to provide what you really need: time-weighted aggregate returns compared with your composite benchmark.

I know of this situation quite well because, a few years ago, I evaluated 20 or more of the leading wealth management firms to see whether they could provide me with time-weighted aggregate returns compared to a composite benchmark. Only a handful of them could do it. Today, a few software vendors offer the service, but it is very expensive for smaller wealth management firms to install and very complicated for the big ones to do so. This is a frustrating state of affairs, and one that's likely to change only slowly.

- Measure your actual asset allocation relative to a target allocation. Your FA can help you allocate your assets to be consistent with your wealth management goals and strategy. When you decide on a target allocation, you should regularly compare your actual asset allocation against the target and, when appropriate, rebalance your portfolio so that it stays close to your target. Also, be certain to reflect your target asset allocation in the design of your composite benchmark.

- Measure cash flows relative to objectives. The FA should track the family's spending rate (or savings rate) to ensure that cash flow is aligned with family objectives and to assess its impact on investment results. For example, if a trust beneficiary is receiving 5% income annually instead of 4% annually, it affects the overall integrity of the family's financial plans. Effective wealth management can and should be measured in dollars and cents. The FA should also track other leakages including taxes paid, fees, and expenses.

- Measure the long-term growth of your financial assets in dollars. Each year, record the actual dollar value of your financial assets as of December 31 and the amount that you either added to or removed from your financial assets during that previous year. Measuring actual dollars is equally vital to measuring percentage gains and losses. Dollar measurements are also easier for most people to intuitively understand than percentages. After all, you can't spend percents!

I have been tracking actual dollar data now for my family for 25 years. It is the indicator that gave me the signal to restructure my family's assets. In recent years, it has been gratifying to see how our family's assets and distributions to family members have grown. Comparing the actual growth of assets relative to our long-term goal is a long-term indicator of success or failure that we evaluate over periods of 10 years or more. For shorter-term feedback, we rely on the percentage data, or we compare the percentage and dollar data to make sure they are sending the same signals. But if the percentage data look good and the dollar data look bad, that's a warning sign that deserves careful and immediate attention.

Tying the Performance Measurement Data Together

Ask your FA to give all five of the previously described metrics back to you in a form that ties actual performance to stated goals. If results and goals diverge, you can (and should) evaluate why. Were the financial markets performing particularly well or poorly, or were there problems in execution? Maybe your goals were too aggressive or are no longer appropriate because of changed circumstances. Collecting this data gives you the impetus to ask good questions of your FA and to keep your wealth management efforts on track. It synthesizes a whole series of decisions down to a few key facts that you can measure to stay on course and to stay focused on your most important financial objectives.

Responsibility #2: The FA Should Assemble and Manage Your Client Records

Having good investment, tax, legal, and administrative records, keeping them secure, and updating them as necessary is a critical service the FA should provide. Instead of sending a box full of unorganized papers to your accountant late in the tax season, ask your FA to assemble and manage the investment tax information you really need. Then have your FA send it to the accountant at the appropriate time (or to you if you're doing your own taxes). Work with your FA to keep important legal and administrative documents in a safe, accessible, organized location and a copy somewhere else. Although some people insist on managing their own records, and others are fortunate to have trustworthy and skilled assistants who can be responsible for this task, I strongly recommend that your FA coordinate this function to do the following:

- Serve as the single point of contact for managing and coordinating all your financial records.

- Collect critical data about you for loan documentation.

- Satisfy the requirements of the U.S. Patriot Act passed in the wake of 9/11. (This act requires specific administrative due diligence of every client, no matter how well known to the financial firm. So, be patient with your FA!)

- Provide performance measurement data on your investments.

- Maintain copies of your trust documents, wills, healthcare powers of attorney, and other important personal documents.

Please keep in mind that the more complex your personal financial situation is, the greater the necessary burden you are placing on your FA. If you are using a Barbell Investing or Index Investing strategy, the cost and complexity of your FA's role is fairly low unless you have a complicated estate plan. But if you use an Active Alpha Investing strategy, the bar rises considerably on both counts, especially when you use alternative investments.

Responsibility #3: The FA Should Coordinate the Work of Specialists

Most wealthy people rely on specialists to help them manage discrete parts of their lives. They use some combination of lawyers, accountants, insurance specialists, stockbrokers, trustees, bankers, philanthropic consultants, and even family counselors to help them manage. Much of the day-to-day work in each of these specialist areas is administrative. In addition, the work that one specialist does often influences the work of other specialists. Unless you are willing to take on the role yourself, the FA should be responsible for coordinating the work of these specialists and for following up with them to make sure that key tasks are completed correctly.

The FA can help you evaluate your wealth management/estate planning advisors. After you choose an FA, he or she should work at the epicenter of your wealth management process. This will help ensure that you're able to execute an integrated wealth management strategy.

A good FA typically has broad experience with a number of private clients and is in a good position to help you evaluate whether there are holes in your wealth management plan and whether the specialists you have hired are performing well. He or she can also provide valuable advice when it comes to reviewing, hiring, and possibly replacing wealth advisors.

This support can be especially valuable in the wake of a liquidity event. At the time of liquidity events, many wealthy people already have lawyers and accountants in place. For business owners in particular, these relationships might go back many years, and the relationships can be very close. Having such trusted advisors in place is a wonderful thing, but the issues that you face after a liquidity event are usually different from those that you faced previously. Thus, you'll need to evaluate how well your existing advisors' skills and temperaments are suited to the new set of demands that will be placed on them in the wake of your liquidity event. An experienced FA can often provide guidance to help you make the right decisions and can be a good source of leads for new hires, if necessary. Whether you keep or replace your accountant, lawyer, or insurance agent, make sure each of them has substantial experience relevant to your new circumstances.

The FA plays a critical role as a communications coordinator. I find that some of the biggest problems in implementing wealth management plans are due to poor communication between clients and their advisors. The best legal or tax advice can be rendered null and void if conceived in a vacuum or misaligned with your individual or family wealth management goals or investment strategy. Because wealth management advice is expensive, it pays to have someone ensuring that your advisors are working in tandem to help achieve your wealth management goals.

Your FA's ability to coordinate the work of various advisors is especially important when it comes to managing complex, long-term execution issues—such as implementing wealth transfer or tax reduction strategies. For example, family partnerships need to have a clearly documented business purpose, and if gifts are made from one family member to another, their value must be properly appraised and documented.

Some of these execution issues require assistance from a lawyer, an independent appraiser, or an accounting firm, but administrative and coordination functions are more appropriately in the domain of the FA. In my experience, (expensive) lawyers and tax accountants are more interested in inventing creative new strategies and generating new business than they are in managing the routine, ongoing administrative details of estate and asset management. So, think carefully about whether the specific task you need to accomplish requires a lawyer who bills at $600/hour or can be handled just as easily (and far less expensively) by your FA!

Responsibility #4: The FA Should Be Involved with Strategic Asset Allocation

Your FA should guide you in allocating your assets to provide appropriate levels of diversification, risk, and growth potential. The goal is to maximize your return potential for the particular level of risk that you feel comfortable taking. Working with your FA, you can evaluate various asset allocation options to find the mix that's right for you.

The historic data that go into these models are used to characterize the return potential or volatility of particular asset classes, or to define how asset classes behave relative to each other. Just because an asset has behaved historically in a particular way doesn't guarantee it will continue to behave that way in the future. In fact, the biggest complaint I heard from private client financial advisors during the financial crisis was that their models broke down. The past simply could not model what was happening in real time.

More sophisticated advisors address this problem by projecting the future, using judgment and experience that may reference the past but is not dependent on it. These judgments then get incorporated into their forecasting models. Because even the best historical data and the best prognosticators can't make predictions with absolute accuracy, either diversification or the ability to withstand volatility in your economic engine is critical to long-term survival and success.

Additional FA Responsibilities #5 and #6 for Active Alpha Investing

Active Alpha Investing is much more complicated than Index Investing. The four FA responsibilities I've just described become more demanding. At the same time, two other responsibilities—manager selection and opportunistic investing—become critical. Both of these functions add considerable execution risk to your portfolio, as well as upside potential. Wealth Strategist Partners focuses intensely on these functions because the stakes are so high.

Having said that, should you charge your FA with these responsibilities?

Many FAs and their firms claim to have skills in one or both of these areas. Financial consultants who work with institutions and very wealthy families also do this work. But in both instances, verifiable track records of people's performances are hard to come by.

Manager Selection

FAs like to recommend that their clients use investment managers— both in-house and third-party—who have demonstrated track records of past investment performance. Clients also respond more favorably to managers who have been doing well. But past results are generally not a good indicator of future returns. In business, you want to back a winner, but when investing, you should seek value for money. Often, this requires that you look for opportunities in places where others don't see them.

How do you work with your FA to transcend conventional market wisdom and correctly identify managers who are going to be winners, not just those who were winners in the past? You need to have the Four A's discussed in Chapter 5, "The Enchanted Forest, the Secret Society, and the Capital Kibbutz," to consistently and successfully choose them. Does your FA have these attributes of acumen, access, alignment of interests, and accountability? It's like horse racing: You can't make much money betting on the odds-on favorite. You have to see opportunity that others don't.

There are no easy answers when it comes to selecting top managers. In addition to reviewing your FA's experience and resources, make your FA prove to you over time that he or she has that rare skill of being able to move insightfully and consistently against the tide.

Opportunistic Investing

The approach to investing client assets in most wealth management firms is governed more by carefully designed processes or the drive to put money to work (capacity) than by the ability to exploit differentiated opportunity on behalf of each client. Given each FAs large number of clients, the wide variety of investment strategies employed, and the personal circumstances of each client relationship, most wealth management firms have little choice but to focus on adherence to process with an overriding emphasis on business risk control and client service. The process just doesn't seem to deliver consistently superior results for client portfolios.

Do a little thought experiment. Imagine yourself an FA who is lucky enough to be associated with a highly skilled investment strategist. In December of 2008, the strategist recommends that all private clients of the firm, including your own, make a big new investment in residential mortgage backed securities ("RMBS") amid the housing market's collapse. Now, your job is execution. You must understand why the strategist is making the recommendation, decide which of your 40 Active Alpha clients should consider such a move, and communicate the rationale for doing so. This requires you to have a detailed understanding of each client's existing managers and asset allocation, investment objectives, risk tolerance, and liquidity. You know it will be tough to make a convincing argument to buy these complex RMBS when their prices are dropping precipitously. In addition, the rationale for making the investment can't be the same for all your clients because each one is unique. In order to raise money to buy the RMBS, you will have to identify specific sale candidates for each client. A few clients will accept your recommendation based on trust. Others will want to do their own due diligence to understand the risks and reward potential more thoroughly—that is, if they aren't completely panicked. I think you get the idea, and we are talking about just one (correct) recommendation here. The numerous, repetitive, yet customized investment processes that are the nature and

---

necessity of most wealth management firms do not lend themselves to generating positive alpha.

Measuring the quality of an FA's skill in selecting managers and opportunistic investing is tough, except with the benefit of a long relationship, the ability to measure results, and your own expertise on the subject. For those reasons, tread cautiously when relying on FAs and their firms to add value in these areas. Explore the facts in detail and ask tough questions. Assess whether your FA has good judgment, unusual—even proprietary—market insight, and the execution skills to deliver alpha within established institutional processes. In the last analysis, manager selection and opportunistic investing are as much art as science, whether you have one client or 40. If you are uncomfortable making these assessments, you are better off using the Index Investing or Barbell Investing strategies.

Evaluating the Success of the FA

To determine how well your FA is performing the responsibilities outlined at the beginning of the chapter, meet with him or her at least once a year to do a comprehensive review of your wealth management plans. In these meetings, review your administrative procedures and your investment performance, update your FA on any relevant changes in your personal life, review any substantive changes in the FA's firm, look for ways to improve your results, write or update an action plan for the coming year, and review success against last year's plan. During these sessions, determine whether you are satisfied with the services you're receiving. Take the opportunity to ask your FA probing questions in the following areas:

- Is each of my investment managers performing as expected? If not, why not?

- Is my aggregate investment performance acceptable relative to stated objectives?

- How will changes in the ownership, management, or compensation systems in your firm affect my account?

- Is the administration of my assets working smoothly and accurately?

- Did I achieve other goals that we agreed on? What are the goals for my account next year?

- Has the risk profile of my assets shifted measurably? If so, what should we do about it?

- What's the likely impact of new tax or trust laws that have been enacted since we last met?

- Do I have the right insurance in place?

- How do changes in my life affect my estate plan?

- How can we improve our collective communication within my family about wealth management issues?

These reviews should not cover new products and services that the FA might want to sell you. Those discussions can take place at another time.

If you are implementing a complex Active Alpha Investing strategy, you will need to meet with your FA more frequently. These meetings provide occasions not just to learn about investment opportunities, but also to probe the thinking and skill of your key advisor and his or her colleagues. With complicated portfolios, there are many issues to discuss and decisions to make. I encourage you to request and review written materials, including a written agenda, investment performance, asset class research, and manager recommendations (including supporting material) in advance of each meeting with your FA. The more prepared you are, the more prepared the FA will have to be, and the more productive the meetings will be.

Sidebar 7.1:   Suggestions for How to Measure Performance

At a minimum, you and your FA should track the following on a regular basis and report results to appropriate family members at least once a year. You should separately track the performance of each entity in your estate that has a distinct investment strategy (i.e., personal investment portfolio, trust, family partnership, retirement plan):

- The aggregate time-weighted performance of financial assets, measured quarterly against a customized benchmark of financial assets over one year, three years, five years, and ten years.

- Aggregate net assets (in dollars) tracked annually and measured against the long-term absolute return goal defined in Chapter 4, "Defining Your Financial Objectives." Measurement periods of less than five years are not useful; a ten-year period is better.

- Actual asset allocation (in percentages and dollars) relative to target percentages, measured quarterly.

- Aggregate contributions to, or spending from, savings in dollars and percents relative to targets. Track this annually, and review the trend over time.

- Annual state and federal income taxes paid on investment assets (in dollars and percentage of assets) tracked annually. Review the trend over time.

- The time-weighted performance of each investment manager, benchmarked quarterly against a relevant index and/or benchmark and measured over one year, three years, five years, and ten years.

- Debt-to-equity structure of each entity or individual, as well as the family as a whole, as appropriate, reviewed annually.

- The liquidity position of each entity or individual relative to contingent or prospective calls on that liquidity, reviewed annually or quarterly as appropriate.

- A quarterly (or annual) "To Do" list and a review of the previous one. This should include an annual list of accomplishments (qualitative and quantitative) as well as objectives.

In addition to the Wealth Strategist, family members and the FA can add additional measures to track other aspects of past performance. A good system of accountability not only is an invaluable financial tool, but also provides ongoing reinforcement of the key values and business principles established in the strategic wealth management process.

Sidebar 7.2:   Common Wealth Management Implementation Errors

Be on the lookout for these common signs that your wealth management plan is not working as it should.

Near-term:

- Your advisor hasn't worked with you to develop an investment policy for each of the discrete entities in your estate (e.g., personal investment portfolio, trust, family partnership, retirement plan) that includes performance goals and a target asset allocation.

- You or your advisor adds alternative investments, especially illiquid ones, to your portfolio, and in doing so you lose the ability to measure your aggregate investment results.

- You want to divide your assets among several wealth advisors to test them head to head. Dividing among investment managers is all right, especially when using an Active Alpha Investing strategy.

- Responsibility for investment performance between you and your wealth advisor is ambiguous.

- Your advisor compares performance against benchmarks of active managers rather than indices, uses indices that don't account for reinvested dividends, doesn't have a composite benchmark to compare against, or changes benchmarks without a major change in your investment policy.

- Your advisor compares performance before fees or sales charges, or exclusive of cash in the portfolio.

- You have high portfolio turnover at either the manager or the security level, you are not accruing unrealized capital gains in a rising market, or your investment tax bill consistently is more than 20% of your gains.

- Your advisors give you multiple options for investment but don't make a firm recommendation for which they are willing to be held accountable.

- A prospective advisor describes "unique attributes" in his or her marketing materials, such as asset allocation skill or the ability to measure portfolio risk, but the professed skill isn't measured in your regular performance reporting.

Medium-term:

- Aggregate performance, net of fees, is below the composite benchmark for three- and five-year periods. The performance of active managers—net of their fees and sales charges—is below their index benchmark for three- and five-year periods.

Long-term:

- Over five to ten years, your assets, as measured in dollars, are significantly below your absolute return objectives, especially if markets have been relatively strong.

Should You Act as Your Own FA?

Some people decide to act as their own FA. If you are an index investor, your family and financial circumstances are fairly simple, and you have the time and inclination to act as your own FA, I encourage you to consider this path after assembling the critical information you need. Firms like Vanguard have a range of index investment products and the ability to offer aggregate investment performance as part of their core service. Alternatively, firms like Morningstar offer a service that allows you to measure the individual and aggregate performance of all your mutual funds. Morningstar charges a fee for performance measurement but it includes a robust package of research information on mutual funds and investing that is useful to advisors and private investors alike. Acting as your own FA can be time-consuming, but with the right tools and the dedication to follow through, it can be rewarding and inexpensive.

Some people with large and complicated asset bases hire a part-time or full-time employee, or an entire family office, to fulfill the FA role. People pursuing a Barbell Investing strategy often designate someone on their finance staff to play the FA role. Alternatively, they might set up a dedicated family office to fulfill the function. (Sidebar 9.3, "What Is a Family Office?" discusses family offices in greater detail.) If you opt for either of these choices, recognize that they require intensive oversight and that implementing good performance/accountability systems can be challenging but is critical to do when millions of dollars are at stake.

Final Words on FA Selection

Up to this point, I haven't suggested that you evaluate the investment management skills of FAs or their firm—even though most FAs work for wealth management firms that tout their investment capabilities. There's a reason for this. I recommend that you keep the role of FA clearly separate from that of the people who manage your investment portfolio. This is especially critical if you are pursuing an Active Alpha Investing strategy. You need your FA to be a scorekeeper, an organizer, and possibly a judge of talent. If the FA must also manage money, it creates a conflict.

If you are using Index Investing or are confident in your own ability to select good managers, choosing your FA and your investment managers from the same firm does have advantages. Administration is easier and often less expensive if everything is under one roof and can be tied together electronically. In addition, the FA doesn't have to judge investment talent, which can be a major source of conflict. Rock-bottom investment fees and low transaction costs also keep the financial relationships pretty transparent and aligned.

Selecting the Right Firm

Now that we've covered how to find the right FA for you, it's equally important to make sure that the right financial-services firm is standing behind the FA.

It's difficult to separate the qualifications of the FA from the qualifications of the firm employing the FA. Nevertheless, there are a number of key issues to consider in evaluating different wealth management firms. For example:

1. Do the firm's skills and experience align with your investment strategy?

2. How transparent are the firm's fees?

3. How robust are the firm's administrative systems?

4. How are FAs measured and incentivized by their firms?

Selection Factor #1: Do the Firm's Skills and Experience Align with Your Investment Strategy?

As I've already suggested, the type of strategy you select—Index Investing, Barbell Investing, or Active Alpha Investing—has a profound impact on the type of firm you'll want to hire. The complexity of your chosen strategy determines the robustness of the infrastructure you'll need in your FA's firm. It also drives the nature of the products, services, and third-party service agreements[2] you should expect from the firm.

Index Investing

One of the beauties of the Index Investing strategy (alone or as part of a Barbell Investing strategy) is that it makes the selection of the FA firm quite straightforward. You will want an FA firm to do the following:

- Have administrative capabilities to handle index funds in their various forms.

- Measure their aggregate performance.

- Rebalance your strategy as different asset classes perform either well or poorly.

You do not need an FA firm to do the following:

- Be well versed in tax efficiency, because index funds are already tax efficient.

- Specialize as a skilled selector of value-added managers, because you are selecting commodity products.

- Be proficient in tactical asset allocation skills, because you have sworn off this level of risk and complexity.

- Get you embroiled in brokerage-type fee structures, because the number of transactions you will have is minimal.

Now, here is the bad news.

Fewer firms will want your business if you index because profit margins for Index Investing strategies are razor thin. Existing providers are loath to cannibalize their very profitable Active Alpha business with low-margin index business. New index-based entrants need huge scale in order for the investment company to make a profit.

What's the solution to this dilemma if you've decided to index? In addition to the direct fees (from less than 0.1% to 0.25%) you'll be charged to participate in the actual index, I encourage you to consider paying a modest fee to your FA firm of between 0.1% and 0.75% of your assets, depending on their size and complexity, if the firm can provide the necessary accountability to support an Index Investing strategy. With this arrangement, you will pay at most half the industry average for such services, but will likely get better performance and service with fewer headaches. If you pursue this approach, I'm confident that this strategy will provide you with an FA firm that will meet your needs for executing an Index Investing strategy or a Barbell Investing strategy.

Active Alpha Investing

Hiring an FA firm to oversee an Active Alpha Investing strategy is much more challenging because your portfolio needs more specialized attention and requires higher-order investment skills to manage it properly. For Active Alpha Investing, you will want an FA firm to do the following:

- Use outstanding accountability systems to track the performance of your diverse portfolio.

- Be well versed in tax efficiency, because you are investing in assets that are highly sensitive to tax implications.

- Specialize as a skilled selector of value-added managers, because you are selecting riskier products that require a mastery of their fickle characteristics.

- Be proficient in opportunistic investment skills, because you will be taking additional risk and the relative attractiveness of asset classes will periodically create opportunities for additional return.

- Evaluate incentive fee structures, because the number and type of investments you have will be highly variable.

The good news is that many firms will want your business because profit margins are lucrative with Active Alpha clients, especially if you use their in-house investment products. When you do this, most firms "bundle" your administrative costs into the investment management fee. There might be cases, however, when you'll want to insist that the FA recommend only third-party managers to avoid conflicts of interest. In such cases, you'll pay separate fees to your FA and to your managers. This is what the Lucas family does because it keeps the FA focused on serving our needs.

Selection Factor #2: How Transparent Are the Firm's Fees?

It's incumbent on you as the Wealth Strategist to evaluate a prospective FA firm's fee structures through what I call the "alignment-of-interests" filter. When applying the filter, I ask two key questions:

1. Will I know all the ways I'm paying the firm?

2. Will the fees I'm charged correlate with the "value-added" benefits the firm provides to my account?

The answer to both questions should be yes! If the answers aren't forthcoming or if either answer is negative, the firm in question doesn't pass the screen.

That's the easy way to evaluate prospective FA firms, but there are many nuances to this process.

Firms that employ FAs, as well as most other financial companies, are remunerated based on four primary compensation models. I've listed them here in order of their attractiveness to you as an investor:

1. **Asset-based.** Advisors are paid based on the size of the assets within their responsibility. Compensation is somewhat tied to effectiveness. If assets grow in value, compensation rises. If assets fall, compensation declines. But asset growth and value added might or might not be linked, depending on the strength of the general markets relative to a portfolio's performance. Investment managers are usually paid this way. It is also my preferred method of compensating FAs, even if it means having a separate fee arrangement with investment managers.

2. **Time-based.** Advisors are paid hourly for their work on behalf of the client. Compensation is not tied to the effectiveness of the work. Consultants and accountants are paid this way.

3. **Transaction-based.** Each time an advisor conducts a transaction on behalf of a client, a commission is earned by the advisor. Compensation can be tied to the apparent value of the transaction to the client, but it is not tied to the actual value of the transaction to the client. Brokerage firms typically charge on this basis.

4. **Spread-based.** Advisors are paid based on the difference between what your funds earn and the expenses associated with managing those funds. A simple example of spread-based compensation involves banking deposits and lending. A bank pays a depositor 2% interest, lends the money at 5%, has 1.5% in costs, and earns a "spread" of 1.5%. But there are many other examples of spread-based compensation, such as "costless collars" and municipal bond trading. The wider the spread the advisor can create, the greater the profit potential.

When evaluating a firm's fee structure, there are other potential costs you might incur:

- **Profit participations.** Some advisors get a share of profits that they generate for clients, particularly in hedge funds and private equity funds. Some tax strategies are priced in part on expected profit (or tax savings). So-called "profit participations" or "carried interests" enable managers to share in profits but not have to suffer losses. Because of the potential for large returns to the manager, without the commensurate risk of loss, profit participations do entice managers to take more risk.

- **Switching costs.** You pay penalties if you sell some products before an appointed time. This penalty period can be one, five, ten, or more years from the date of purchase. Almost all investment products, except no-load mutual funds, have significant switching costs. Life insurance and annuity products are particularly prone to high switching costs because they incur high upfront sales commissions that must be amortized over time. Any investment with a significant unrealized gain has a switching cost because capital gains taxes become due.

- **Hidden compensation.** Wealth management firms have other sources of "hidden compensation." They include mutual fund marketing fees (called 12b-1 fees), brokerage fees, fee-sharing arrangements with third-party separate account and hedge fund managers, and in-kind services in exchange for directing clients' trading activity to certain brokers (the latter are known as "soft dollar" arrangements). Still other fees can include corporate finance and merger/acquisition fees, directors' fees, and profits from engaging as a principal in a transaction (i.e., stock trades and derivatives trades). Don't be bashful about asking a firm to commit in writing to full fee disclosure.

Some financial service firms, especially large conglomerates, charge their clients using several compensation models—all at the same time. If you analyze other fee components—performance features, switching costs, and hidden compensation—you'll find that these can either increase or decrease the alignment of interests. Suffice it to say that the more ways a firm charges you for services, the more difficult it is to keep the interests of advisors and client aligned.

Selection Factor #3: How Robust Are the Firm's Administrative Systems?

An efficient administrative infrastructure is critical to managing the alignment of interests among your family, your FA, your FA's firm, and your investment managers. Creating a culture of accountability among all parties to acknowledge and monitor the alignment is extremely important in protecting your interests. It also signals when interests may be diverging. Whatever the practical impediments are to creating accountability, work through them as best you can with your FA and his or her firm.

Here are some of the problems you will encounter. The wealth management firms that most easily pass muster on the alignment-of-interests test often fail most easily on accountability. The reverse is also true. Small, independent wealth management firms that have fewer potential conflicts of interest to manage typically are not big enough to justify the cost of complex, automated administrative and reporting systems. Large firms such as Morningstar, Charles Schwab, Advent, and LPL Financial have developed platforms to efficiently manage the back offices of these independents. These systems are well-suited for administering and reporting on portfolios of securities and mutual funds. But they are not yet robust enough to provide all the support needed for alternative investments. You should feel free to ask whether a current or prospective advisor uses one of these systems, and why.

The financial conglomerates, especially investment banks, have the most sophisticated reporting capabilities and arguably the most sophisticated full-service product offerings, but there are potential conflicts of interest embedded in almost everything they do. It is hard for you to feel assured that they are consistently putting your interests first.

Issues of alignment and accountability aren't huge hurdles to deal with if you are indexing or investing only in mutual funds. You can find small firms that have adequate systems, and you can structure your relationship with big firms to avoid most conflicts. However, if you use alternative investments as part of an Active Alpha Investing strategy, finding a solution that gives you both accountability and alignment of interests is very difficult. In addition, very few firms, large or small, track long-term historic asset values and cash flows to help clients understand long-term, dollar-based trends. With a little arm twisting, you might be able to convince your FA or accountant to do this for you. In our family, we have to track this data ourselves and we find it enormously useful. We also do "shadow accounting" to double-check the accuracy of our FA's systems and procedures, and our own.

We are all stuck with a difficult challenge of finding optimal administrative solutions. This problem represents a wonderful business opportunity. Indeed, the standard for industry leadership is wide-open here. I hope that one or more firms will aggressively address this opportunity in the next few years and that clients are wise enough to recognize its value.

Selection Factor #4: How Are FAs Measured and Incentivized by Their Firms?

To be successful, FAs have to make money for their firms if they want to keep their jobs. At the same time, they should add value to their clients. In an ideal world, these two goals are symbiotic. However, most firms don't even measure the value that FAs provide to their clients, and if they did, the exercise would be complex and imprecise. Value to the client can come in many forms: creating positive alpha through good manager selection, identifying hidden risks in a client's balance sheet, giving good asset allocation advice for an Index Investment strategy, or pointing out that the client is spending too much money. Most firms, however, don't spend much energy measuring their value added to clients. Some firms don't even measure how often clients leave the firm.

By contrast, measuring the revenue (or profit) contribution of FAs is simple, precise, and closely scrutinized. Firm managements typically track it at the individual and/or team level. Often, this information is publicized within the firm to encourage competition among FAs. Recognition, bonuses, and discretionary awards are given for exemplary performance. These incentives create constant pressure to perform.

Fortunately, most FAs pride themselves on service to their clients and want to do the right thing for their customers. I've known a number of FAs over the years who go out of their way to get things done for their clients, despite the predictable institutional roadblocks that arise from time to time. Most of these advisors have served at their firms a long time and have developed loyal clients over the years. They build strong personal relationships, meeting with their clients at summer homes or joining them on fishing trips or for golf outings. In return, these loyal clients actually provide their advisors with an element of job security. Happy clients mean a stable revenue stream. Of course, because it is so hard to measure the value added to clients, good service and a strong personal relationship are often the best ways to keep clients happy.

The combination of company pressure to perform and the difficulties of providing strong accountability to clients presents a real challenge to highly conscientious FAs. Below are three real-life examples of FAs from three different firms dealing with the peculiarities of their job.

FA #1: Eve was such a good client advisor that a few years ago she was lured from one major boutique wealth management firm to another. The terms of her non-compete agreement prevented her from soliciting her old clients, and she and her new firm actually abided by that agreement. The new firm promised her resources to build a team and to support her business development efforts. But then the economy suffered a downturn and, in the face of industry contraction and a new management team, profitability and cost reduction became the priorities of the firm. Each month, the firm compared the revenue and profit contributions of each client advisor and distributed the results to all the team leaders. Eve and her scaled-back team were always at the bottom. Despite the fact that Eve enjoyed high customer-satisfaction ratings from clients, she decided to leave the firm after a year of ever-increasing stress to meet the firm's expectations for revenue growth. Even though her employer didn't literally push her out the door, the pressure to meet performance expectations simply became too great.

FA #2: George was completely dedicated to his clients even though he worked for a huge financial firm. He carried two cellphones at all times and was always on the road. His clients could call him 24/7, and they received plenty of "face time" when they wanted it. George was careful about how he managed his book of business and would, from time to time, hand off smaller and time-consuming relationships to a colleague. This enabled him to maintain service levels and profitability.

George was a real stickler for process and timeliness, much to the chagrin of the middle- and back-office specialists at his firm whom he regularly chewed out because he knew how to expedite things for clients when staffers erected roadblocks. Years of working inside the firm before becoming an FA had taught him the firm's systems and processes backward and forward.

Even though George's firm had been subject to mergers, systems changes, and numerous reorganizations and "adjustments" to his compensation plan over the years, he managed to shield his clients from the turmoil. While the rest of his firm struggled to keep client attrition down to acceptable levels in the 2000–2002 bear market, George never lost a single client. In 2003, the firm went to a bonus system that was payable entirely at the discretion of management. Ostensibly, this was done to improve teamwork, but it also had the benefit of helping the firm to manage its earnings because bonuses were a line item in the firm's budget. Finally, managing the tension between serving the client and meeting the firm's expectations got the better of George. When the financial markets started to recover, he quit. In the first edition, I speculated he would turn up again as the founder or co-founder of an independent advisory firm. I was right—George is now enjoying his new entrepreneurial endeavor and wonders why he didn't make the move sooner.

FA #3: Martha worked for a large brokerage firm during the second half of the 1990s advising private clients on their portfolios. The firm has a highly entrepreneurial culture that offers advisors wide latitude on the advice they give as long as their revenue numbers look good. This firm is one of many that tracks advisors' performance on the basis of net new revenue, but does not measure client attrition.

Through a referral, Martha attracted a successful entrepreneur as a client. This client's firm had spun out several million in excess cash that the client needed to invest. In addition, the company had tax-deferred profit sharing and pension plans that needed to be managed. Martha recommended a selection of variable annuities invested in stocks. One of the expressed benefits of annuities is that the assets grow on a tax-deferred basis. She recommended variable annuities for the company's profit-sharing and pension plans, as well as for her client's taxable accounts.

The cost of the annuities plus management fees approached 4% per annum, sucking up all the tax benefit for the client in anything but the most robust stock market environment. By contrast, an equity index fund of equal amount would have been nearly as tax efficient and had an annual fee about 95% lower. Furthermore, recommending that variable annuities get placed inside a tax-deferred vehicle was inexcusable.

The sales commission on the annuities Martha sold to her client enabled her to make a very tidy sum upon closing the deal. Furthermore, when her client committed to the products, the switching cost to change to other alternatives would further cut into his profits, essentially locking him in for seven or more years.

For a couple of years in the late 1990s, the rapid rise in the stock market obscured the impact of the high costs the client was paying to be invested in annuities. But when the bear market hit, the full impact of the misguided strategy became apparent. The client suffered severe losses and fired Martha's firm. She, however, had already made out like a bandit and was ready to move on to the next new prospect. Five years later, the client was still trying to extricate himself from these highly priced, poorly performing vehicles.

All the previous examples are true, though the names have been changed to protect privacy. All these advisors are, or were, at the top of their game and, with the exception of Martha, went to great lengths to balance the demands of their companies with their own very high standard of service to their clients. But despite considerable personal sacrifice, and in most cases financial success, each FA had a very hard time maintaining balance.

Most advisors are dependent on a single employer, but have numerous clients. When pressures to perform increase, all people, financial advisors included, tend toward economic self-interest. All other things being equal, this gives the employer the upper hand in molding employee behavior. The more aggressive the employer and the greater the level of advisor remuneration, the harder firm managements tend to push. Customers need to be protective of their own interests.

It's the responsibility of the Wealth Strategist to provide a proactive counterbalance to the business pressures of firms and the natural human tendencies of individual employees. In some cases, the Wealth Strategist must stand up to the advisor, and in other cases, he or she needs to informally partner with the FA to pressure the FA's firm for better client support.

Sidebar 7.3:　The Case for Corporate Trustees

Many wealth management strategies involve the establishment and management of trusts. On the assumption that trusts will be part of your integrated wealth management strategy, how should you choose a trustee?

Being a trustee is a serious responsibility that can be technical in nature and carries with it substantial potential liability. There is inevitably a significant administrative component as well. Trustees can be either corporations or individuals. I am a strong believer in using corporations, especially for trusts that are for anything other than your own benefit. Corporate trustees are usually more expensive than individual trustees, but the professional expertise and the administrative capabilities you receive are usually worth the cost. Corporate trustees embed a notional liability insurance charge in their fees because they do get sued by disgruntled beneficiaries. Individual trustees can get sued, too, but they usually accept the role as a favor to a friend or family member. They rarely have the experience and structure in place to protect themselves legally in cases of disputes. Do you want to saddle a friend or family member with this responsibility?

There are two additional benefits to using a corporate trustee, benefits that I would argue are even more valuable. The first is that they have "infinite lives." They don't die unexpectedly, get sick, or leave town on extended vacations. They provide a sense of stability and long-term perspective that is useful. Their other great benefit is their ability to say no to beneficiaries in a dispassionate, unemotional way. Family relationships are complicated, and corporate trustees can act as objective and legalistic arbiters of disagreements or misunderstandings. Most people don't expect them to have a heart if it conflicts with their fiduciary duty to fulfill the grantor's wishes or to execute administrative responsibilities within the law. If there are family feuds, spendthrift children, or financial guardianship issues, and even if the family is functioning well, inserting a corporate trustee into the mix adds valuable perspective, professionalism, and administrative skill.

To guard against trustees becoming complacent, I recommend that you put a process in place to remove the trustee without cause at any time during the life of the trust. In our case, a majority of selected family members may remove a trustee without cause. A trusted lawyer, accountant, or family friend can also be a good "trustee remover."

Hiring an FA

As I said at the beginning of the chapter, hiring an FA is your most important wealth management decision. Assuming that you have followed the Strategic Wealth Management Framework to this point, you're ready to write a fairly detailed job description for your FA in the context of your values, family situation, and financial strategy.

After you have written a job description, the next step is to identify firms that are most likely to meet your needs. If you are looking for an FA to help you with indexing, firms like Vanguard, BlackRock, Northern Trust, or Pimco might be places to start. If you want personalized service but also index-type products, Dimensional Fund Advisors certifies independent wealth managers to distribute their products. If you have substantial wealth and are looking for customized indexing capabilities, add Parametric Portfolio Associates to your list. Sometimes you have to dig deep within a firm to learn that it actually does offer indexing capabilities. Goldman Sachs, Fidelity, and JP Morgan, among others, also have indexing capabilities, but they aren't always well advertised. If you are looking for an FA to help you with Active Alpha Investing, many of the aforementioned firms offer active management, as do many more large and small firms.

In recent years, Family Office Exchange (FOX) has done some good work evaluating multi-family offices and helping their members to find the right fit for their needs. They have built an Advisor Directory of leading advisors based upon serious due diligence and their member's recommendations. You can check them out at www.familyoffice.com. FOX is a useful, independent resource if you are looking to hire an FA. I encourage you to take a look.

Regardless of the strategy you are pursuing, I suggest building a list of six or eight firms that you think can meet your needs. Make sure your list includes different types of organizations, including independent financial boutiques, not just big brokerage firms or mutual fund companies or banks. Do your own research or use the FOX Advisor Directory to identify a few specialized wealth management firms or independent planners so that you can study a range of offerings. If possible, get good references for specific advisors within larger firms. Review your list, go to each firm's website, and try to narrow it down to three or four preferred providers.

After you've compiled your preferred list, prepare a written Request for Proposal (RFP) that includes the FA's job description, information about yourself and your financial and family circumstances, and a series of questions that you would like each firm to answer. To help you out, I've included a list of sample questions in Sidebar 7.4. When the RFP is complete, assemble the names and contact information of specific individuals within each firm, preferably a business manager in wealth management. Set up telephone interviews to learn more about the firms using your RFP as a guide. Compare what you've learned about each firm and advisor, and try to whittle down your list to one or two top contenders that you want to meet with personally. Save the more subjective questions or those that benefit from more expansive answers for these in-person meetings. If after the meetings you're not happy, go back to your broader list. You might even expand it somewhat. The selection process is a good learning opportunity. Although you want to be respectful of people's time, you also want to make an informed decision. When you find a firm you like, make sure you meet with the person or people who will be assigned to manage your relationship, not just a marketing specialist. All the while, ask yourself: Are these people I can work with? Will these people be the ones who will actually work on my account, or are they salespeople or senior managers? Are they comfortable with the way I want to manage my assets and with the job description I have for them? The best advisors will be evaluating you as well. So, be open and balanced about your own issues and expectations. It's in everyone's interest to make sure the fit is good. Ideally this relationship will last a long time and be fruitful for client and advisor alike.

Sidebar 7.4:   The FA RFP

Putting together an RFP is a key step in preparing yourself to identify the right FA for you. Here are questions and requests you should address to prospective service providers as part of that process:

- Can you provide brochures describing your wealth management services and financial products? If possible, please include the firm's annual report, including financial statements. (Getting several years' reports will give you insight into the stability and priorities of the organization. Read between the lines; these are polished marketing documents.)

- Who owns the firm?

- Can you provide relevant organizational charts for the firm and its private client group?

- What constitutes a typical team serving each wealthy client? How many clients does the typical private client team serve? Who do you recommend for my relationship? How long has this team been working together at your firm? How many new clients have been added to this team in each of the past five years? How many have left in each of the past five years? (Please send a résumé of each of the key people whom you recommend to work on my relationship.)

- How does the firm track the amount of value-added that the client service team provides to its clients? What does it do with the information it collects?

- How do you make strategic asset allocation decisions on behalf of clients? How do you evaluate risk? Are your models based on forward-looking or backward-looking information? Before-tax or after-tax information?

- How do you help clients choose managers? Do you receive any incentives to recommend certain managers over others? If so, what are they? What track record do you have to demonstrate your manager selection skill?

- What fees do I pay the firm? Does the firm receive any other income from my assets other than direct fees, including but not limited to brokerage fees, banking fees or spreads, sales charges, 12b-1 fees, or indirect compensation from service providers that you recommend to me?

- How much professional personnel turnover has there been in the private client group in each of the past five years? How are your key client advisors compensated? On what basis are their bonuses calculated? How do you measure client satisfaction?

- Please send a sample of your typical client-reporting package. Can you calculate the time-weighted total return for a total portfolio of public assets including stocks, bonds, and mutual funds? If alternative investments, including illiquid investments, are included, does your system still have the capability to measure aggregate time-weighted rates of return?

- Can you create customized benchmarks using market indices to compare against the actual performance of each manager and the aggregate portfolio? Are any upgrades to your accounting and performance measurement systems planned within the next two years? If so, please describe them.

- Describe the administrative services offered by the typical client service team other than portfolio administration and performance measurement. Summarize your procedures for ensuring accurate and timely execution of administrative services. Do you have online administrative services that I can access?

- Can you provide at least three client references at the appropriate time?

The Lucas Family Experience of Selecting an FA

Before we chose our new FA in 2001, we had the same individual serving us for seven or eight years. He was almost part of the family, and if he had received better support from his organization, we would probably still be working with him. He had developed strong personal relationships with each member of the family. He got his firm to do things for us that it did not do for anyone else—using third-party investment managers, putting alternative investments into irrevocable trusts, and creating a partnership with our family to make investment decisions.

But he couldn't fix his firm's reporting infrastructure, and even with his support we were always fighting the system. Because he had built such strong personal relationships, my family trusted him. This made it particularly difficult for me to convince the family to take action. But finally I prevailed, and the search ensued for a new FA.

We needed an FA equipped to handle an Active Alpha Investing strategy, complete with alternative assets and tactical asset allocation. We wrote up a detailed description of our wealth management strategy and the capabilities we sought in order to implement it. We wanted a corporate trustee that embraced complete open architecture, could provide the necessary support for accountability, and was comfortable with multiple asset classes, including alternative investments.

We sent out RFPs to eight carefully selected firms. Most were large banks with well-established trust departments; a few were large family offices that were trying to attract additional clients (multifamily offices). We also approached several investment banks that had trust departments. We explicitly told each firm that we would ask it, if selected, to sign a detailed Memorandum of Understanding (MOU) committing it to deliver on those things it promised in the RFP.

The search for a new FA proved to be eye-opening. First, when the marketing people realized we were serious about the key stipulations in the RFP, most said they could not deliver both the complete open architecture and the accountability structure we sought. And several insisted on managing up to 50% of the assets internally, a proposal that we rejected. Eventually, we did find three firms in this elite group that claimed they could fulfill all of our specifications. After interviewing two of them in detail, we chose to negotiate with one. In the late stages of negotiation, this particular firm backed away from claims it made in the marketing presentation about its performance measurement capabilities. (We ultimately agreed to pay an extra fee to an affiliated consulting firm to get what we wanted.) The second surprise was the takeover of this firm in the midst of our negotiations, even after representatives had assured us they intended to remain independent.

Despite the surprises and midcourse adjustments, out of this process we retained a new FA firm that delivers to us today in many ways:

- There is alignment of their interests with ours (if our assets do well, their fees rise; if our assets do poorly, their fees fall).
- We know precisely how they are paid.
- The accountability systems in place are adequate.
- The firm has a sophisticated suite of services that support our Active Alpha Investing strategy.
- The firm pays its people a competitive wage.
- They oversee a tax-managed index portfolio for us.

The new FA firm does have one key deficiency: Turnover of personnel resulted in four relationship managers over a period of three years. Fortunately for us, we have a stable family office, so when our FAs turn over, it is less disruptive than if we didn't have our own infrastructure or if we had to change firms each time.

Roll the clock forward to 2012 and once again we have recently completed a new search and changed FAs. Whereas the first merger with our old FA was tolerable, the second one was not. Despite the personnel turnover serving our account, we had liked our old FA firm and found them capable. But we could not get comfortable with the new owner and the owner's vision for the business. The questions we asked and what we looked for in the replacements were very similar to what transpired a decade earlier. Because we track the industry pretty closely and we have very specific requirements, we focused immediately on just two firms and ultimately chose one. That was really the only difference in process. I hope this relationship will last.

Conclusion

This chapter has described the pivotal roles that the Financial Administrator (FA) and his or her firm play in helping the Wealth Strategist implement wealth management plans and strategies.

Most potential FAs will tell you they are great investors. But what you need is a great administrator who has your interests, not an employer's interests, as his or her top priority.

Now, let's move on to Chapter 8, "Taxes Can Be Your Ally!" where we'll discuss taxes and how best to minimize them for purposes of optimal wealth management results.

Chapter 7: Issues to Discuss with Your Family

1. How do you track the performance of your investments? How can you improve on your current process?

2. Do you currently employ financial advisors to help you implement your financial goals? If so, do they have the requisite qualifications outlined in this chapter?

3. Have you had experience with financial advisors that proves they have your best interests at heart? If not, can you imagine selecting new advisors to assist you?

4. Are you convinced that the more advisors you have, the harder it might be to fulfill your financial goals?

5. Have you ever measured your asset base at the end of each year? If not, do you have the information and skills to do so?

6. Have you ever known what fees you actually pay to your financial-services firm? Do you know how to go about better discerning how fees should be charged to you?

7. Do you think it's possible for a Financial Administrator to put a client's interests first, while still serving the firm in which the FA is employed?

8. After reading this chapter, do you have enough confidence to issue a Request for Proposal (RFP) to financial-services firms seeking professional assistance?

9. Have you changed your mind regarding your preferred investing strategy after reading about the varied qualifications required of an FA to implement each of the three investment strategies?

Endnotes

1. The CFA Institute is a member organization of investment professionals committed to leading the global investment profession by setting the highest standards of education, integrity, and professional excellence. As part of their program, they led the establishment of a global standard for how to measure investment performance: the Global Investment Performance Standards, or

GIPS. These standards are regularly reviewed and periodically updated to allow investors to measure performance in the fairest possible way and to accurately compare the performance of various managers. For more information about GIPS, go to www.gipsstandards.org. For more information on the CFA Institute, go to www.cfainstitute.org.

2. Many firms that sell third-party products negotiate service agreements with the firms whose products they sell. Agreements often include revenue and cost-sharing clauses, as well as terms for handling client information and joint marketing efforts.

8

Taxes Can Be Your Ally!

"Over the long term, benign neglect really does pay off."
—**Charles D. Ellis, author of** *Winning the Loser's Game*

I t should come as no surprise that taxes rank as either #1 or #2 on the list of expenses for wealthy Americans. Today, taxes are my family's second-biggest leakage behind spending, and without careful planning, they would be the biggest. In 2013, in all likelihood taxes on the wealthy are going to go up, possibly a lot.

By comparison, many institutional investors—pension funds and endowments, for example—with billions of dollars in investments don't pay any taxes at all.

So what can you do responsibly to minimize your taxes?

Although tax efficiency is a critical element in your investment strategy, most investment managers don't concern themselves much with tax minimization because doing so doesn't reap them any bottom-line benefits. After all, they are evaluated and paid on pretax performance by almost everyone. But I'm here to tell you that evaluating your after-tax results is important. Managed well, taxes also can be your ally in the strategic wealth management planning process.

Under the U.S. tax code, the wealthier you become, the more control you have over how much you pay in taxes and when you pay them. There are also numerous incentives in the tax code that work in your favor to reduce risk and to help your assets grow more quickly. Most of the incentives I discuss in this chapter are likely to remain in any new tax bill, though some of the details will no doubt change. This chapter gives you the framework you need to ensure that taxes stay front and center in your wealth management strategies, resulting in the highest net level of return possible on your investments. Check with your tax and financial advisors about the current state of affairs and its impact on you before you make any decisions.

Where Do You Begin?

There are enough tax regulations out there to fill a library. U.S. taxpayers are subject to the U.S. tax code with its federal regulations, fifty different state tax codes, and thousands of county/city/town tax codes. I simply cannot address the minutiae of all of these different rules, and you certainly didn't buy this book in search of mind-numbing tax analysis.

To keep your "eye on the big prize" (tax minimization and tax efficiency), I can tell you that the structure of the U.S. tax code offers some very attractive incentives for wealthy investors and creates disadvantages in other areas. Consequently, for you, the Wealth Strategist, there are five key takeaways from this chapter:

1. Understand that U.S. taxing authorities are, in fact, your investing partners. I'll explain why.

2. For taxable investors, it's valuable to be a long-term, equity-oriented investor.

3. You can add value to your bottom line through tax management.

4. Retirement and deferred-compensation plans are great pretax savings tools, but don't overcommit yourself to these vehicles.

5. Don't put after-tax money into variable annuities and retail life insurance savings policies.

It's worth exploring these key takeaways with your financial administrator and your accountant and incorporating them into your wealth management strategy. In the rest of this chapter, I will explore each of these points in detail. Sometimes the math is a little complicated, but it helps more numerate readers to understand the issues more clearly. In these cases, I separate the detail from the concept so that you can choose how much you want to immerse yourself. For better or worse, a significant part of wealth management is quantitative.

Takeaway #1: U.S. Taxing Authorities Are Your Investing Partners

In previous chapters, I've talked about your partners in the wealth management process—accountants, lawyers, and investment managers. I have not included the Internal Revenue Service or your local taxing authorities in this list of wealth management partners—until now.

Personal income taxes were legalized in the 16th Amendment to the U.S. Constitution, and the first modern income tax law was enacted in October 1913. Since the end of World War I, the top Federal marginal tax rate has been volatile, with a high above 90%, a low of 28%, and a current rate of 35%. In 2013, it is currently scheduled to rise to 39.6% on earned income. In its early years, the top marginal rate affected only the super-rich, but today the majority of people reading this book are likely to pay taxes at the top marginal rate, even in retirement. For sound economic reasons, the short-term capital gains tax rates now mirror income tax rates. But next year, they are likely to be 3.8% higher because of the new Medicare tax applied to most investment income.

By contrast, since 1929, the top marginal long-term capital gains tax rate has been steadier, ranging from a high of 40% to a low of 15%, which happens to be the current rate. This is a much narrower and lower range, particularly when you consider that the rate has been meaningfully above 30% only for brief periods. Since 1929, the long-term capital gains tax rate has been lower than the top marginal income tax rate in all but two years. Next year, unless Congress acts, Federal long-term capital gains rates will go back to 20%, plus the 3.8% Medicare tax. Dividend tax rates will rise from 15% to 43.4%, almost a 200% increase. What is harder to assess at this point is the impact that the Alternative Minimum Tax (AMT) rate has on your current tax rate and what it might be next year. There are a lot of moving parts with potentially big impacts!

Today, federal income taxes are the largest source of federal government revenues, about 45% of the total. This is over ten times the revenue typically generated by capital gains taxes. With gaping deficits today, the government needs a large revenue boost. It is impossible at this time to predict which combination of income tax and capital gains tax changes, plus spending and entitlement reduction measures, will be instituted. Stay close to what is happening in Washington and use the framework in this chapter to help you think through the implications for you.

Despite all the current confusion, for wealthy investors and business owners I prefer to think of U.S taxing authorities as investment partners, as opposed to adversaries. I also view that partnership in unconventional ways, which I describe in the following paragraphs.

First, when you are designing a wealth management strategy, it's important to remember that although the government sets the rules for how to calculate taxes in the tax code, the government in fact acts like a silent partner. Each taxpayer is left to apply the code's rules to his or her own advantage. (More on this in Takeaway #2.) Our own actions and decisions have an enormous impact on our tax liabilities!

Second, unlike accountants, lawyers, and investment managers who make money off your assets through fees regardless of how well your investments do, tax authorities benefit only if you generate profits. If there are no profits, or profits are deferred, Uncle Sam doesn't get paid.

Third, in exchange for taxing you, the government provides you with a wide range of services including defense, emergency services, a system of law, economic management, Social Security, and community infrastructure, including roads and schools. All these are critical to ensuring a stable society, guaranteeing free commerce, and enabling you to get wealthy in the first place. Just how many billionaires do you know in the Sudan? Even in Western Europe, the rate of wealth creation isn't nearly as high. I rest my case.

Takeaway #2: Be a Long-Term, Equity-Oriented Investor

The tax code offers strong incentives for investors to think and act long term.

Long-Term Investments Are Taxed at the Lowest Rate

Today, the top short-term capital gains tax rate is 35%, which means that if you sell a profitable investment one year or less from the day of its purchase, you are taxed at this rate.

By contrast, today's top long-term capital gains tax rate is 15%, a full 57% lower, and you don't pay the tax on the long-term gains until you sell. Also, most dividends on stocks, at least at the moment, are taxed at the same low rate, even in the first year, although you pay tax every year on dividends.

The longer you hold an appreciating investment, the more advantages there are:

- Deferred capital gains taxes are like interest-free loans.
- "Benign neglect" pays off.
- Deferred capital gains taxes provide downside risk protection.
- You might never have to pay capital gains taxes.
- Investing in equities lowers the tax rate on "spending money."
- Declining capital gains tax rates have been a bonanza to long-term investors, but that might soon stop.

The combined benefits of holding assets for the long term are substantial, so long as the assets are appreciating in value. To explain the details, I must delve into some basic accounting theory and a few numbers. I encourage you to try to follow along, even if numbers are not your strong point. After all, it is your money, and taxes are a big leakage.

Deferred Capital Gains Taxes Are Like Interest-Free Loans

Taxes on long-term gains can be deferred until an asset is sold, even if it's 86 years later, as in the case of my family's ownership of Carnation stock. The unrealized gains over 86 years of ownership meant that there was a large accruing, but unpaid, liability to the IRS on our family's balance sheet.

It's like getting no-interest loans from the government! It also has some other attractive features. First, at no point does the government have the authority to say, "We are calling your loan." You have the right to let the free "loan" continue to be unpaid for as long as you want, as long as you don't sell the underlying asset. Second, in most cases, the size of the loan varies proportionately with the success of the investment. The bigger the gain, the bigger the loan.

"Benign Neglect" Pays Off

The concept of benign neglect is best portrayed by a mathematical example. Let's start by looking at two investors who pay federal taxes on long-term capital gains at the full 15% rate. Each buys the same asset for $100,000.

The first investor holds it until it is sold for $1,000,000, for a 900% percent increase in the original investment. He pays taxes on the $900,000 gain (15% capital gains tax rate times $900,000 equals $135,000) and is left with $865,000.

The second investor gets impatient, sells early, and generates $200,000. He pays the $15,000 in taxes on his $100,000 gain and is left with $185,000. He then realizes he has sold too soon, but manages to buy back $185,000 of the asset at the same valuation. It then increases five times in value for a total of a 900% return, just like the first investor. After paying federal taxes of 15% on the $740,000 gain, the second investor is left with $814,000.

The second investor's impatience cost him $51,000 (the difference between $865,000 and $814,000).[1]

Additionally, if the second investor had executed his first sale within one year of buying the asset, he would have paid a 35% tax ($35,000) instead of a 15% tax ($15,000). After he has reinvested, participated in the rest of the price appreciation, and paid the 15% long-term rate on the rest of his gains, the total value of his investment would be $726,000, a far cry from the already diminished $814,000. Clearly, the cost of paying short-term capital gains is high, which is why long-term investing is almost always better for taxable investors.

Lastly, let's look at two more hyperactive investors who sell (and repurchase) every time the stock increases by $100,000 in value. In other words, over the course of the 900% increase, they each buy and sell nine times. One investor pays only long-term capital gains tax at the 15%

rate because he always waits at least one year to sell and repurchase. The other investor pays short-term capital gains tax at the 35% rate because he always sells and repurchases within one year.

How much are they left with after the 900% appreciation? The first investor is left with $743,963. The second investor generates only $490,668! Interestingly, the second investor's major loss is not because of the higher tax rate. It is the lost opportunity to earn profits on money that is paid each year to the government.

Figure 8.1 provides a summary of these five examples.

The Cost of Acting Short Term

	Investment	Pre-Tax Return	Net Return	Cost of Acting Short Term
Long-Term Hold	$100,000	900%	$865,000	$0
Intermediate Sale	$100,000	900%	$814,000	$51,000
Short-Term Sale	$100,000	900%	$726,000	$139,000
Multiple Long-Term Sales	$100,000	900%	$743,963	$121,037
Multiple Short-Term Sales	$100,000	900%	$490,668	$374,332

Figure 8.1 High turnover adds a lot of cost to the portfolios of taxable investors.

You can clearly see the benefit of being a long-term investor. Most investments are not likely to return 900% over 2, 5, or even 10 years. But over 20 years, a 900% return equates to 12.2% per year, and over 30 years to 8% per year. Many investments over a longer time frame can and do generate these types of returns. So, the costs of not thinking long term are very real.

The flip side of the long-term incentives offered in the tax code is that investment income and short-term capital gains are expensive luxuries. Before you invest in assets that generate high levels of current income and short-term gains, it is prudent to compare the estimated after-tax performance of these assets relative to other more tax-efficient alternatives.

The Alternative Minimum Tax law uses a different methodology for determining your taxes, one that eliminates a number of (usually favorable) deductions and adjustments to your taxable income (state income tax and property taxes among them). If your AMT liability exceeds your regular tax liability, you will be subject to AMT. Millions of taxpayers are getting hit by the AMT each year.

The AMT rates are still somewhat lower than standard rates. They are 26% on the first $175,000 of AMT income and 28% for income over that amount. The standard 15% rate for individuals on long-term capital gains and dividends also applies under AMT. So even under AMT, you are given strong incentives to be a long-term investor.

Before a liquidity event, many people generate enough earned income and have few enough deductions that their standard tax rate is above the top AMT rate of 28%. After a liquidity event, many of the same people have higher itemized deductions that don't qualify under AMT, lower salaries, and more unearned income. Also, they might own certain investments that have income subject to AMT that are not subject to the regular tax. In short, it's tougher to avoid AMT after you have accumulated significant and diversified wealth.

Many private investors allocate a portion of their assets to municipal bonds because they are tax-exempt. There are, however, many types of "muni" bonds, and not all of them have the same tax treatment. Bonds that are general obligations of a municipality ("GO Bonds") are exempt from federal tax—including alternative minimum tax. For bondholders residing in the same state, GO Bonds are usually exempt from state tax. However, another common class of muni bonds called Private Activity Bonds, which typically fund specific qualifying projects, are not exempt from alternative minimum tax. These bonds often trade at higher yields than GO Bonds, but for those who are in the alternative minimum tax bracket, the net of tax yields might be lower. Many muni bond funds invest in Private Activity Bonds as a way of increasing their stated yield. It is important to make sure that the tax strategy of the fund is consistent with your own tax position.

Deferred Capital Gains Taxes Provide Downside Risk Protection

The U.S. tax code provides downside protection for the investor. Realized losses from one investment can be used to offset gains from another investment. There are some details that complicate this generalization,[2] so it is important to work with an accountant to make sure that the offsets are appropriate. Generally speaking, profits and losses from stocks, bonds, hedge funds, and other vehicles that invest in public companies can be used to offset each other.

My family and I review our assets every fall to see whether there are losses that we want to realize to reduce our net tax liability for the year. Sometimes, we can replace one mutual fund or stock with a similar one, lowering our tax burden without significantly changing our overall portfolio or incurring significant transaction costs. It's an easy thing to do. It can save real money and it involves insignificant risk if executed prudently.

Another benefit of downside protection that is rarely discussed is that your silent partner, the government, loses disproportionately when appreciated securities decline in value. Taxes are payable only on profits, not on the total value of your investment. If one of your high-performing investments has a reversal and declines, say, 30% in value, the deferred tax liability declines by more than 30% because the profit has declined more than the total value. Your share of the profit (net of deferred tax liability) declines by less than 30%. This phenomenon happens only in taxable accounts. In a retirement plan or annuity, a 30% decline means a 30% decline no matter what.

The downside protection offered by the tax code is more powerful for stocks than it is for bonds. All but distressed bonds trade in a range that is within 20% of their $100 par value. As such, the level of capital gain or loss, and the associated capital gains tax, is fairly small. Stocks, on the other hand, can grow many times in value, accruing huge unrealized gains in the process.

Equity mutual funds and hedge funds that frequently turn over their portfolios also get much less benefit from the downside protection than investment vehicles with buy-and-hold strategies.

I have never seen a wealth management firm incorporate the downside protection of taxes into their asset allocation models. If they did, they would recommend that their clients increase exposure to long-term equity-type investments (including real estate) relative to bonds, hedge funds, or other tax-inefficient investments, especially as unrealized capital gains build within the portfolio.

For a few years after a major liquidity event, most people don't have many unrealized gains in their investment portfolios. If this is your situation, this has the effect of increasing your risk because you can't get the downside protection from taxes. Any losses you incur cannot be used to offset realized gains until you generate additional gains sometime in the future. In earlier chapters, I have urged you to be methodical when putting money into investments in the wake of a liquidity event. This is just one more reason to take your time, increase your risk profile in parallel with your own experience, and resist the temptation to put your newly liquid assets to work quickly.

You Might Never Have to Pay Capital Gains Taxes

If you play your cards right, you don't ever have to pay capital gains taxes. Here are four techniques that are straightforward and simple to execute. They are solidly embedded in the tax code (though obviously subject to change), and they can save you millions of dollars:

1. **Don't sell.** Neither my great-grandfather nor my grandfather paid capital gains tax on the majority of their Carnation stock because they didn't sell it! Forward-thinking estate planning enabled them to pass the stock from generation to generation, continuing the tax-free compounding of the stock's value. It was only when the company was sold in 1985, 86 years after the first case of evaporated milk rolled out of the factory, that capital gains taxes on the stock became due!

2. **Invest in tax-managed equity mutual funds.** I recommend that people invest in "tax managed" equity mutual funds offered by Vanguard and others that have never triggered a capital gains tax liability—even though a number of the stocks in the fund have been sold. The managers of these funds make an active effort to sell the stocks that have declined below cost. They then use those losses to offset against gains in companies that had to be sold because of a merger or takeover. The Lucas family employs a similar tax-managed index portfolio to do the same thing, but it is structured as a separate account, just for us. The minimum investment is higher but, unlike with a mutual fund, we can use the losses generated in our portfolio to offset against gains generated in our other investments. So long as we don't sell, and especially if new cash comes into these vehicles, we are likely to pay little or no capital gains tax on these investments for decades.

3. **Donate.** Rather than selling a stock and paying tax on the gains, we periodically donate it to either a nonprofit organization or a family foundation, and take a tax deduction. Then the nonprofit sells the stock. Because it is a tax-exempt institution, no capital gains taxes are owed.

   Donating appreciated securities is significantly more attractive than donating cash because you get the tax deduction on the amount you would have received, net of tax, if you had sold the stock yourself. Plus, you get a deduction on the amount that would have gone to the government in the form of taxes. In short, you don't pay taxes on the gain, and you can use a "supersized" deduction to lower your taxable income.

4. **Death and taxes.** If one owns an appreciated asset at the time of death, there is a further capital gains tax benefit. When the asset is distributed out of the decedent's estate, it receives a "stepped-up basis." (The stepped-up basis might disappear in larger estates if Congress reforms the estate tax.) Essentially, the accrued capital gains taxes are not payable by the estate, and the recipient of the asset receives a cost basis equal to the value at the time of death. The asset is subject to estate taxes, but they are calculated without regard to unrealized capital gains. Smaller estates will

suffer no estate tax bill. However, the estate tax can be substantial in multimillion-dollar estates.

Investing in Equities Lowers the Tax Rate on "Spending Money"

If you are spending money from your investments, how much you spend and what types of investments you use to finance spending will affect how much you contribute to government coffers.

If your spending money is generated by realized long-term capital gains or dividends, it is taxed at 15%. If it comes from interest income, a variable annuity, or a retirement plan, it can be taxed at 35% or more if you include state and local taxes. In places like New York City or California, the combined rate can approach 50%.

The tax efficiency of your investing will dictate the tax efficiency of your spending. By investing in stocks and accruing the capital gains, you can substantially lower the drain on your assets from spending. For example, on $100,000 per year of spending there is a net benefit of roughly $36,000 if your spending money comes from long-term profits and dividends on stocks rather than from corporate bonds, distributions from Social Security, annuities, or 401k retirement plans.

Declining Capital Gains Taxes Have Been a Bonanza to Long-Term Investors, but That Might Soon Stop

Today, if the government were in the marketing business, it would be touting the current capital gains tax rates as a great "bargain sale." When rates were dropped from 20% to 15% a few years ago, they became the lowest since they were instituted 76 years ago.

This cut in the capital gains tax was instituted at a time when the economy was really struggling to get back on its feet. It was intended to have a stimulating effect and, for wealthy Americans, it did. When the tax rate dropped, the size of the "loan" from the government to an investor with a million dollars of accrued, but unpaid, taxes (before the decline in rates) immediately dropped by $250,000 (a five-percentage-point [or 25%] drop on a 20% base times $1 million). This money went from a government IOU straight into that investor's pocket. Talk about free money! For investors who suffered through the bear markets of 2000–

2002 and 2008–2009, and didn't have any gains, there was no immediate benefit from the tax cut. But it did encourage them to look favorably on being equity investors because they would get to keep a higher percentage of future profits.

It is likely that tax rates will rise again soon. Under these circumstances, the math in the preceding paragraph works in reverse. But the power of the "free loans" is so great that capital gains taxes would have to rise considerably to negate the benefit of the free loans, so long as your asset continues to grow over the long term. My bottom line here: If you own securities with large unrealized gains, sell only if you are a seller for fundamental reasons, if you need the money in the next year or two, or if you think there is going to be a major hike in long-term capital gains tax rates.

Takeaway #3: Improve Investment Results Through Tax Management

Though it seems counterintuitive, you really can add value to your investment portfolio by managing your taxes well. And you can do it with a high degree of certainty. Here's how.

Sidebar 8.2: Aggressive Tax Strategies Are Risky

The tax code is open to interpretation; the greater the complexity of someone's tax situation, the greater the room for interpretation. Aggressive tax strategies can keep a great deal of money in an individual's pocket that might otherwise go to the government. Even though the IRS audits less than 1% of all tax returns, and the odds of losing in an audit are smaller still, aggressive tax strategies are usually complicated. They also restrict your flexibility to deal with the unexpected and typically carry a substantial administrative burden.

Before embarking on aggressive strategies, do your homework thoroughly and choose selectively. I would start by asking some questions in the context of a potential IRS challenge:

1. Why do I need the extra money? Are the dollars big enough to matter?

2. Is there a less risky way to accomplish most of my objective?

3. Can I defend my position robustly? Documentation and process are really important. Also, carefully negotiate the wording of any opinion letters from lawyers or accountants to limit the caveats. If the caveats are too broad to make you comfortable, your interests are not aligned with those of your advisor. He or she will be paid up front while the risk burden falls largely on you.

4. Can I afford to lose a challenge?

5. Will other family members affected by a challenge or adverse ruling be my allies or become my enemies? Will my actions cause them to be audited as well? Consequences can include lost time, stress, legal fees, back taxes, interest, and penalties.

If your answers sound equivocal or negative, the red flags should go up.

There are other potential risks of aggressive tax strategies besides IRS challenges. Any tax strategy is risky if it requires you to establish a tax liability today that must be paid for with a volatile asset at some point in the future, particularly if the assets and liabilities involved are significant relative to your total estate. The outcome is terrific if the asset's value keeps rising, but if the opposite happens, it can be disastrous. In extreme cases, people have had to declare personal bankruptcy. Unfortunately, income tax obligations are not eliminated in the bankruptcy process.

Complicated tax strategies are administratively intensive. During the process of setting up the strategy, lawyers and accountants are usually very good at defining the infrastructure required to justify and support the strategy. However, someone needs to implement the infrastructure and keep it operating, often for a decade or more. Over longer time spans, lawyers, accountants, and administrators change or get busy doing something else, or clients balk at paying high hourly rates for essentially administrative duties. However, the viability of the strategy and the conditions set out in legal opinion letters are dependent on effective administration. Before executing such a strategy, be prepared to see through the mundane details over its complete life.

After a complicated strategy is put in place, it is expensive or impossible to turn back the clock. Yet, as we have already discussed, tax rates are unpredictable. What appeared to be a good decision a few years ago might, with a changed fact set, no longer be attractive. In fact, it might create all sorts of new, expensive, and time-consuming problems.

Hire Only a Few Broadly Diversified, Tax-Efficient Managers

If you use an Active Alpha strategy, most wealth advisors recommend that you hire a number of different managers. As part of a complete portfolio, you might be offered a large-cap growth manager, a large-cap value manager, a small-cap manager, and an international manager, and four or five others as well. Your advisor might explain that each manager is an expert in his or her particular space, and that with multiple managers you have the ability to shift your asset allocation opportunistically, or if a manager doesn't work out you can simply replace the name in that "box." Even if your advisor advocates an Index Investing strategy, he or she might still recommend this approach to investing, which is often referred to as "style box" investing.

Institutional managers have been successfully pursuing the style box approach to investing for decades. But most institutional investors don't pay taxes and you, of course, do.

Let's take a look at what happens if you invest using this approach. The value manager buys a stock that has come on hard times. Then the company starts growing again, and its stock recovers. Now the value manager sells the stock at a profit about the same time that the growth manager thinks, "Hey, this is an attractive growth stock," and buys it. Your portfolio hasn't changed, but you have paid taxes and transaction costs unnecessarily. Although these costs might be immaterial for a large institution, they can be quite substantial for an individual investor. If you keep selling your winners, you don't accumulate accrued taxes. If you don't accumulate the accrued taxes, you eliminate much of your ability to share investment risk with the government.

How do you combat this problem? When you assemble a series of tax-efficient managers—whether active or indexed (passive)—don't choose very many. The more managers you choose, the less tax efficient your overall portfolio will be because there will be more buying and selling going on. In particular, don't choose a growth manager and a value manager if you can choose an appropriate alternative that does both. Likewise, don't choose a large-cap manager and a small-cap manager if one will do. As the previous example attests, companies regularly move between growth and value portfolios as their fortunes change. In fact, if you own growth and value index funds, it is almost inevitable. The same is true of small- and large-capitalization portfolios.

Frankly, if you are using an Index Investing strategy, you need and want only one U.S. equity portfolio that replicates the whole market. You can, in fact, own one global portfolio. However, if you prefer to manage the ratio of domestic to international holdings, it's okay to own separate international and domestic portfolios because companies rarely change their country of domicile.

As you can plainly see, one of the beauties of maximizing tax efficiency is that it actually simplifies your investment strategy considerably while simultaneously adding a lot of value.

Save Early

Why do I encourage young college graduates earning modest salaries with outstanding student loans to put money into retirement plans that they won't use for 40 or 50 years? It all has to do with what Einstein called the "eighth wonder of the world"—the power of compounding. And it has a lot of implications when it comes to paying your taxes.

Every $1,000 that you put into a retirement plan in your twenties, and that has the ability to grow for 50 years free of taxes in an equity investment, could be worth $100,000 when you retire. If you don't start saving for retirement until you are 45, the value of that $1,000, compounding at the same rate, might be worth only $10,000. As you can see, you gain a tenfold difference in return simply by starting 20 years sooner. In my own case, I am about 60% through my career, if I work until 70 years of age. In the first six years that I worked after graduating from college, I deposited as much as I could afford into my retirement plans, about $50,000 in total. I put the maximum amount allowed into my IRA and my 401k plan. Fortunately, I didn't have college loans to pay off, had a reasonably well-paying job, and had an employer that offered an attractive retirement plan. After I left the company, I kept the money I had saved in a segregated retirement savings plan. Today, the asset is worth more than $1 million. If it grows at an average of 9% per year from now until I turn 70, the original $50,000 investment will be worth about $5 million, 100 times the original amount! Those first six years of savings, from age 21 to 27, will have taken care of all my retirement spending needs, and then some.

As with the Carnation stock, my retirement plan is an investment that grows consistently over many decades and is not held back by spending or the payment of taxes. Even better, my retirement plan is not investing only in a single company but in a broadly diversified portfolio consisting largely of equity securities. The only unfortunate thing is that I will most likely have to pay income tax rates on the distributions rather than comparatively low capital gains tax rates.

Today, however, the government offers a Roth IRA—a great savings tool for retirement that wasn't available to me in my 20s. It doesn't give you a tax deduction when you invest (which isn't such a big deal if you are in a low-income tax bracket), but after your money is invested, you don't pay any taxes, even at the time of distribution! If you're young, financially capable, have a low tax rate, and otherwise meet the eligibility requirements, I would invest first in a Roth IRA, up to the full amount available. If your tax rate is high, take a more balanced approach, employing your regular IRA or 401k plan and your Roth IRA.

High Management Fees and Low Returns Are a Bad Combination!

No one likes to pay an investment manager high fees in return for poor performance. When this happens, you suffer doubly unless you are using a mutual fund because your taxes are calculated before fees are subtracted. Most wealthy investors cannot deduct investment management fees from their gross income for tax purposes.[3] For example, if you invest in a hedge fund that earns 5% (gross of fees and taxes), you pay tax on the full 5%. At a 30% notional tax rate, this leaves you with a return of 3.5%. But, after subtracting investment management fees of 2%, you are left with a measly return of 1.5%, an effective tax rate of 50%, not 30%!

This is exactly what happened to us once. We hired a technology manager who picked stocks and held them for the long term. Portfolio turnover was very low. For a while, the manager performed well and accrued large unrealized capital gains as he let his winners run. Even though the manager's fee was 2%, we thought he had special insights that, coupled with good tax efficiency, more than made up for the high fee. But then the market reversed and the manager suffered along with the rest of the sector. Finally, after almost eight years, we sold the investment. Over the period, the gross rate of return, before fees, was a little more than 6%— acceptable under the circumstances of a down market. But net of fees and taxes, the return was a pathetic 2%. The manager earned as much from our money as we did! And because the fees were high and our returns were low, the government also took a disproportionate share of our meager profits. If we had sold this investment when the technology sector was performing well, the poor tax treatment of management fees would not have been a big deal, and the tax efficiency would have looked very attractive. But we got crushed. High management fees and low returns are truly a bad combination!

Takeaway #4: Don't Overcommit to Retirement and Deferred-Compensation Plans

Many people use retirement plans and deferred compensation plans because they assume that the tax-deferral benefits make them superior investment vehicles regardless of all other factors in the decision-making process. They are conditionally wrong.

Many retirement plans and deferred compensation plans are great savings vehicles because they allow you to delay paying taxes on what would otherwise be taxable income for years, sometimes decades. In addition, gains are not subject to tax until they are distributed from the plan. When assets are distributed, they are taxed at the income tax rates (not capital gains tax rates) that apply at that time in the future.

This creates an analytical challenge. Is it possible to be worse off for having put assets into a retirement plan or deferred compensation plan than to have simply paid the taxes at the time the money was earned and then invested the net proceeds? The short answer is yes, if income tax rates rise significantly between now and the time that your tax-deferred assets are distributed. Answering how much they have to rise is less straightforward. There are a number of variables that are extraordinarily difficult to predict, such as whether the investments outside of a plan will perform better or worse than those in the plan or when you will withdraw the assets. But the most important variable is how tax rates will change. In 2005 I said, "If the top marginal income tax rate rose by just 10 percentage points, the rise would negate the benefit of many retirement plans." Right now, it's slated to go up in 2013 by 8.4 percentage points. Other, potentially countervailing factors in this analysis include how much long-term capital gains taxes will rise and how tax efficient your investment portfolio is.

In addition, there are issues about liquidity. When you put assets into a retirement or deferred compensation plan, there are often penalties for removing them prematurely. These plans are much less flexible when it comes to handling the vagaries of life than if you own the assets directly. Because it is impossible to predict tax rates way into the future, I propose that you diversify your tax vehicles, just as you diversify your investments.

A Framework for Making Decisions

The following factors influence the attractiveness of specific tax-deferred vehicles:

- **The tax status of contributions.** It is better to contribute pretax earned income to a tax-deferred vehicle like many retirement and tax-deferred compensation plans. However, some tax-deferred vehicles like annuities, Roth IRAs, and life insurance savings plans cannot be funded with pretax dollars.

- **The tax status of distributions.** You have to weigh the tax treatment of each tax-deferred vehicle. For example, because Roth IRAs can be funded only with after-tax dollars, growth in value and qualified distributions from the Roth IRA are not taxed. This is a pretty good deal if you qualify, and management fees are low. When annuities distribute, part of each distribution is taxable as income and part is considered a return on capital and is not taxed. Beneficiaries of life insurance proceeds are not taxed, but if your life is the one insured, it doesn't help you very much (though it could prove lucrative for members of your family). If you surrender a policy for its cash value, the difference between the gross cash value and the net amount contributed to the policy is generally subject to income tax. Retirement-plan distributions are entirely taxed as income. If distributions are taken earlier than intended (usually before age 59 1/2), an additional penalty is levied by the government.

- **Future tax rates.** Given the current state of government finances, U.S. demographics, and historically low federal tax rates, the odds are good that the tax rate applied to your tax-deferred assets at the time they are distributed will be higher than the current income tax rate. Most readers of this book are likely to be in or near the highest marginal tax rate after retirement. For them, high post-retirement income tax rates make tax-deferral plans less attractive, especially if long-term capital gains tax rates don't climb as much as income tax rates. If you own assets in a tax-deferred plan, the cost of unwinding the plan (in anticipation of future increases in tax rates) before you reach retirement age is high.

- **Investment strategy.** If you are using an Index Investing strategy, the value of a tax-deferred plan drops significantly because you are already deferring most of your taxes. But if you are an Active Alpha investor in the Secret Society or the Enchanted

Forest and you are regularly buying and selling, these vehicles allow you to defer any tax payments until the time of withdrawal.

- **Age.** The closer you are to retirement, the lower the value of the deferral mechanism. Many plans require you to begin liquidating by the time you are 70 years old. If you are within 10 years of retiring, weigh carefully the trade-offs of putting more money in a retirement plan versus paying the income tax now. You might prefer to have your money in a completely flexible form rather than maybe saving a little tax.

- **Expenses.** Some retirement plans have administrative costs that taxable accounts do not have. These costs counteract the tax benefit, especially in portfolios that generate low investment returns.

- **Switching costs.** If an investor needs access to cash or the investments in his or her tax deferral plan are not performing well, it might be desirable to access cash within that plan. Many plans have some flexibility for investors to withdraw or borrow assets without penalty. However, withdrawing more than a limited percentage of the assets can be expensive. The government taxes people (sometimes with penalties added) who withdraw assets from a tax-deferral plan prematurely.

There is a real trade-off between the flexibility of owning assets directly versus owning them in a tax-deferred plan. This is a complicated subject, even for wealth management experts. Unfortunately, there are lots of incentives in our financial system to encourage people to overuse tax-deferred vehicles and not a lot of incentives for advisors to encourage a reality check. Therefore, you must take charge to get good advice.

Takeaway #5: Don't Put After-Tax Income into Variable Annuities and Retail Life Insurance Savings Plans

If I am an advocate of retirement and deferred-compensation plans, why do I discourage people from investing after-tax dollars in tax-deferred savings plans, such as annuities and life insurance savings plans? There are a couple of reasons.

First, even a modest hike in income tax rates can eliminate the benefits offered by a retirement plan, a deferred-compensation plan, or an annuity. Second, many of these structures have high administrative costs (on top of investment fees) that hack away at your investment return. Life insurance is a little different because there is no tax payable when a policy distributes a death benefit. And there might be some estate tax benefits, unless Congress repeals the estate tax completely. However, the cost of life insurance savings plans, and especially retail products, can eat up all of their tax benefits, especially in an environment where investment returns are modest.

If you show the preceding couple of paragraphs to an insurance agent (annuities are also sold through insurance companies), he or she will tell you that I am biased against his products. The agent will likely give you the following arguments against my view:

- The beneficiaries of life insurance don't have to pay tax on the benefits they receive.

- Capital gains taxes are likely to go up.

- Bonds have been good investments, and you should own bond-like investments.

- You will be in a lower tax bracket when you retire.

After you hear all of these arguments for buying life insurance, ask the insurance agent to compare the returns from his or her products (after fees and taxes) against diversified index funds (with or without tax loss harvesting). Have the agent do various scenarios, check the math, analyze the assumptions, and decide for yourself whether you think there is value in these products.[4] I think you will come to my conclusion.

If, after doing this analysis, you still think that the tax-deferral benefits of these products are good, read the fine print about surrender charges imposed if you cancel the policy. Then turn to the section that discusses insurers' unilateral ability to raise your costs. Although there are limits on their ability to raise your costs, there is still a lot of flexibility in the contracts I've seen. The agent will tell you that they have never raised the costs to their clients, at least in their memory. But remember, for the last 30 years, we have been in a bull market in bonds. Because bonds are the primary asset on life insurance companies' balance sheets, the companies have had the wind at their back throughout the careers of most insurance agents. If interest rates just stay where they are for an extended period, times will get tougher for life insurance companies, and some might feel compelled to raise their fees to policyholders in order to keep their shareholders happy. Retail policies are typically written with prohibitively high costs for switching vendors unless you've had your policy a long time. (Private placement life insurance may be a beneficial estate and tax management tool for a select few, but the minimums to achieve wholesale pricing and terms are too high for most people.)

If you still like life insurance's attributes, remember that low interest rates and tight credit spreads, like we have today, really eat into the profitability of life insurance companies. So if you do buy life insurance, monitor your firm's credit rating and other indicators of balance sheet weakness. With many types of insurance, you become a general creditor of the insurance company, even though your money is invested in a diversified investment portfolio. In the past quarter-century, a defaulting insurance company has been a rare event. But it has happened. Ask a life insurance salesperson about Executive Life, Mutual Benefit Life, and Monarch Life, all of which became insolvent in 1991 when interest rates were considerably higher. What happened to these insurance companies was similar. Their bond and real estate portfolios performed poorly, and then policyholders started to surrender their policies in large numbers, and finally the receivers had to be called in. If the bond market becomes bearish, we could see a similar scenario play out again.

Even if policyholders (or their named beneficiary) eventually receive the money owed to them after the bankruptcy is sorted out (it took eight years or more for Mutual Benefit), a delay in payment of months or years can cause significant financial hardship. If you have done all of your analysis and still believe that one or more of these products is right for you, don't put your personal balance sheet at risk by exposing it to a single general creditor, no matter how secure it appears to be.

Finally, don't put variable annuities into a retirement plan, IRA, or other tax-deferred vehicle. You don't need the tax-deferral benefits of an annuity in these vehicles. And there are many other ways to access high-quality investment vehicles that are cheaper and have no surrender charges. In short, a variable annuity in a tax-deferred vehicle is a high-cost redundancy, regardless of what happens to future tax rates.

Conclusion

As you can see, my perspective on taxes and their implications is quite different from that of many in the financial services industry.

Most wealth advisors encourage you to buy lots of investment products, regularly switch out underperforming managers, use bonds to diversify risk, and encourage the use of annuities and life insurance as savings plans.

My goal in this chapter has been to convince you to manage your taxes efficiently when you invest, limit the number of investment products you own, hold them for the long term, deemphasize bonds, and avoid annuities and life insurance savings plans.

If you do these things, you will pay less in taxes, make more money than the majority of people who invest in financial assets, and get good value for the money that you pay to your advisors and the government.

With the extra time and additional resources you have as a result of more efficiently managing your taxes, the next three chapters should hold appeal for you. I'll be talking about what I consider to be more important than anything I've been discussing so far: using your wealth to contribute to your community and empower your children.

Chapter 8: Issues to Discuss with Your Family

1. Overall, do you think that the U.S. tax structure is fair?

2. Are you convinced that a buy-and-hold investment strategy can reap substantial tax benefits, or do you think that active trading is more lucrative?

3. Do you ask your advisors about the after-tax effects of their investment recommendations? Do you measure whether the results actually come through as expected?

4. Are you bearish or bullish on the long-term health of the economy? How does this affect your tax management strategy?

5. How can you use the power of compounding to improve your financial circumstances?

6. Are you committed to life insurance savings plans as a sound investment? If so, why?

7. Are there opportunities for you to donate appreciated stock instead of cash to support your philanthropic objectives?

8. Have you asked your retirement consultant or insurance agent how their recommendations would be affected by an increase in income tax rates? How do you assess their replies?

9. Do you use various portfolio managers with different investment styles (for instance, large-cap growth, large-cap value, mid-cap, and small-cap)? What's the likelihood that some of these managers are selling just as others are buying, creating unnecessary turnover, higher transaction costs, and lower tax efficiency?

10. Do you approach taxes aggressively ("I am determined to go to great lengths to pay as little as possible in taxes")? If so, how has this benefited you or been to your detriment over the years? What are the unintended consequences of this approach?

11. Is your family prepared to support you if your strategy is contested by the IRS?

Endnotes

1. The $51,000 cost is far more than just the difference between getting an "interest-free loan" from the government and having to take out an interest-paying bank loan for the same amount. It comes from the foregone profits on the $15,000 of accrued but unpaid taxes to the government. Alternatively, the second investor could take out a bank loan for $15,000 and reinvest a full $200,000 in the company. If the stock continues to rise, as it does in this example, then the only cost of selling early would be the interest cost on the loan.

   However, if the stock declines in value, the first investor's liability to the government declines accordingly while the second investor's liability to the bank remains at $15,000 plus interest.

2. "Passive activity" rules prevent matching the losses from certain investments, typically related to oil and gas exploration and production or real estate, that generate passive losses against gains from the sale of stocks or bonds. Generally, passive losses can be used only to offset passive gains.

3. This is true of separately managed accounts, limited partnerships, and most other commingled funds. However, mutual funds are taxed differently: Taxes are calculated on profits generated net of fees. This has the effect of making mutual fund management fees fully deductible.

4. Some agents might decline to project mutual fund returns, citing that it is illegal under federal securities law for securities salesmen to make return projections for mutual funds. In most cases, life insurance is governed under separate, state laws that allow such projections. If the agent refuses, do the calculations yourself or ask an accountant to help you.

9

Promoting Entrepreneurial Stewardship

"My keenest desire is that the country's opportunities and its possibilities remain open and available to my son and to my grandchildren and to their children after them, as well as to all other young men and women who have high ideals and are willing to make sacrifices for their attainment."

—E.A. Stuart

As you've learned in previous chapters, the Lucas family's financial goals are firmly multigenerational in focus. To that end, I've described what it takes to achieve ambitious returns on your investments. I've also talked about how to develop tax strategies and pursue other proactive steps to preserve your family's wealth—not only for your lifetime, but for multiple generations.

The missing subject so far in our discussion—a critical factor in preserving and growing wealth over time—is something I refer to as "entrepreneurial stewardship." I think entrepreneurial stewardship goes right to the heart of family purpose, the most important of the three key value drivers in the Strategic Wealth Management Framework. It can be an essential element that energizes families to maintain a common purpose across generations. It is also an ingredient in optimizing the human capital of each individual family member. For my family, it is a core value.

Some wealth advisors encourage multigenerational families to write family mission statements and family constitutions. They build governance structures to help the families make decisions. The third-, fourth-, fifth-, and sixth-generation families that I've worked with around the world need formal structures because of the number of people and households involved. As a practical matter, they need a representative form of government to function. I don't address the intricacies of these structures in this book, but this chapter is essential to making them work in practice.

Entrepreneurial Stewardship

In 2010, I wrote an article with David Lansky, Principal Consultant at The Family Business Consulting Group, titled "Managing Paradox."[1] We noted that healthy, wealthy multigenerational families embody and manage a number of paradoxes. The most important paradox is that family success ultimately resides in the actions of descendants and beneficiaries, not in the success of the founding entrepreneur. Another paradox of multigenerational wealth is that the best way to keep a family together is to set its members free. If our families can empower the individual members of each generation to take risk, to draw strength from failure, to seek continuous improvement, and to be useful to others, the individuals will flourish and so will the family. The more you are able to unleash the power of human capital in each generation, the less they will need your money. Entrepreneurial stewardship, itself a juxtaposition of opposites, is the key to resolving the paradoxes of wealth.

Typical entrepreneurs have little to lose when starting out, other than reputation and sleep. They usually have few resources but are ambitious and have a vision for making the world a better place. They are completely focused on the task at hand. Most are "command and control" managers. We tend to think of entrepreneurs as business owners, but entrepreneurship takes many forms and operates in many walks of life. Great insights everywhere are usually the result of an entrepreneurial hunger.

Stewards, by their very nature, are different. They start from a position of privilege and responsibility to others. If they are shepherding their own wealth, they have a lot to lose if they manage poorly, so they focus on preservation. They do this by diversifying risk and protecting their downside. They are much more comfortable with consensus decision making.

Entrepreneurial stewardship is a blend of these two seeming opposites. You must be ambitious, but as a member of a wealthy family, you have access to money, contacts, and other resources that most entrepreneurs could only dream about. In business, the benefits are clear, but they also apply in other contexts. Being a great teacher, author, or interior designer while having supplemental income to raise your family benefits the community, your children, and your spouse. Your supplemental income might enable you to choose to teach rather than feeling compelled to do something more remunerative but less satisfying. As an entrepreneurial steward, you have lofty goals, but you also understand the downside of taking too much risk to achieve them. You recognize that diversification helps to protect capital, and you know that to achieve success in a competitive world, you need to focus. That's the beauty of Barbell Investing in the context of entrepreneurial stewardship—you balance diversification through indexing with focus through building your growth asset.

The most successful entrepreneurial stewards integrate their vision to serve both their careers and their family. They design their lives to do their job well and to nurture the family's human capital. This requires an adaptable leadership style: sometimes leading from the front like an impassioned entrepreneur, sometimes leading from behind like a shrewd parent. Lao Tzu, a 6th-century BCE Chinese philosopher, captured the essence of the subtle leader: "one who is never seen, never heard, and never felt, but is revered for one thousand years by his followers for his excellent leadership."

Many highly successful people are challenged to shift their mind-set from being in control to enabling others to take control. To do this, the senior generation in families must come to terms with giving up power and crafting a new relationship with their wealth in which they view personal wealth as family wealth and view their legacy as residing in the actions of descendants and beneficiaries, rather than in their own actions.

Udders and Herds

You know that cows have played a central role in our family's lore for over a century. A cartoon drawn years ago, now hanging in our summer home, depicts my grandfather when he was CEO of Carnation, milking a cow. Instead of milk, dollars are flowing into his pail. Underneath, the caption reads, "All I have I owe to udders."

The cartoonist was half right. Carnation's slogan was "Home of Contented Cows." It's true that our family relied on and served those "suppliers," as well as the firm's customers and employees. Collectively, these key constituents of the business's success are the "udders" to whom the cartoonist refers. But the family was definitely not milking the cow, at least metaphorically. Through representation on the Board of Directors, senior management, and deep into the organization, we fed and cared for cows, strengthened the herd, and helped it grow stronger and larger. That's what made Carnation so successful and what built our family's fortune until the company was sold to Nestlé 86 years later.

Successful family-controlled businesses like Carnation have clarity of purpose that is respected in the marketplace and is the basis of their stakeholder relationships. Our family embodied the corporate culture and benefited from its visibility and acceptance in the marketplace. Family members who were involved day-to-day in the business developed experience and deep expertise. Wealth creation over years and decades was the result, but it was not an end unto itself.

So often when family businesses are sold, family cultures shift from feeding the cow to milking it. Selling the business and becoming a "financial family" risks a fundamental and potentially damaging change in the family's culture. No longer activist shareholders or active managers, a family might become inward looking. The family's clarity of purpose can get fuzzy. There is no longer a public face or the threat of competition to hold the family accountable. And there aren't customers. The family's focus shifts from serving the customer to being the customer. How well is my financial advisor or family office taking care of me? What's happening to my distributions? Am I getting my fair share of the family pie?

In my view, a successful multigenerational family culture should focus on empowerment to serve others, not entitlement or ease. The simple fact is that it is as hard to maintain and grow wealth after you have it as it was to generate it in the first place. It is an uphill battle to generate returns robust enough to overcome the tug of spending, fees, taxes, inflation, and numerical growth of most families. The math clearly shows that each generation must create a strong economic engine (or more than one!) and the means to manage it, or else the wealth will erode.

Empowerment is compelled by more than math and money—it's about the satisfaction that comes from being useful. Who knows whether the next generation will have within it talented wealth creators who are invested in the family? Maybe you have great violinists, environmentalists, teachers, or politicians instead. Maybe there are simply quality people of average talent. But they can all affirmatively address the question, "Am I useful?" If the answer is yes, they are likely to lead fulfilling lives and the family's purpose will be served.

Building a successful family business, nurturing its growth, and selling it at just the right time make you an outlier. Producing multiple generations of wealth creators is even more unusual. But a focus on human capital—talent development, risk taking, and an appetite for hard work—should be at the forefront of every decision the family makes, especially after the family business is sold.

If you are not careful, your very success sows the seeds for future failure. After you shift from being a business-owning family to a financial family, the odds of failure get even higher. Financial advisors hold out the promise that they can maintain your wealth indefinitely so you can focus on other things. They imply that you no longer need the intellectual capital, the business resources, and mostly the hard work to keep a good thing going, because they're doing it for you, in perpetuity. They might be right for years or even a few decades, but when it comes to multigenerational wealth management, they are flat-out wrong. Each generation of all but the very wealthiest families needs to create new economic engines, or perpetuate and grow existing ones, if they don't want their wealth to dissipate in a generation or two. It won't happen any other way. Don't let your financial advisor or your own good fortune focus you on the udder. Instead, use your financial security and a spirit of entrepreneurial stewardship as opportunities to strengthen the herd.

"Fly First-Class; Your Children Will"

So reads a finely needlepoint pillow I came across recently at the home of a trust lawyer who has decades of experience working with wealthy families. I loved the humorous expression of tension between cost-conscious first generation and an entitled second generation, but is that really the message we want to send? When it comes to fostering financial responsibility, I've learned to extend the time horizon we use to evaluate wealth management decisions, and to assess carefully the trade-offs between short-term spending and long-term growth. For the past several years, for example, I've been trying to convince my family that the rate at which we distribute money from our collective investment vehicles is too high if we want to maintain our goal of maintaining per capita wealth across generations. On the one hand, I feel like a "fun sponge" by proposing that everyone give up something very concrete today to meet an abstract goal 30 to 50 years in the future. On the other hand, given the best information we have, it is what prudent stewardship suggests we do.

Fortunately, we have all worked hard to understand the context within which we must choose our distribution rate. We have investment performance data going back nearly 20 years, so people can see what long-term means in concrete terms, and understand long-term outcomes. Seven years ago, we took an incremental step by modestly reducing our spending rate at an opportune time. When the financial crisis hit, we all tightened our belts again to preserve capital in a tough time. It was a great lesson; we learned, and our children learned, that budget management and periodic pruning is best practice, not something to be scared or ashamed of.

You Have to Take Risks

As I noted earlier in this book, preserving and growing wealth takes as much discipline, imagination, and persistence as is required to amass wealth in the first place. Multiple forces at work in our economy—taxes, inflation, spending, and stock market volatility—can rapidly erode your wealth. Therefore, it's important to search wisely for investment opportunities, to seek risk when good opportunities avail themselves, and to be appropriately cautious when the environment is dangerous. This is the only way your family's economic engine will perform well enough over long periods to overcome all the leakages.

To generate adequate returns after your own working years are over, it's also important to nurture successful entrepreneurs and wealth stewards in the next generation of your family. For you, as Wealth Strategist, this entails instilling values of entrepreneurism and self-sufficiency in all family members, nurturing a select few (family or otherwise) to assume hands-on responsibilities of business oversight and/or wealth management, establishing effective family governance, and finding ways to support all family members in the pursuit of their individual passions and goals toward being useful. This is the key to ensuring that all your children live vibrant and fulfilling lives, while ensuring your family's continuing legacy and heritage. It is true whether you still own your family business or you sold it decades ago.

Think Twice Before Selling

Many people, especially in America, believe that selling their business is the crowning accomplishment of their career. The sale crystallizes the value that's been created by running the business over a lifetime—or several generations—and it lays the groundwork for a comfortable retirement and maybe generations of family wealth.

To be sure, there are times when selling the family business is the right decision. Perhaps business logic (your business's difficult competitive position is not apparent yet to others, and you can't fix it on your own), or exogenous factors (political uncertainty), or personal reasons (unresolvable family tensions) dictate the sale. Having all your eggs in one basket, and for many an illiquid basket at that, is risky.

On the other hand, people underestimate the risks of selling and overestimate their ability to make money in the financial markets afterward. At this critical decision point, business owners don't understand that in trading a business asset for a financial asset they are simply trading familiar problems for new, unfamiliar ones. They are encouraged to move ahead by financial advisors—whose self-interest is well-served by investment banking fees and a pile of cash to manage—who espouse the prudence and value of becoming diversified financial investors. I've seen it time and again with families I advise in the aftermath of liquidity events and to whom I teach wealth management.

Wealth creation from successful business ownership is generated from earnings growth, profitability, and cash flow. Many pragmatic, focused business owners expect 10% or higher annual growth from their business (the recent financial crisis notwithstanding). When thinking about selling, these same people often gloss over the fact that financial assets have grown at a significantly slower rate and it's really tough to beat the market. Although my crystal ball is as foggy as it's ever been, there are sound economic reasons to expect this pattern to continue.

If your business is strong, stable, and conservatively financed, staying in the business might create substantially more value than investing in financial markets. Carnation Company was founded by my great-grandfather in 1899. As the business grew, it diversified by product and geography. The business wasn't cyclical and it held little debt. Even in tough times it almost never lost money, and technological obsolescence wasn't a major factor. It grew at an average of 13% over the 86 years before it was sold. This return wasn't eye-popping, but it sure beat the capital markets overall, and over a very long period. Remember, too, that there is great value in not realizing those deferred taxes.

If you've been a successful entrepreneur or executive, be aware that your training and intuition in business have *not* prepared you to be a successful investor. Building businesses creates value for the owners, but also for suppliers, employees, and often customers. Investing is a zero-sum game. To outperform in the market, you have to take that value added away from someone else.

As a business owner, you are used to riding your winners and culling your losers; successful investors often do the opposite. Success in business is persistent and builds momentum; the returns of financial investments tend to revert to the mean. As a business owner, you are used to taking action when times are tough; successful investors understand the value of riding out the difficult times, often doing very little until the climate improves (Warren Buffett says he sometimes wishes he spent more time at the movies). Lots of people see the value of their assets fall and then sell just as the market starts to turn up again.

You've developed information systems and intuition to measure your business's performance, enabling you to see impending problems early and to respond quickly. Data flow in financial investing is overwhelming, and only a tiny fraction of that information is actionable in a way that makes you money. Furthermore, disorganized data tends to play on emotion and confuse rather than educate. I try hard to control tightly the quality (and quantity) of investment information I receive. I have also had to design my own analytics because the standard fare just doesn't give me what I think is most relevant.

Maybe the most important reason to think twice about selling is that, unless you find a way to perpetuate a culture of entrepreneurial stewardship, selling will have a major impact on your family's culture. A Latin American family I work with speaks of the family's heart being ripped away when the business was sold. The business, particularly if it has thrived over several generations, gives definition, pride, and a raison d'être for your family. Time and again, I have seen examples (including in my own family) in which the sale of the business causes family ties to weaken. This is often a natural response as family members—who might feel that they've been yoked together involuntarily—enjoy their new-found freedom and autonomy. The effort required to counteract that centripetal tendency is enormous, and requires a heavy educational component. Working in a family business, it is relatively easy to "walk the talk" of hard work and the value of success (as opposed to wealth). That changes when the business is sold. For whatever reason, spending becomes harder to control when your primary occupation changes from running the business to managing your investment portfolio.

So, what can you do? Think Barbell! The key is to recognize that diversifying and selling are two different things. If you sell, consider using some of the proceeds to buy and operate new businesses that you understand. If you continue to own your business, redirect excess cash flow to finance expansion into new geographic locations, different products, or new types of customers. You also can deploy your business's excess cash flow into financial markets. If you invest in assets that are not correlated with the success of your primary business, you will achieve diversification, greater liquidity, and the opportunity to gain experience managing a small portion of your wealth in financial assets—all of which will considerably lower the risk if and when you do decide to sell your core business.

How do you get started? It begins with awareness of your own unique circumstances.

Reorienting Yourself

If after careful consideration you've sold your business, or if your business is now generating excess cash, or if you've just inherited wealth, you will quickly discover how it changes your life circumstances. For example:

- You now have investment income to pay for life's necessities, so you don't need to worry about "making a living" to put food on your table or to pay for the kids' college tuition.

- You have access to capital. Maybe not enough to launch a multi-million-dollar start-up by yourself, but you're not financing your business or your family on a credit card, either!

- You might have a track record of business success and a wide-ranging network—both of which can be platforms for future financial, social, and business success.

- You have the luxury of time. If you don't find a great opportunity this month, there's also next month—and next year! The luxury of time also enables you to pursue nonfinancial interests like serving the community, writing poetry, running a marathon, or collecting art.

In short, life as you know it has changed dramatically. You're now materially comfortable—perhaps more than you ever imagined you'd be. You're now in a unique position to pursue your personal goals and desires, help others, and contribute to society. So what will it be? You can use your good fortune to create more wealth or to make your mark in the arts, science, culture, good citizenship, or social advocacy. You have untold opportunities now, so go for it!

When you become wealthy, you can easily live quietly and in a leisurely manner. But, being wealthy also means having the opportunity to explore personal passion or professional interests that you never had the time or the capital to pursue. Unfettered by the need to earn a conventional living in order to put a roof over your head and food on the table, you have much more choice. As examples:

- Several wealthy friends of mine run successful private equity firms, helping small businesses to grow and prosper. Knowing that they are influencing the fortunes of the newest entrepreneurs by passing on their economic savvy to fledgling companies and promoting new technologies is profoundly satisfying to them. Plus, they are creating a lot of value and earning a lot of money!

- My brother is a practicing family doctor who loves to teach. He does both because he knows he adds great value in places where it is very difficult to attract highly qualified professionals. He schedules his time carefully so that he can be totally committed to his wife, four kids, two dogs, chinchilla, and multiple other pets.

- My cousin is a dedicated philanthropist who chairs two well-run foundations. He's passing on wealth in the more traditional sense, as well as championing causes that are dear to his heart.

- In my case, in addition to my investment work, I've played leadership roles in two organizations focused on strengthening primary and secondary education and community support systems for children. I'm trying to pass on my family's commitment to education and children so that our society can be better equipped to compete and so that individuals will have the educational tools to lead more fulfilling lives. I also use my investing skills for the benefit of these institutions.

Many of us fortunate to earn or be born into wealth have faced the "dilemma" of overwhelming choice. You may feel like you can buy anything and do anything. Looking back on my career, it seems logical and progressive. Thinking back, however, I remember distinct moments when overwhelming choice was very difficult, and I made some costly decisions as a result.

I think the freedom to do anything and the freedom to do nothing is the greatest fear that wealthy parents have for their children. They fear that choice will be confusing and wealth will be demotivating, even destructive. Let's see now how entrepreneurial stewardship can be an antidote to the freedom of wealth.

Growing Up In Privilege

As every young person does, I had to find my way through the ups and downs of adolescence and young adulthood. Being from a wealthy family does not change those rites of passage. In high school, I worked hard, got good grades, and had a good shot at going to an elite college. But I also was overweight, couldn't hack "hell week" on the freshman football team, and was socially awkward. Failure and criticism were regular occurrences, but I persevered. By senior year, I was chairing a ski racing league and competing in the expert class. I even had a date for the senior prom!

I applied to, and was accepted at, my father's alma mater, Princeton. But I took a great liking to Dartmouth. At the time, my father was a Trustee of Princeton, but when I was fortunate enough to be given the choice, I opted for Dartmouth. My father was very disappointed and angry that I did not heed his will. I didn't fully realize it at the time, but this was the first major independent decision of my life. I wanted to own my college experience and to know that I deserved it. By choosing Dartmouth, I knew that my successes and failures would be my own and would in no way be influenced by my father's position at Princeton. I wanted to compete on an even playing field.

Many of us who are raised in privilege and want to succeed try to test ourselves independently of our family history and circumstances. I don't know whether being born into a family of privilege ever made my classmates or colleagues talk about me behind my back or wonder about my capabilities. But I've always felt an urge to prove myself independently as a way of feeling comfortable being the beneficiary of my parents' wealth.

In my own way, by choosing Dartmouth I started on the road of entrepreneurial stewardship, and in the fullness of time my parents supported my desire to prove myself independently. Some wealthy children graduate from college and go directly into their family business to work beside their fathers, mothers, aunts, or uncles. I think this is often a mistake. This early life choice can stamp out entrepreneurial fires and restrict the development potential of those young people. In many cases, it would be better if such individuals created lives for themselves outside the "family orbit" and perhaps built careers and track records of success in other businesses or other arenas. Doing so enables them to discover who they really are and to own their own lives, achievements, and failures. If they ultimately return to a family business, they do so with a lot of valuable life experience and with greater authenticity and ownership of the lives they have chosen to embrace.

Education and Entrepreneurial Stewardship

Getting good grades and taking on leadership roles outside the classroom are important in our family's culture. It was a high priority in my house when I was growing up, and my own children know that we expect them always to do their best in school.

Sidebar 9.1: Do Your Children Need to Be Wealth Strategists?

As hard as we try, our children aren't all going to be good wealth stewards. Some will develop extraordinary talents that have no economic benefits and could even be talents that are expensive to nurture. Some will be spendthrifts without the sense or the self-control to exhibit financial discipline or to hold a job. Others might be gullible, marrying the wrong spouse or trusting an incompetent or deceitful advisor. A few might have physical, mental, or emotional issues that prevent them from taking care of themselves.

As these situations arise, it's important to handle them on a case-by-case basis. Sometimes the challenge is temporary; other times it is lifelong. Often, it is impossible to tell what the timeframe will be. Situations like these demand flexibility, creativity, and patience.

Effective financial management can be structured with a combination of family emotional support and an objective, rules-bound corporate trustee to provide needed financial stewardship. That way, financial discipline is separate from family emotional support. In rare cases, it might be necessary for the family to walk away from a member who is unwilling to fulfill his or her part of the contract to participate constructively in the family. If you happen to have this situation, try to leave a door open in hope that the future will be better.

Sometimes entrepreneurial talent skips a generation. If you are the Wealth Strategist and this turns out to be the case, you might have to rely temporarily on a trusted advisor or corporate trustee to act as interim Wealth Strategist. Or you might simply continue in the role until your grandchild (or grandchildren) is ready to take on the responsibility.

Think back on how you created or inherited wealth. What characteristics made you a success? What are the characteristics of other successful people around you? Maybe your family really does have the makings of entrepreneurial stewards in the next generation. Your challenge, and your opportunity, is helping your children to discover their true talents.

Education, however, means more than formal schooling or peer networking. Wealth Strategists need to supplement formal education by teaching young family members how to save and manage money—even to save for retirement. Parking money from that first job into a Roth IRA is one of the greatest investments in deferred gratification that a young person can make. In our society, there are enormous incentives to spend money today rather than to save it for tomorrow. Saving for retirement fosters great discipline, teaches the power of compound interest, and can create strong values of responsibility and accountability in one's family. If you can pass on the value of financial responsibility and prudence to your heirs, you pass on a sense of the power of money and the importance of using it wisely. That's why I'm such a passionate believer in the importance of introducing young people to investments, saving, and compound interest at the appropriate age and why I discuss this with my own children.

It's also why I think it's important to give young people the chance to experiment with small sums of money at a relatively early age and to make some mistakes with it. I certainly did, and the experience taught me that money is a finite resource to be protected and used wisely.

Possibly the most important educational tool you can provide your children when it comes to managing wealth is the math of Chapter 4, "Defining Your Financial Objectives." When I first put pencil to paper, I had no idea how hard it was to grow *and* spend wealth. It's easy to convince yourself that once you are wealthy, you have a right to remain so. The math is simple, and the math says "no way." When I discovered this, the implication was profound: we have to re-create the wealth in each generation if we want to keep it. This realization has motivated me, it motivates my children, and it should motivate you. The foundation of entrepreneurial stewardship is the math in Chapter 4. Teach it well.

Family

The stereotypical image of a wealthy family is that of a closed system, open only to those who are born into it. This simply isn't true. With each new generation, every family is refreshed and sometimes redefined through marriage, and sometimes adoption. New opportunities for enriching the family's human capital and harnessing entrepreneurial stewardship abound.

Most wealthy families have a strong-willed wealth creator, a seminal figure, who—even if long dead—might still strongly influence the family's shared values. Having said that, family culture changes as long-established cultural norms evolve with every new generation. Each new marriage of a family member interweaves one's family tree with other family trees, bringing outside influences into the original family, forming new values, and reinforcing or replacing existing ones. These choices invariably dilute the founder's influence as ever-increasing numbers of family trees merge into the fold. At the same time, the founder's expanding lineage broadens his or her influence. Extended families must accept, adapt to, and even embrace the addition of new family trees and all the richness they bring.

The patriarch and originator of the Carnation family, E. A. Stuart, set the tone in our family. That tone was reinforced and modified by E. A.'s son, E. H., who adopted my mother. Needless to say, my life would be entirely different had E. H. not made the choice to accept my mother and her sister as his own. When "the girls" married, E. H. accepted their husbands into Carnation. As they proved themselves, they became valuable members of the company's senior leadership team.

Within my own generation, our nuclear families have expanded in ways that add richness and texture to our lives. All my siblings are married, and our spouses have brought to the family their own histories, heritage, and ways of doing things. We have carried on the tradition of creating families that go outside the narrow orbit of the biological family system. One of my brothers adopted a child with complicated health issues. At the time of the adoption, I worried for my brother and his wife because of the demands I thought they were imposing on themselves and their young family. They didn't see this as a risk, but instead as a great opportunity. Watching their kids today, I know they were right, and we are all better off because of their decision.

My nuclear family has broadened its religious and ethnic boundaries in ways that are wonderful. The grandparents of my wife and soul mate, Susan, were Jewish immigrants from Eastern Europe. They came to this country with stories of struggles to overcome adversity, in part because they were immigrants and in part because of prejudice against Jews in this country and the Old World. In the two generations her family has been American, they have added to their heritage stories of hard work, devotion to family, small-business successes, commitment to education, and service to their communities. By celebrating the lessons from her heritage, we encourage our children's own ambitions and reinforce a standard for us all to live up to. I am as grateful for her traditions as I am for my own. All of our children are now Bar or Bat Mitzvahs. A dear friend expressed to me how moved he was by this tradition because it gave us the opportunity, in front of all our friends and family, to celebrate our love and admiration for our children.

As a large, complex family, we struggle with changing circumstances and our inability to fully satisfy all members all the time. We act in insensitive ways, get mad at each other, and fight. At times, people have opted out. My Aunt Ethel used to say that people are toughest on those to whom they are closest. Different times and circumstances have also presented opportunities for family members to reconnect. At some points, choice enabled people to pull apart, and at other points, it brought them back together. Reconciliation can be powerful, and it's my hope that all readers of this book will stay open to its healing nature.

I think what has gotten us through the arguments, hurts, and different agendas can work for you too. We are learning to be better listeners and more sensitive communicators, plus we work to maintain the presumption of goodwill. We work hard to reinforce shared values and purpose while better appreciating our individuality, airing differences constructively, seeking common ground, and supporting each other personally and professionally.

Parenting

When I was growing up, I was fortunate to know a woman who raised four boys in privilege in New York. I called her "Mrs. B" as a sign of respect and admiration. She was the daughter of a minerals tycoon, and in the summers she used to take her four young boys to a fabulous family lodge on a private lake in the Adirondacks (when they weren't traveling to Europe to explore another branch of their family tree). Each of her boys is very different, but they are all industrious, creative entrepreneurs. They are also just great people and good friends with each other.

A year or two before she passed away, I asked Mrs. B her secret to great parenting. Her answer was simple and elegant. She said that she was completely dedicated to encouraging each of her children to be a unique, independent person. She endeavored to support each son in the pursuit of his individual passions. She looked past the privilege, past the "important" people in her life, the fancy dinners and exotic vacations, and focused intensely on each of her children as individuals. She tried to understand them and support their agendas, not use them as an instrument of her own.

Another friend, Howard Stevenson, a professor at Harvard Business School and co-author of the popular book about success *Just Enough*, has seven thriving adult "children." With all his responsibilities as an entrepreneur, professor, fundraiser, and author, he makes sure to set aside the time and energy necessary to be a good father as well. He knows that the gifts of his time and presence are more important to ensuring the future success and happiness of his own children than is any monetary reward or professional fame he achieves in his own highly successful and fulfilling professional life.

My greatest parental mentor is my mother. She has four children and she has been, and continues to be, there for us. She was very involved in our schools when we were growing up. She easily put 100 miles a week on her car shuttling us to and fro, even though she officially drove carpool only once a week. She kept mum when we put Alice Cooper or Black Sabbath in the 8-track tape deck. When my brother was in the fifth grade, she made a friend of his walk the last several blocks home for swearing too many times in the back of our station wagon.

Now in her mid 70s, Mom is still "showing up" a lot. Even though we have lived far apart since I was 17, she still helps me if my father and I aren't communicating. And now she's showing up for my kids too. Not long ago, she took our three children and my nieces and nephews to the Galapagos Islands in Ecuador.

A lot of what Susan and I value as parents we've learned from our own parents, Howard Stevenson and Mrs. B. Even though Dad was on the road a lot when I was growing up, we still had lengthy summer vacations together, and my mother was always involved as a volunteer in the schools that my siblings and I attended. Both of them showed up a lot—certainly for the most significant moments of my life, and those of my siblings. But we also had dinner together almost every night. Family meals were the times when we all talked about our victories and frustrations of the day. It was such an important time of being together that my parents almost never went out to dinner when I was growing up. Susan and I work hard to live up to their example.

When it comes to giving things to one's kids, I think most parents would agree that they would rather instill the will to excel in their children than transfer wealth if they could do only one or the other. In the Lucas family, we as parents are indebted to our children, not the other way around. Our children mean everything to us. The more we can help them succeed at whatever they choose to do with their lives, the greater our sense of purpose fulfilled. That's why we owe them!

Sidebar 9.2: On Not Being the Client

One of the most surprising aspects of affluent parenting is how difficult it is to find opportunities for our children *not* to be the client. Susan and I are consciously trying to raise productive, responsible, hard-working kids. Our three very fortunate children can recite (probably in their sleep) our "privilege always comes with responsibility" mantra. Nonetheless, our kids—who work hard in school, clear the table after dinner, babysit in the neighborhood, and save up to buy the "extras" they want—are clients in most aspects of their lives.

The literature on raising privileged children often refers to school, with its (relatively) objective assessment and competitive allocation of rewards, as an antidote for the toxic mix of entitlement, infallibility, and immunity from consequence. At their excellent schools, which are both rigorous and rich with opportunities, our children are supported and exhorted to do their best. Pressure to perform is high, and competition for top college spots is keenly felt, even in middle school and early high school. They each have struggled and—we hope—earned their successes and owned their failures. But their school environment—like those at many fine private and public schools—is explicitly organized around their well-being and, to a lesser extent, our satisfaction.

This same pattern holds in organized sports, music lessons, and summer programs—all the stuff of privileged childhood. They attend all their sports practices, even when it's cold and rainy. They babysit for family friends and neighbors, even when their friends are going to the movies. We are proud of their responsible, conscientious behavior, their efforts, and the risks they take. But they are clients in all these settings. The family friends for whom they babysit are both kindly solicitous of their well-being and highly motivated by the neighborhood scarcity of available teenagers. Even the (generally) substantial and useful community service activities at their socially responsible schools and congregation are organized with an eye toward maximizing their learning experience and improving their awareness.

Through all of this, hard as we try to minimize and separate it from their experience, our don't-miss-a-thing kids know that we are paying tuition and instruction fees, are actual or potential donors, and have ready access to the adults in charge. And—accurately or not—they hear about other kids getting a place on the team, or getting a part in the play, or avoiding the consequences of bad behavior because "their parents are really rich" or "gave a lot of money for the new building."

When our daughter was 15, she worked for the summer answering phones in a local small business office. She was proud to have a job, and liked earning a paycheck. But it wasn't much fun, and she was pretty mad at us for insisting that she do this while her friends were on Teen Tours or service trips, or at the beach.

She learned two valuable lessons. The first happened when she opened her first paycheck. She had diligently kept track of her hours and had done the multiplication necessary to calculate her check. She was well on her way mentally to spending the portion of her check that we didn't insist she put in the bank. Of course she knew in theory that everyone who works pays taxes. But imagine her shock—and indignation—when she learned that taxes were subtracted from her total, too!

The second lesson emerged over several weeks. People in her office were pleasant and helpful to her, and glad that she was there. She had plenty to do, most of the time, and felt reasonably useful. But she often brought home vague complaints about work—nothing she could put her finger on, just a feeling that something wasn't quite right. We listened to her describe this uneasiness and, eventually, we all figured it out: Quite appropriately, no one at the office was particularly concerned about her job satisfaction. Her work was organized around what needed doing, and her gratification and personal development were not part of the calculus as tasks were parceled out. Her supervisor focused on whether she completed the job adequately, not what she learned from it. For the first time, she was truly, authentically, not the client. In fact, quite the reverse: She was working to satisfy a supervisor and customers who were her clients.

Why is this important? Because telling children that the world does not revolve around their concerns sticks only if they experience that reality. Because a lot of the stuff of productive adulthood is

> done in the service of clients and without the prospect of immedi-
> ate reward, whether those clients are bosses, lenders, customers, or
> infants. Because the confidence and independence that can come
> only from learning to make their own way will make them better
> stewards of their good fortune.

Family Meetings

When was the last time you had a "family meeting" to discuss finances, complete with written agendas, flip charts, and bottled water? These meetings are key to communicating the mathematical challenge of growing and spending wealth, explaining the benefits of deferred gratification, and reinforcing the culture of entrepreneurial stewardship.

In the Lucas family, the family office organizes regular meetings so that adult family members (including spouses) can all participate and share their views as an important part of the family's wealth management activities. Everyone understands that their individual interests are well served by the family office and that there are tremendous benefits from working together to manage our collective wealth. In addition, the family office has a responsibility to listen to, and be sensitive toward, the individual circumstances of family members and, where practical, to support them.

Family members who participate and benefit from the family office must also meet certain expectations. First, each of us is expected to participate in that annual family meeting, where we discuss the family's affairs in a respectful, open, and informative way. Second, we are all expected to contribute to the costs of running the family office. Third, we share a common belief (one supported by facts and regularly addressed) that our long-term interests, both individual and collective, are being served by Wealth Strategist Partners and the family office.

In recent years, we've started inviting the next generation to parts of the meeting. We talk about the web of affinities that define our family. We talk about the companies that we invest in. We listen as each family member in turn shares their own accomplishments and challenges since the last meeting. They are being brought into the family system, and in future years they will shape it. Plus, their involvement brings new challenges and opportunities to make the meetings fun and interesting for all.

Entrepreneurial Stewardship in Families

In multigenerational family enterprises, those family members who demonstrate the interest and skill to manage family wealth face a difficult challenge: It's a tough job because there is a lot to lose. You can weaken or lose the family's economic engine (and the social standing that goes with it), and you will be held responsible by those family members who entrusted you with their assets. If you are extraordinarily successful, your significantly enriched relatives might not truly appreciate your business or investment skill.

Choosing leaders for the family's economic engine and legitimizing their authority is one of the most important challenges that family enterprises face. Ideally, we would all like a leader who is fully tested and experienced. In practice, this is a challenge. The more a family's economic engine grows and prospers, the more complicated and harder to manage it becomes. The more complex it is, the fewer people (family or professional) there are who have the skills to manage the complexity. Families need to recognize this when selecting and holding accountable leaders of the family enterprise. The complexity of your economic engine may grow faster than the capacity of family members to manage it. I've seen circumstances where a business's success has outstripped the founding entrepreneur's ability to manage it. The same can be said a generation or two down the line. This high-class problem is something to be proud of, but also wary of! You want family leaders of your economic engine to be challenged, but you also want them to be up to the task. Family leadership under any other circumstance is not a good idea, and it's probably time to look outside.

If you have skilled entrepreneurs and stewards within the family, how should they be chosen? Specifically, should they be selected by the senior generation or their own generation? Certainly in the early years of leadership, legitimacy can be derived from the senior generation, but eventually the legitimacy must come from peers. It's best to start building that legitimacy early on. It makes for a much more stable situation after the senior generation is no longer with us.

Good governance is also an important element of leadership selection and accountability. Business boards of directors that include both family and nonfamily members who are actively engaged are extremely beneficial: to hold the leadership accountable, to provide knowledgeable independent wisdom, and to support that leadership in times of stress. If you are a financial family, the same logic applies to having an investment committee regularly review the investment policy and results.

Sidebar 9.3: What Is a Family Office?

At different points in this book, I mention our family office. Somewhere between 2,000 and 3,000 families in the United States each have a dedicated family office to coordinate governance, financial administration, and sometimes the investment of some or all of a family's financial assets. Most family offices get involved in organizing tax, legal work, and even bookkeeping. Some of the larger offices provide concierge and other support services for some or all family members. I've seen family offices responsible for as little as $50 million (though at that size they rarely make economic sense), and I've seen them with 50 or more employees and billions of dollars to oversee.

Our family office manages administration, governance, and business communication with the family. My brother William plays the lead role. He coordinates our quarterly communications about all our activities and prepares an annual report for the family that is second to none. Every report weaves together financial results with family culture and values, humor, discussion topics, and financial education. This report forms the basis for our annual family meeting, for holding Wealth Strategist Partners accountable for investment performance, and for strategic review of the family enterprise. He also spends a lot of time helping other family members to think through their personal financial issues. He does not do their work for them, though I know that sometimes this would be easier. Instead, he plays the role of educator and troubleshooter. He sees his role as promoting self-confidence, independence, and (subtly) a fuller appreciation of the value that the family office brings. He is also training future family leaders for long-term governance responsibility.

Family offices usually get established for two reasons. Almost always, wealth owners see them as a useful construct through which to organize a complicated lifestyle. They are administrative, tax, and estate-planning hubs. Family offices also oversee, and sometimes manage, the economic engine of the family enterprise.

Wealth Strategist Partner's clients have outsourced the investment function to us. But they still administer their financial assets. They retain control and oversight while delegating day-to-day investment responsibility to professional investors whose interests are well aligned with their own.

Outsourcing the function of Chief Investment Officer is a growing phenomenon among family offices, I think because the past decade has clarified how important and how tough the job is. The family office community is learning that the cost of a B-grade in-house CIO is not salary, it is the adverse impact on performance. On the other hand, outsourcing is not for everyone. Some families already have the talent they need, and they want to oversee and manage their economic engine. I see this most often with business-owning families, real estate families, or those that have specialized skills or market niches. They can exploit their competitive advantage and reinforce the spirit of entrepreneurial stewardship.

Family offices, especially those that provide a lot of lifestyle support, can inadvertently encourage dependency and risk aversion. Dependency develops because the office is there to help, to take the burden of responsibility out of the wealth owner's hands, and even to manage family "toys" or make airline reservations. What's more, a dependency culture might subtly discourage family members from accepting responsibility for driving the family's economic engine as hard as it must be driven to maintain wealth across generations. The more comfortable you become as "the client," the harder it is to embrace the discomfort of risk and, ironically, its potential rewards.

Successful family leadership and governance seeks to balance the needs and aspirations of the individual with those of the whole family. This is where instilling a sense of entrepreneurial stewardship is so important. Leadership by example is critical, preferably intertwining the take-charge attributes of an entrepreneur with the revered and subtle approach of a Lao Tzu steward. A parent who is not a good steward of wealth is unlikely to pass a sense of stewardship on to the next generation. Good stewardship in this context is about defining your culture, managing the economic engine, controlling leakages, and living the values that reflect the importance you place on family.

Nepotism

Nepotism, the favored treatment of one's relatives, can mean bailing someone out or pushing them to new heights. The former implies some weakness; the latter bestows a sense of confidence to achieve. I have seen many parents—wealthy or not—misuse nepotism. Creating a sense among family members that they can expect—or need—nepotistic favors to get ahead fosters a sense of dependency and dampens entrepreneurial fires. This behavior often reveals itself in the way money is distributed in a family. Encouraging adult family members to be dependent on the family's wealth is a classic example. This arrangement reinforces negative, dependent behavior, with both parties buying in. It ultimately weakens the family.

A healthier form of nepotism involves helping a family member explore new opportunities. There is often an implied or stated contract that spells out what is expected in exchange for accelerating the family member's trajectory forward. Beneficiaries of this kind of nepotism recognize the need to prove to the family that they are capable of achieving what they pursue. They are, after all, asking for family support in achieving their dreams or realizing their passions. With success, they can gain the respect and admiration of family and colleagues who supported them in their endeavors from the beginning—financially and/or emotionally.

Using nepotism to share entrepreneurial risk or to help increase the odds of success stimulates entrepreneurial behavior while simultaneously exhibiting the power of family stewardship. We see the power of this healthy form of nepotism quite visibly in two political families of national prominence: the Kennedys and the Bushes. Powerful economic engines support both families, and in both cases a powerful older generation has been instrumental in propelling a younger generation forward to fulfill personal and family ambitions for public office. Neither

John F. Kennedy nor George W. Bush is likely to have experienced the political success that he did had his family not played an active nepotistic role behind the scenes. This type of healthy nepotism expresses itself in America's financial and industrial families as well, though it is less visible in the public eye.

Fairness

Is nepotism granted to one child fair to another? This important question has no simple answer. In the fascinating book *The Millionaire Next Door,* there is a chapter titled "Economic Outpatient Care." The authors point out that in many millionaire families, there is an inverse relationship between the amount of financial support that parents give each of their children and each child's skill in managing his or her finances. As a result, those with the least ability to manage money often receive the most money. If this practice is established early, occasional bailouts become regular handouts, and repeated mistakes with money on the part of certain family members drain family assets, sap those individuals of self-esteem, create resentment by other family members, and foster lifelong dependencies. Economic outpatient care can become chronic and debilitating, to both the donor and the beneficiary.[2]

As one of four siblings and a parent of three children, I find the fairness issue very difficult. Just how do you want to position wealth with each of your children? How do you foster an attitude of empowerment in a child versus an attitude of entitlement? It's a tough call.

The healthiest way I can address the issue is to think of it this way: It is the giver's responsibility to determine fairness. It is the recipient's responsibility to use any generosity that he or she receives in an appropriate way. If I bothered to struggle with whether the actions of my parents toward me have been fair, I would tie myself up in knots. I also realize that I simply do not have an adequate perspective to understand the whole picture here. Who am I to judge how my parents have interacted with me around the issue of money and how they use their own resources? Frankly, I have more interesting things to think about.

When our children were younger, my wife and I were regularly accused of being unfair. As parents, Susan and I don't believe that fair means equal. We think our job is to help each of our children grow and flourish in his or her own way. Because they are all different, we expect to treat each one differently. If we do our job well, our fairness will eventually become apparent to them. Now that our children are approaching adulthood, unfairness accusations seem to have taken a back seat. Let's hope they stay there.

Conclusion

In wealthy families, long-term success depends on nurturing a culture of entrepreneurial stewardship. Entrepreneurial stewardship reinforces the key value drivers in the Strategic Wealth Management Framework and, guided by the Eight Principals, they build a virtuous circle of innovation and growth in successful family enterprises.

My great-grandfather's question, "Am I useful?" is so simple yet elegant. How you and your family approach the question, how you think about serving customers, how you strive for continuous improvement are the things that give life and family purpose.

Weighing the benefits that result from managing wealth collectively is another factor in shaping family culture and purpose. Our family has found that, through its collective efforts, we have improved our financial circumstances significantly. As a result, each of us has more freedom to pursue entrepreneurial stewardship in our own way. At the same time, we have developed a capacity to work in tandem toward common goals. We are also building the next generation of family leaders. Our success in these endeavors will determine our ability to continue to build our family enterprise and maintain our family purpose over coming generations.

In Chapter 11, "Putting It All Together: Multigenerational Planning and Wealth Transfer," I discuss how to transfer wealth from one generation to the next while reinforcing the values of entrepreneurial stewardship. I describe simple actions that can have positive impact for decades to come—and even longer.

But first, in Chapter 10, "Making Philanthropy Part of Your Strategic Wealth Program," I address some of the opportunities and challenges of using your wealth for the betterment of society.

Chapter 9: Issues to Discuss with Your Family

1. What do you consider to be the pinnacle of success in your life?

2. Have you charted your family trees, and what have you learned by performing such an exercise?

3. Is your family culture a closed system or more of an open system? What are the pros and cons of your current family culture, and are you open to changing it? How do you reinforce the positives and deemphasize the negatives?

4. Are you taking risks beyond the financial realm to encourage entrepreneurial stewardship within your own family?

5. What does the term "social capital" mean in your own life? How do you leverage it to the benefit of your family and the wider community?

6. How have you chosen to be involved in your family's/children's lives so that your entrepreneurial goals are communicated and values are transmitted? How do you create the glue to strengthen ties with and among your children and grandchildren as they become mature adults?

7. Who are role models for you in your community? How have you reached out to them to network and to learn more about their family culture and values?

8. Do you believe that nepotism can be a good thing, or do you regard it with suspicion? Why?

9. Are there members of your family who cannot or will not assume independent financial status? If so, what are you doing to deal with this situation?

10. Do you define fairness as treating each person on their own individual terms, or do you think that fairness means treating everyone equally?

Endnotes

1. Stuart E. Lucas and David Lansky, "Managing Paradox," *Family Business Magazine*, March 2010. For more information on David Lansky and The Family Business Consulting Group, Inc., contact www.efamilybusiness.com. For more information on *Family Business Magazine*, contact www.familybusinessmagazine.com.

2. Thomas J. Stanley, Ph.D., and William D. Danko, Ph.D., *The Millionaire Next Door: The Surprising Secrets of America's Wealthy* (Longstreet Press, 1996), 141–74.

10

Making Philanthropy Part of Your Strategic Wealth Program

philanthropy: 1. good will toward all people; esp: effort to promote human welfare 2. a charitable act or gift; also: an organization that distributes or is supported by donated funds.

—The Merriam-Webster Dictionary[1]

Philanthropy and service to others are deeply rooted in our family purpose and are important elements of the Strategic Wealth Management Framework. From a young age, E. A. Stuart, a practicing Quaker, gave generously of both his time and his money, in good times and tough times. So when in 1937, in the midst of the Great Depression, he formed The Elbridge Stuart Foundation as a charitable trust, it was simply a continuation and formalization of a lifelong mission. Four years later, he established a second foundation in memory of his wife, Mary, to whom he was married for 55 years. From then until the sale of the Carnation Company in 1985, millions of dollars in grants from these foundations were made to strengthen local schools, libraries, churches, and boys' and girls' homes in communities where Carnation operated. The company's leadership felt strongly that it had a responsibility to make these largely rural communities as vital as possible. A board of directors made up of company executives, including members of the Stuart family, was responsible for allocating the grants and following up with grantees to monitor and encourage their hard work.

Back when these foundations were formed by my great-grandfather, there were fewer than 12,000 charitable tax-exempt entities of any kind in the United States, and most of them were operating as charities, not foundations. Today, there are more than a million charitable tax-exempt organizations in the country. Of that total, there are 76,000 foundations in the U.S. that have accumulated assets over $600 billion. They distribute $46 billion per year to social services organizations, educational groups, healthcare organizations, environmental causes, the arts, places of worship, and other philanthropic institutions.[2] Proudly, I say that E. A. Stuart was in the vanguard with other great entrepreneurs and philanthropists of his time.

Since the Carnation Company was sold in 1985, the two foundations cited previously, plus another one started by E. H. Stuart, have been merged into the Stuart Foundation. We have also narrowed the foundation's focus. Today the foundation is dedicated to children and youth in the states of California and Washington, and it supports improvements in the public-education system and the child-welfare system. We focus on these two states because they were the primary residences of Carnation and the Stuart family. There is now a professional staff of experts managing the Stuart Foundation, and since Carnation was sold, the foundation has given away more than $250 million. I invite you to visit the foundation's website at www.stuartfoundation.org to learn more about this organization of which I am so proud.

Why People Give

From biblical times, there have been stories of wealthy people who decide to follow a life of poverty and give away all of their worldly assets. Possibly the most striking example is that of Buddha. He was the son of a king who gave up worldly pleasures to seek enlightenment as a monk. Today there are some extraordinary people still following this course, Buddhist and otherwise. Often, their stories of selflessness and service to others aren't very well publicized.

Some people are philosophical about their giving, as expressed in some of my great-grandfather's memoirs. In a statement he wrote upon founding the first foundation, he notes: "It has been my privilege and pleasure to have led a busy, and I trust, a useful life.... [Now] my keenest desire is that [America's] opportunities and its possibilities may remain open and available to my son, my grandchildren, and their children after them, as well as to all other young men and women who have high ideals and are willing to make sacrifices for their attainment."[3] He adds: "One of my profound observations during all these years is that communities are industrious, progressive, and successful when the individual citizens are industrious, progressive, and successful."[4] I'm sure that there are many other philanthropists who feel much as my great-grandfather did, and I admire them all for proactively sharing their good fortune with others.

I think most wealthy people engage in philanthropy for one or more of the following reasons:

- They want to make a profound impact.

- They believe that privilege and good fortune demand responsibility to others.

- They want to acquire social capital.

- They feel some guilt over their good circumstances.

- They are driven by the inspiration of others.

- They want tax relief.

Making a Profound Impact

Many wealthy people get great satisfaction from the impact of their gifts of vision, time, and money, and they rise to the creative challenge of making their gifts effective. Great institutions have been funded through philanthropy. The Rockefeller family was instrumental in financing the creation of our national park system and in founding Rockefeller University (one of the finest graduate research institutions in the country); the University of Chicago; and Winrock International, an international development organization.

Groups of people sometimes come together with a vision. In 1992, a small group of people came together to build an endowment for National Public Radio, which at the time had 9 million weekly listeners. Just a few years later, I bought into the vision and joined the effort, becoming a member of the board of the NPR Foundation. Together with other members of the foundation, we transformed a financially insecure foundation with no assets into one with $250 million in assets, and we are in the midst of raising funds for a new, desperately needed headquarters in Washington, D.C. Thanks largely to the dedication of

NPR's leaders, correspondents, and Public Radio stations across the country, NPR's weekly audience now tops 27 million listeners.

Believing That Privilege and Good Fortune Demand Responsibility to Others

John D. Rockefeller proclaimed his family's commitment to social responsibility in a plaque located in the middle of Rockefeller Center in New York City for all to see. "I believe that every right implies a responsibility; every opportunity, an obligation; every possession, a duty." Many others share Mr. Rockefeller's belief that those of us who are fortunate have a responsibility to help others, as individuals, as communities, and as nations. And they act on it in small ways and large. For many people, this sense of responsibility is inextricably tied to their religious or ethical belief system. This was certainly true of E. A. Stuart.

Responsibility to others takes many forms. At one extreme, people fight to reduce disease and poverty. They support institutions like food banks, shelters for battered women, AIDS clinics, and children's hospitals. At another end of the spectrum, people recognize and support exceptional drive and talent. The Pritzker Prize in architecture, the Golden Apple teaching awards, the Rockefeller Genius Awards, and the MacArthur Fellowships are just a few examples of philanthropy in which people give back by identifying and rewarding greatness in fields that make our culture and humanity stronger. Money, public recognition, time, and compassion are all the tools of thoughtfully offering goodwill to others.

Acquiring Social Capital

There is nothing wrong with giving away money as a means to acquire social capital. Some people do this by giving money to support charitable organizations and accepting invitations to lavish dinner parties as a reward. (Typically, attendance entails getting your name and sometimes your picture in the newspaper.) Other people lend their names as honorary chairs of charity fundraisers with which they have only modest hands-on contact, but whose causes they love dearly or to which they're sentimentally attached.

There are still other ways in which societies reward the rich and powerful with social capital. In England, you are knighted. In France, you can earn the Legion of Honor. In China, you rise within the Communist Party. In Monaco, it's about gaining access to the right boat slips and parties in Monte Carlo!

Although the motives for giving in such cases can be mixed, especially when a "reward" is attached, the end result is that such giving does support worthy causes. And I applaud people whose generosity ultimately benefits deserving organizations!

Feeling Guilty

Among inheritors of wealth, some people are motivated (unfortunately) by a sense of guilt. When a person's inner conflict can be turned outward, both the donor and the grantee are likely to benefit from the donor's act. Philanthropy at its best starts from the soul. From there, it typically radiates outward in expressions of exuberance, passion, and compassion for those who are less fortunate.

Being Inspired by Others

Sometimes committed leadership inspires people to give because they admire people who "live a cause." Christopher Reeve, Mother Teresa, Nelson Mandela, and Princess Diana are all examples of exemplary public figures who have inspired people to support worthy causes with time and money—whether to cancer and spinal cord research, the elimination of poverty, political freedom, AIDS education, or the elimination of land mines. You don't have to be a famous figure to inspire others to give. You just need a vision and the heart to see it through.

Wanting Tax Relief

Some people give because they don't want the money to go to the government. The tax benefits of philanthropy date back to 1917 when they were codified into the tax code, a mere four years after the income tax was first instituted. At that time, there were very few charitable tax-exempt institutions in the country. Uncle Sam clearly had a foresighted policy of wanting to encourage giving in return for tax relief.

Today there are numerous ways to give away assets and receive tax benefits. Each philanthropic option varies in its tax ramifications based on the types of assets you contribute, the amount of control you retain, administrative expenses, and your desire to remain anonymous.

In all cases, you can receive a deduction of the amount of the gift from adjusted gross income (AGI) on your tax return, up to certain limits. So, for example, if you report an AGI of $100,000 and you make a donation valued at $10,000, it reduces your taxable income to $90,000. There are limits on the size of the deduction, as a percentage of AGI, that you can take in any one year. But you can roll forward any unused amounts.

Maximizing the Tax Benefits of Giving

From the tax man's perspective (and by definition), making a donation means that you are offering a gift. You are not receiving goods or services in exchange for the gift. If you do receive something of substance in exchange, it's not a gift. It's a business transaction. That's why if you go to a charity dinner, a portion of your contribution goes to paying the cost of the dinner and is not tax-deductible. To receive tax benefits, you must make a donation.

When you are offering a gift, it is almost always more advantageous from a tax perspective to donate appreciated securities (held longer than one year) than to donate cash to qualifying philanthropic causes because if you give cash, you get a tax deduction only on the after-tax value of your gift. However, if you give appreciated securities, you get an income tax deduction based on the gross market value of the gift. Here is an illustration of how this works: If you give appreciated stock with an initial cost of $1 and a current market value of $10, you get a $10 tax deduction and you don't pay a tax of $1.35 (assuming a 15% long-term capital gains tax rate) on the accrued profit of $9.

By giving away the stock, you get a $10 tax deduction, you choose the recipient of your largesse, the government waives its claim to the $1.35 in capital gains taxes you would otherwise pay, and it redirects all the tax it would otherwise receive to the same worthwhile cause. If you plan to make charitable gifts, it's just one more reason why owning a diversified portfolio with an equity bias makes sense. Whenever a stock does really well, you can donate it instead of selling it and never pay tax!

Making Bequests

If you make a charitable donation as a bequest, it reduces the size of your estate by the value of the bequest. If you are subject to the estate tax, this gives you an opportunity to reduce the value of your estate, thereby reducing or eliminating your tax liability. Because estate tax rates have traditionally been high for wealthy people, there is considerable value for individuals to include philanthropy as part of their estate plan.

People who have a financial goal of maintaining purchasing power don't want to run out of money. To protect themselves, they defer a portion of their philanthropy until death to give themselves more of a financial cushion.

But other people have plenty of cushion and should consider making donations now to reduce their taxable income and their taxes. If they give to an endowment, the donated assets have more time to grow tax free. A nonprofit recipient can use the gift, or the income from the gift, to do good works right now, rather than having to wait a month, a year, or a decade until the decedent's estate bequeaths it. And you, the beneficiary, get to enjoy the value that you've created. Your leadership and your expression of passion can influence other people to rally around the cause and make greater contributions themselves.

Other Options

There are at least two charitable structures that integrate philanthropic goals with estate and tax planning. These structures, called charitable lead trusts (CLTs) and charitable remainder trusts (CRTs), are more complicated and require detailed legal and tax advice. In each case, you fund an investment vehicle that makes annual distributions for a period of years or until a specific event occurs, such as your death or the death of your spouse.

With a CLT, the cash flows must be directed to tax-exempt charitable organizations, but at the specified time the remaining principal is distributed to your children or grandchildren. With a CRT, the reverse occurs. The cash flows go to a person and then the remainder, at a predetermined time or upon the occurrence of a predetermined event, must go to designated charities.

The CLT is used as a way to transfer assets from one generation to another while limiting the gift and estate tax bite—an alternative to life insurance plans. The future trust appreciation going to your family escapes estate tax. The taxable value of the assets transferred to your family—which they will receive in the future—are discounted using IRS present value formulas. The CLT can often result in less income tax being paid to the IRS, because trusts can deduct charitable giving against taxable income without the "percentage of gross income" limitations to which individuals are subject, as discussed earlier in this chapter. The value of the assets in the CLT (that will eventually be distributed to your family free of estate tax) can be estimated based on some assumptions about the financial growth of the assets.

The CRT is a way to secure your financial well-being or that of a loved one, usually until death, while reducing your income tax bite. This is because you receive a current charitable deduction for your future gift to charity (discounted by present value formulas), and you are entitled to an annual annuity payment. If you contribute appreciated assets to your CRT, and then sell those assets within the CRT, you will also reduce or delay capital gains taxes. The CRT does not pay income taxes and the annuitant pays taxes only on the amount received each year, which can be taxed at capital gains rates. This allows diversification of a large stock holding without current taxation on the full gain. Many high-flying stocks have been contributed to, and then sold by, CRTs with their annuitants enjoying many years of payments secured by a diversified CRT portfolio. The potential attractiveness of either of these vehicles is based on a number of factors. If you think such techniques might be of interest, I strongly encourage you to discuss them with your advisors.

In addition to thinking about the tax and societal benefits that will accrue from such trusts, also consider how you and your family will oversee the effective management of these trusts over a period that could span decades.

The CLT and CRT can integrate wealth management and philanthropic strategies. For example, in 2004, Harvard University got an innovative private letter ruling from the IRS allowing individuals to invest the assets of their CLTs or CRTs alongside those of the university's endowment. There is a catch, though: As part of the arrangement, Harvard must be the trustee and sole charitable beneficiary of the assets. On the other hand, Harvard's endowment has one of the best track records of any endowment in the country. If its track record continues, this arrangement would be very beneficial both to the university and to those individuals who partake. Harvard is so excited about this offering that they will even help you to set up a qualifying trust.

Harvard has another program for people who want to make a partial donation to the university. Harvard will still act as trustee but the assets are invested in a series of Vanguard tax-efficient (think index) funds. If past is prologue, these assets won't perform as well as Harvard's endowment. But if you have a CRT, there's an interesting tax dimension. Given the way Harvard manages its endowment, the tax rate on distributions to a taxable individual like you would be about double the tax rate on distributions from the Vanguard program. So, although you might not get the same asset growth in the latter program, your taxes would be lower, so, all other things being equal, your spendable income, at least for some years, would be considerably higher.

A number of other universities have since followed Harvard's lead and received the benefit of similar IRS rulings.

Final Thoughts on Why People Give

If I had to summarize my great-grandfather's public service and philanthropy, I would say he was motivated by all the reasons I've cited—depending on the specific situation. E. A. Stuart believed passionately in perpetuating the strengths and values of American culture by empowering individual citizens through his philanthropic work and in everyday business. He always thought very long term, as evidenced by his explicit reference to "unborn generations of my descendants," whom he hoped would benefit from this land of opportunity. He established his foundation as a perpetual trust to embody this perspective.

How to Be Philanthropic

A Wealth Strategist has four principal structural options for allocating funds to philanthropic causes. Ranked from simplest to most complex, these are the options:

1. Direct donations
2. Support organizations
3. Donor-advised funds
4. Private foundations

Direct Donations

You can make direct tax-deductible contributions to qualifying institutions under paragraph 501(c)(3) of the tax code. You can learn about whether a nonprofit organization is a qualifying institution, and about filings that every nonprofit must make to the IRS, at www.guidestar.com. When satisfied that the organization qualifies, you can make a tax-deductible donation and, if desired, can stipulate how you want your contribution used. Know that after you make the donation you lose control over its use, although all reputable charities take donor intent very seriously (most would not stay in business very long if they didn't). Practically speaking, most direct gifts are made for current use, and donations can be made anonymously.

Support Organizations

Some operating charitable institutions have endowments whose sole purpose is to provide financial support to that institution. The most well-known endowments are those of colleges and universities, but they exist also in larger cultural institutions, religious organizations, and even nonprofit media outlets like National Public Radio. Most of the grants to support organizations are made to an endowment. Sometimes the donor specifies some specific purpose for the cash flow from the endowed gift; other times, it is left up to the institution. Donations can be anonymous.

Donor-Advised Funds

Community foundations pioneered the concept of letting people give money to a foundation and then indicate to which (type of) organization their contributions should be directed. Fidelity, Vanguard, Schwab, and others picked up on the concept and developed donor-advised programs, giving the donor some flexibility for how funds should be invested and where their "fund" should be donated. If you are donating appreciated securities, you can expect that Schwab, Fidelity, or Vanguard will sell the securities immediately; some community foundations, if requested, might retain the security in a segregated account. In either case, you will get a tax deduction at the time you donate to the program and at the same rate as if you made a direct donation. Also, you can defer making grants for a number of years so that assets can accumulate tax free. Grants can be anonymous.

Private Foundations

Foundations are the most flexible, but also the most complicated, way of doing planned giving. Although a foundation's governance structure is separate from your own assets, you can sit on your foundation's board, designate the characteristics of other board members, and set the procedure for selecting them. This makes private foundations the best way to control assets after they have been donated, either because you want to hold onto donated stock or because you want to direct the donations of the foundation. The tax benefits of establishing a foundation are almost as good as those of as the alternatives.

Private foundations are required to distribute at least 5% of their assets each year, either in the form of grants or in qualified expenses. Because of this restriction, they can't compound their tax-free growth at the same rate as donor-advised funds or support organizations that choose to distribute less. Also, they must file an annual report (Form 990) with the IRS and pay a modest excise tax. This filing becomes public information.

If you are considering making a donation of less than $250,000, it is probably not practical to set up your own foundation because the administrative costs and substantial reporting requirements will outweigh the benefits. If you are committed to this alternative, you should review a service offered by Foundation Source that lowers the cost and complexity of setting up a foundation at www.foundationsource.com. A foundation cannot make anonymous gifts.

Amount of Control You Retain

I am concerned by a recent trend in giving. Today, more and more donors are demanding to support specific programs rather than giving general operating support. Their argument is that supporting programs creates a greater level of accountability within the nonprofit, and this is true up to a point. But it can have adverse consequences. Program-based fundraising puts a larger administrative burden on organizations because nonprofits must make solicitations in many different forms and prove their success using many different formats to satisfy the idiosyncrasies of individual donors. The ensuing larger administrative costs can reduce fundraising efficiency, taking dollars away from where they are needed most.

Also, because of the popularity of program-based fundraising, it becomes difficult for many nonprofits to raise money to support general administration, executive salaries, and basic infrastructure. Finally, program-based fundraising sometimes encourages organizations to engage in financial "shell games," wherein nonprofit executives move money around on the organization's balance sheet, both to satisfy the whims of individual donors and to meet the overall operating goals of the organization. This behavior actually undermines accountability and diverts the focus of the organization away from its primary mission.

For these reasons, I am a big believer in providing general operating support to well-run organizations with clear missions. Excellent management teams know where to spend and invest their resources!

Desire to Remain Anonymous

Some people desire to be anonymous when it comes to philanthropy, but I advise people to be on the record with their generosity. I encourage "on-the-record giving" because the donor's leadership encourages others to give to a cause as well. So, before you tick the "Anonymous" box, think carefully about whether you are maximizing the benefit to the organization(s) you are supporting.

Occasionally, there are reasons why you might want to be an anonymous donor. People might assume that, as a major named donor, you have disproportionate influence on the organization. This often isn't the case, but the appearance of influence can still be awkward for you or for other family members involved in the organization.

Innovations in Effective Philanthropy

With so many institutions engaged in philanthropy and so many dollars at work, it is no surprise that there is a lot of innovation in philanthropy today. Organizations like the Center for Effective Philanthropy, the Council on Foundations, and academic institutions like the Northwestern and Harvard business schools are studying best practices and searching for new ways to make the nonprofit sector more effective and fundraising more satisfying to donors. The most creative ideas are in venture investing, social impact investing, advances in accountability, public-private partnerships, life cycle debates, and governance. I can't resist a quick shout out for Howard Stevenson's new book, *Getting to Giving: Fundraising the Entrepreneurial Way*. It's a valuable read for anyone who wants to donate or raise money effectively. Howard combines his decades of experience teaching entrepreneurship and raising over a billion dollars for Harvard Business School and other organizations in an incredibly thoughtful way.

Venture Philanthropy

The $46 billion that U.S.-based foundations give away each year sounds like a lot of money, but it pales in comparison to, say, the approximately $50 billion annual budget for public primary and secondary education just in the state of California. Some philanthropists try to leverage their relatively small dollars by applying some of the principles of venture capital to grant making.

They look for new ideas that appear attractive and, if proven effective, can be scaled up. They conduct research to gather as much information as possible about the idea, to discern whether components of it have been tried elsewhere, and to determine what aspects of the idea still need to be crystallized. They then look to fill out the team of committed and talented people to manage a pilot project. If it is successful, they roll out the concept. In the field of education, the Gates Foundation's support of the Khan Academy (www.khanacademy.org) is a great example of venture philanthropy. If you haven't visited the Khan Academy website, or seen TED Talks by Salman Khan on YouTube, you should. You could be witnessing the beginning of an education revolution.

Sometimes, a need is recognized but no solution is yet evident. A philanthropist might pay for a group of experts to come together to "hatch" a solution. Then, there is more research, a pilot, and expansion as appropriate. This type of philanthropic work is particularly prevalent in the medical field.

Venture philanthropy is very exciting, risky, and hard work. If successful, it can have a big impact on society, but because it is done in the form of grant making, there is no economic return to the funder. For example, the NPR Foundation was started as a venture capital operation, and has been very successful. The Stuart Foundation has helped to hatch a number of successful organizations in the fields of education and child welfare. The beauty of this type of philanthropic investing is that you can often begin your initiative with a fairly small amount of money. Currently, the creative and risk-seeking aspects of venture philanthropy are beyond the skill of many established charities. However, I firmly believe that venture philanthropy as a component of corporate and institutional philanthropy will grow in importance in the years to come.

Impact Investing

Impact investing is about investing a foundation's assets, not about grant making. The theory goes that a foundation uses cash flow to the tune of only 5% of its assets each year to support public service. What if it dedicated a substantially larger portion of its balance sheet to investing in socially worthy ventures in hopes of generating a financial return as well as a social return on those investments? This is the idea of impact investing. The idea really started out as a way to use foundation and endowment capital to express an institution's values—for example, no tobacco or no apartheid.

Over time, the concept has developed further. Should a foundation interested in the environment invest in fuel cells, solar technology, or methane-reducing feedstock for cattle? Should a hospital endowment invest a portion of its assets in the commercialization of biotechnology?

Would reasonable people agree that these investments constitute part of a prudent portfolio of investments?

There appears to be a trade-off between maximizing economic profit and values-based investing, in large part because it turns out that many "sin" stocks have been high-performing long-term investments. This could theoretically create a conflict for fiduciaries (trustees) between maximizing the value of their financial assets and fulfilling the mission of their institution. In practice, thoughtful exclusion of certain assets now does appear to be a widely accepted (though not required) practice in the foundation world.

My favorite example at the moment of impact investing is the UNREAL Brands, makers of UNREAL Candy. UNREAL candy tastes great, yet it has no corn syrup, no artificial ingredients, no preservatives, real cacao, and a fraction of the sugar of M&Ms, Milky Way, Reese's Peanut Butter Cups, or Snickers Bars. I also find that I have less craving for a second helping. UNREAL is the brainchild of Michael Bronner, founder of Upromise and Digitas, and his son Nicky. The Bronners don't pretend that candy is good for you, but they are trying to help address the child obesity problem by providing a healthier alternative to the typical choices. Try some; you might even share it with your children!

UNREAL might be a good financial investment, too. But, as a general rule, investing material portions of a foundation's assets in an unorthodox way that is not likely to generate a reasonable rate of return is an issue. Foundation trustees are obliged to represent the public interest in the execution of their responsibilities. (That's why foundations don't pay much tax. Furthermore, if individuals put their own money at risk, any losses are tax-deductible.) If trustees invest prudently, it could be the case that alignment of the foundation mission and the investment of its assets are mutually reinforcing. But if the investment approach is not prudent and is not designed to generate a reasonable return at reasonable risk, trustees could be open to litigation. These issues have not been well-tested in court or in the realm of public opinion, so if you want to engage in Impact Investing, please do so cautiously and consult with an informed attorney.

Advances in Accountability

Historically, public service organizations have struggled with accountability. Their goals are often intangible, long-term, subject to personal taste (what is good art?), and hard to measure. Well, accountability is coming to philanthropy. Today, more than ever before, grant-making organizations are demanding specific performance commitments in return for the money they offer organizations. These commitments can be measured in myriad ways: hours spent, people served, secondary infection rates (for hospitals), nutrition per meal served, user satisfaction, teacher accreditation rates, and the list goes on.

The spotlight of accountability (even on investment performance) is shining on nonprofit, charitable, and philanthropic boards of directors. Increasingly, membership on such boards is bringing with it specific performance criteria and fiduciary responsibilities: to participate regularly at board meetings, to oversee the organization's financial performance and performance against mission, to give a minimum designated amount of money to remain on a board or to raise that money from other people, to recruit other qualified board members, and to provide specific business expertise. National Public Radio and many organizations today do annual evaluations of board members to assess individual contributions to board activities. Increasingly, if nonprofit board members are not fulfilling fundraising responsibilities or other aspects of their nonprofit board "job descriptions," they are being asked to step aside.

Public/Private Partnerships

Another trend in philanthropy is the formation of public/private partnerships. In such cases, private foundations or operating charities partner with government organizations to deliver services more effectively than if each operated independently.

This theory capitalizes on the innovation of the private sector and couples it with the infrastructure and money in the public sector to serve specific communities more effectively and efficiently. These partnerships take many forms, and each one is established to address a specific set of issues. Some partnerships have finite lives and are project-oriented, whereas others continue successfully for many years.

In Chicago, the Ounce of Prevention organization has effectively partnered with government organizations for a number of years to bring educational and social services to at-risk newborns, infants, toddlers, and their parents. In California, the Stuart Foundation partners with a number of county-level organizations to improve social services for children in foster care and to help more of them find permanent, safe homes. We also work with district- and state-level organizations to improve educational outcomes for children in public schools.

Large philanthropic institutions that work extensively overseas—such as the Gates Foundation, AmeriCares, and the J. Paul Getty Trust—work directly with governments and quasi-governmental organizations to do research and deliver services around the world. These organizations exchange research and share resources to solve problems that neither could do alone.

Life Cycle Debates: Perpetual or Limited Life?

There is a current debate over whether private foundations should be required to have limited lives. As mentioned earlier, private foundations must distribute at least 5% of their assets each year, but this figure includes both grants and most administrative expenses. Foundations with permanent lives incur substantial annual administrative costs (typically between .5% and 1.5%) to maintain the perpetuity, so direct grants might constitute only 3.5% to 4.5% of a foundation's assets each year. Some people question whether this lower level of distributions to serve the public good justifies the foundation's favorable tax treatment. Yet foundations have many ways they can add value "beyond the grant." They organize convenings and build networks to help nonprofits share information and learn best practices. Foundations that become respected in a particular field give a "seal of approval" to grantees, and sometimes help them raise money from other foundations and individuals. Some foundations provide free or paid consulting to grantees, sometimes supported by data and analysis that the foundation has collected and studied. At the Stuart Foundation, we aim to have our non-grant-making activities make at least as much of an impact as our check writing.

Another debate is over obsolescence and donor intent. Most people who establish foundations or endowments create governing language giving future trustees flexibility to change the foundation's focus if the original focus ceases to be relevant. This creates the risk that future trustees apply funds in ways that the donor did not intend or might find objectionable. On the other hand, donors who write overly restrictive language into governing documents risk the possibility that their organization becomes obsolete. I think that most foundation founders want to find a balance that keeps the foundation's activities relevant while remaining true to their founding vision.

Given the changing nature of social and community needs, it's healthy to have an ongoing debate about the role and function of foundations. Julius Rosenwald, a great philanthropist and a founder of Sears Roebuck, stipulated that his foundation must distribute all of its assets within 50 years of his death. Other philanthropists, like Joan Kroc, made their philanthropic commitments late in life to specific operating charitable organizations. Today, younger entrepreneurs, many of whom have made large direct donations to causes, have done so as part of embarking on second careers in philanthropy. Many have made a life shift—from a focus on entrepreneurship in business to a focus on entrepreneurship in public service. Instead of creating and running foundations, they are rolling up their sleeves and using their business skills to manage or start operating nonprofits or to become fundraisers, teachers, volunteers, and mentors.

Governance

Foundations are formed and financed privately. But after they are brought into being, theoretically they exist for public benefit. As we've discussed, in exchange for the tax benefits of endowing a foundation and its tax-exempt status when it is established, the government insists that foundations support qualifying nonprofit activities and do so responsibly.

The Sarbanes-Oxley Law, passed by Congress in 2002 to bring more discipline to corporate governance, has had repercussions far beyond America's corporate boardrooms. Leaders in the foundation world are assuming that their turn will be next. Some states, like California, have responded to Sarbanes-Oxley by legislating additional governance requirements for foundations and their boards. Inevitably, these changes add cost, complexity, and the potential for liability to foundation directors and managers. Fortunately, today's direct donations, support organizations, and donor-advised funds offer attractive and simple alternatives to foundations for individuals and families that want to engage in planned philanthropy.

Foundations have a unique and privileged position in American governance, and it is susceptible to both the perception and the reality of abuse. Foundations do not have paying customers, they don't need to raise money, and they don't have shareholders. Many foundations have no independent board members. The market mechanisms and checks and balances that constrain most other organizations in our economy do not exist for foundations. The only checks on their autonomy are the ethics of the people who run and oversee them, the requirement that they disclose key (financial) information publicly, and their duty to file the Form 990 each year with the IRS.

From a policy standpoint, it's important that families continue to receive nonfinancial incentives to keep managing the $600 billion that currently resides in America's foundations. We need to keep families engaged in foundation management and prevent the burden of regulation from becoming overly cumbersome.

At the same time, prudent levels of governance should be legislated to minimize abuse of foundations' special status. In coming years, policymakers will have to wrestle with ways to make governance more transparent without disrupting the good work that foundations do.

Philanthropy and Family

As you might have noticed, family is central to my makeup. I look at life through the lens of my family and am always searching for links that circle back to strengthening the family. Philanthropy, for me, is in part about seeking connections to family. Because there is no longer a Carnation business to tie our family together, philanthropic pursuits and public service have become a shared passion that binds members of my family together.

Another family, the Lehman family, has used philanthropy to bind its members together and to perpetuate the values of the family company. The Lehmans are one of three families that built a company called Fel-Pro into one of this country's leading auto-parts companies. One of the bedrock beliefs of the company's leadership was that a workforce that is respected, listened to, and supported by top management far exceeds in productivity any costs incurred by creating a more humane and supportive workplace. Before the company was sold to Federal-Mogul in February 1998 for $720 million,[5] it was ranked as one of the best companies in the country to work for. Auto-parts manufacturing has always been a tough, competitive business, and Fel-Pro's human resources (HR) strategy was both a commercial success and a point of pride.

After the sale of Fel-Pro, the Lehman family set up a charitable 501(c)3 organization to promote best practices in human resources for small- and midsized companies. They called the organization Winning Workplaces. It offers a series of "Tool Kits" (at modest prices) that explain best practices in numerous areas of HR. To ensure proper recognition of outstanding practitioners in the field, the family partnered with *Inc. Magazine*, and before that *The Wall Street Journal*, to establish awards for the top small-company workplaces. More than 300 supporters attended an awards dinner only a few short years after the organization was founded. Four generations of Lehmans also attended. (Maybe good HR policies are correlated with longevity!)

The Winning Workplaces board consisted of several family members from the two senior generations, as well as a number of independent experts. Although the family financed most of the start-up costs, it successfully reached out to others to share the cost, and the rewards of being useful. In time, other organizations sprang up and followed Winning Workplaces lead to help small and mid-sized businesses succeed and provide new and satisfying careers to its employees. Top workplace competitions proliferated, too. Eventually, the field has become crowded enough that Winning Workplaces made another bold decision. The work they set out to do has been achieved, so they decided to suspend operations. The tools they provide are still available at www.winningworkplaces.org and are downloaded by the hundreds.

The example of public service through entrepreneurial stewardship that was established by the senior generations has been embraced by generation three. However, the G3 family members are expressing that mission in new ways that are most meaningful to them. They are leaders in their local community, in Teach For America, and in building an innovative hospital ship on Lake Tanganyika. Human and financial resources of the family have been redirected to support the third generation's expressions of the family's philanthropic mission. I admire the Lehman family very much for all they've accomplished, individually and collectively, and for their willingness to embrace change—a hallmark of flourishing multi-generational families.

In summary, foundations and operating nonprofit organizations can reinforce family purpose through public service in similar ways that family businesses can through commercial enterprise. They are both about being useful and serving others. Philanthropy provides another forum for family members to explore common values through individual and shared interests, and another means to galvanize the family.

Philanthropy and Children

Many of our religious institutions and schools teach us at a very early age to engage in what Judaism calls *tsedaka*. All major religions encourage tithing and/or other forms of philanthropy and community outreach. We cannot start too early to impart to our children the values of goodwill and serving others.

Starting when they were quite young, each week, my own kids put a portion of their allowance into their *tsedaka* boxes, and when the boxes were full, they thought carefully about how they wanted to give away the money. Today they have become active in community service, tutoring, developing a database of public high schools for a local charter school, and working for the Chicago Council on Global Affairs.

Although I am a big believer in engaging children early and often in public service, I encourage restraint when it comes to the power of the pen. Giving away material amounts of other people's money is a position of power that I don't think is constructive for children. In addition, money in a foundation does not make it a "teaching tool" for younger members of the family. Children don't need to disperse other people's money to experience the joys and challenges of public service, and there are better places to learn how to budget or manage investments. The responsibilities of managing a foundation, deciding how to allocate its grant money, and holding grantees accountable is work best left to mature adults.

Family Foundations

When deciding whether to set up a foundation within your family, you need to ask these vital questions:

- Does the foundation have a mission?
- Do you have assets that need to be managed in a particular way?
- Do you have the scale to amortize the costs appropriately?
- Are you going to make charitable grants to people and organizations that are not registered 501(c)(3) organizations?
- Do you want the foundation to have a specific and independent identity that will enhance your mission?

If the answer to all of these questions is yes, a foundation is probably the right way to go. Keep in mind that foundations are expensive to administer and must maintain corporate records, file Form 990s on an annual basis, manage their assets, and do basic due diligence on grantees. Larger family foundations need permanent staff to evaluate grant proposals and manage a public relations program. These administrative costs can easily exceed 1% of a foundation's assets every year, or one-fifth of their required distribution. They are also modestly less tax efficient than other philanthropic structures.

In multigenerational families, foundations are often established with a bequest. This technique shrinks the size of one's taxable estate and minimizes the impact of estate taxes. Carefully crafting donor intent and having extensive discussion about governance with the next generation will make the difference between the foundation's flourishing and its being considered a burden by the next generation. If you are considering this option, I urge you to establish a foundation today at a reduced size and work through the issues of governance and focus with your family. This will give you all the experience and confidence to fully fund the foundation with a bequest. You can also encourage your spouse or children to add more assets in the future.

Direct Service

There are many advantages to rolling up your sleeves and getting involved in direct service to nonprofit organizations. I guarantee that it will make you a better philanthropist because you will better understand the organizations you support and their constituencies. You will also build a useful network. Mostly, it is gratifying to take the opportunity to give of yourself to organizations and to make a positive impact on individual lives.

You feel that emotional impact the most when you are working on the frontlines of an organization. You can broaden your impact (without giving up that frontline experience) if you also provide managerial leadership or committed board-level service. Again, there are many advantages to serving on the boards of nonprofit organizations. You can use your business skills to help organizations function more effectively. You will become more familiar with governance issues that are peculiar to nonprofit organizations. In some cases, you will learn about, and perhaps contribute to, how organizations invest their financial assets. You will see organizations that you believe in from the inside, and you will get into a rich flow of information that will help you and the organization make more informed decisions. Plus, it is fun.

Conclusion

My great-grandfather believed strongly that being wealthy carried with it a responsibility to live a useful life—as a moral obligation, as a show of respect for his ancestors, and as an example for his children. As James Marshall, author of my great-grandfather E. A. Stuart's biography, noted, his "great wealth was truly in what he gave, and not what he retained, for his personal estate at the time of his death was very much less than what he had given and set aside for others during his lifetime."[6]

I have tried to live this philosophy in writing this book and in striving to be an active philanthropist, a responsible family member, and an entrepreneurial steward of my family's assets. Incorporating philanthropic values into an integrated wealth management strategy remains a lifetime goal. I hope that you share this perspective and that this book will lead you to fulfilling that dream for yourself and your family.

Chapter 10: Issues to Discuss with Your Family

1. Do you have a public service mission? Why or why not? What is it?

2. Do you think that any one reason for being philanthropic is more valuable or legitimate than others? If so, why?

3. How do you feel about anonymous gift giving?

4. Have you purposefully used philanthropy to maximum legal tax advantage? If not, why not?

5. What is the right structure for your philanthropic activity? Are you using appreciated securities to make donations?

6. Do CRTs and CLTs hold appeal? Do you have the right advisors to help you pursue these options?

7. What gives you confidence that the organizations to which you donate use the money well? Have you ever asked an organization to provide data that enhances your trust in their stewardship? Have you considered getting involved as a volunteer or board member?

8. If philanthropy and community service are important to you, what have you done to educate, encourage, and support your spouse, children, or grandchildren in these areas?

Endnotes

1. *The Merriam-Webster Dictionary,* 1998 Edition, p. 391.

2. The Foundation Center, Foundation Yearbook, 2011.

3. Elbridge A. Stuart, "Statement." The Elbridge Stuart Foundation, November 30, 1937, pp. 5 and 7.

4. Ibid, p. 7.

5. PricewaterhouseCoopers, Global Automotive Deal Survey, 1998.

6. James Marshall, *Elbridge A. Stuart, Founder of Carnation Company.* Western Printing and Lithograph Company, 1949, p. 199.

11

Putting It All Together: Multigenerational Planning and Wealth Transfer

"I must study politics and war that my sons may have liberty to study mathematics and philosophy. My sons ought to study mathematics and philosophy, geography, natural history, naval architecture, navigation, commerce, and agriculture in order to give their children a right to study painting, poetry, music, architecture, statuary, tapestry, and porcelain."

—John Adams, second President of the United States

Good estate planning means constructing a valuable financial, family, and social legacy. It's the successful outcome of implementing the Strategic Wealth Management Framework for your family enterprise.

Several of my relatives have had a profound impact on my desire to build on our valued legacy. My great-grandfather E. A. Stuart integrated his love of family into his company, the trusts he established, and his philanthropy. My Aunt Ethel taught me that wealth has nothing to do with how much money you have and everything to do with "how" you leave a lasting legacy. My mother's effort to encourage open communication about the difficult issues of estate planning has been one of her hallmarks in our family.

In our family, estate planning is not a private affair, and it never really has been. Even as a child, I remember getting an envelope under the Christmas tree from my grandparents that had a Carnation stock certificate in it. I didn't really understand what was going on at the time, and the envelope, when presented, quickly found its way into my mother's purse. But over time, I began to understand and appreciate my grandparents' generosity.

Now that we are adults and have families of our own, my siblings and I have been included in our parents' estate planning. Good communication is making my parents' plans more effective, but it also provides great learning for us as we plan our own affairs and prepare our children to be wealth strategists.

The Estate Planning Road Map

My estate planning road map focuses on three fundamental points: ensuring that the core needs of each generation are met, reinforcing family harmony, and empowering subsequent generations. The road map consists of six sequential steps, with each step building on the preceding one to assemble a complete plan. Each step is defined by a goal with accompanying techniques you can use to accomplish that goal. More important, the road map reinforces the culture and values needed to sustain family wealth across generations. Here are the six steps:

1. Anticipate and communicate about your eventual demise.

2. Focus on defense; let your heirs worry about offense.

3. Deal with family houses and other "legacy assets."

4. Perpetuate the family's economic engine.

5. Prepare estate plans to create income streams.

6. Accomplish the must-dos.

This road map is remarkably simple and flexible, as any good estate planning process should be. You want to avoid, at all costs, estate plans that involve rigid legal structures, administrative overload, positions that are inadequately defensible to the IRS, and whopping legal bills. A few families of means opt for great estate complexity because the tax savings appear substantial and they have the infrastructure to manage the complexity. Even then, however, I recommend strongly that they take into account that they will be dealing with multiple generations, expanding family size, a changing and unpredictable future, and wide-ranging aptitudes for managing this kind of complexity. Such complexity can undermine family harmony and cost a lot of time, money, and Rolaids to resolve.

Whether your estate plans are simple or complex, following these six steps should go a long way toward making them more productive. When interviewing prospective trust and estate lawyers to advise you on the details of your plans, make sure they are experienced in this type of work and have impeccable technical skills. Don't cut corners in this important aspect of your wealth management plan.

Step #1: Anticipate and Communicate About Your Eventual Demise

Your first responsibility when it comes to multigenerational planning is to make sure your own house is in order. You want to do this for your own peace of mind, but you also want to do it for your children. It might seem obvious, but making sure that you are well taken care of in your later years relieves your children of a huge potential burden. Being wealthy puts you in a much better position than most people to give this gift to yourself and your children.

Putting your own house in order means the following:

Financial security. Make sure that you and your spouse (if you are married) have enough financial resources to last your lifetimes. Your Financial Administrator should be able to help you model how much wealth, and in what form, you will need to be financially secure. By regularly reviewing your financial position throughout retirement and by budgeting carefully, you can make appropriate midcourse corrections.

Research. Investigate services that provide a range of senior living alternatives, offer research on aging, and work with families to resolve issues of aging. Continuing Care Retirement Communities (CCRCs) offer healthy seniors an active community life with flexible medical and other support services that our minds and bodies eventually need as we age, all in one location. Information on health like the *Harvard Health Newsletter* or the *Mayo Clinic Health Newsletter* can provide valuable suggestions for maintaining and improving the ways you take care of yourself, as well as information on cutting-edge research on medical breakthroughs that could affect you.

Effective communication. Communicate periodically with your children about your wishes for your estate, your health management, and your loved ones. They need to know your desires because there might come a point when you won't be able to fulfill them without help from others. Topics include these:

- Articulating whether you want to stay in your "family house," move into the "doorman phase of life" (i.e., an apartment), investigate independent senior living communities like CCRCs, acquire in-house nursing care, or move into a quality nursing home.

- Discussing end-of-life issues and death. Americans do not like to talk about their own death. There is something in our culture that has stigmatized it. I don't know why it is the case, but I have lived in Britain and France, where people view death as a natural part of life. If you start the conversation early, it is not a conversation about an anticipated event, only an inevitability. The conversations don't have to be somber or morose. In fact, a good dose of humor is useful. Get rid of the stigma, and try to enjoy the conversation. You won't regret it and neither will your children.

- Managing your healthcare if you cannot manage for yourself. The law relating to end-of-life health issues varies from state to state and regularly changes. The moral issues are both personal and societal. The more guidance you can give your children about how you want to deal with end-of-life issues, the more likely your wishes will be fulfilled and the less moral burden you place on them.

- Talking with your family about your estate plan, and about bequests you will make to friends or institutions, helps to establish expectations. It is easy, particularly in our mobile society, for adult children to be unaware of their parents' bonds of friendship and companionship. Someone you view as a dear companion could be viewed by your children as an opportunist or gold digger waiting for you to die so that they can inherit your wealth. If you choose to differentiate among your children in your will, isn't it better to be able to explain to them why you are doing so rather than leaving the job to your estate's executor?

We have all read about contested wills, and we all know people who have endured emotional struggles about end-of-life issues. Good communication lifts these burdens from the next generation in the way that good asset management lifts the financial burden. These truly are valuable gifts.

Legal preparation. You will want to prepare advance directives and healthcare powers of attorney to give someone—usually your spouse or children—authority to make medical decisions on your behalf, if you are unable. Advance directives make clear an individual's wishes with regard to the use of life-prolonging procedures, such as use of ventilators and feeding tubes. The Terri Schiavo affair, so much in the news in 2005, only brings home the hard reality that making firm and concrete end-of-life plans can ease burdens of guilt and responsibility for one's family. In most states, an advance directive is all that is needed for a physician to act without fear of legal recriminations if patients are not capable of advocating for themselves. The absence of an advance directive leaves open the possibility that a terminally ill patient will be kept alive against his or her wishes as family members, physicians, lawyers, and sometimes politicians debate what to do.

A power of attorney provides a legal means for people who become mentally or physically incapable of administering their own affairs to turn over decision-making responsibility to the person or people of their choice.

Therefore, it is important for you to have both a healthcare power of attorney and an advance directive in place while hoping you never need to rely on either. If you have not already done so, I encourage you to discuss this issue with your lawyer and with your family. Don't wait until a crisis point to do this. Every adult should have these conversations with the people they trust and with competent legal counsel.

Backup. If you do not have a spouse or children, or your relationship with them is such that the actions cited so far are not appropriate, you will need someone else with whom to share your wishes and to act in a fiduciary capacity for both financial and health issues. Some wealth management firms and most trust and estate law firms provide services of this nature. Finding someone who is skilled and whom you can trust, literally with both your life and your livelihood, is a very important decision. Make the decision sooner rather than later and take the time to develop the relationship, even if it costs some money.

Step #2: Focus on Defense; Let Your Heirs Worry About Offense

One of the first questions people ask about transferring wealth to their children is "How much should I give them?" No wealthy parent wants their heirs to become "trust fund babies" who do not lead productive or fulfilling lives. Asking "How much?" is the wrong question. Asking "How?" is the right question, as in

- "How should I transfer wealth so that it empowers my children and creates new opportunities for them?"

- "How should I transfer wealth so that they can learn to be effective stewards of their good fortune?"

- "How should I transfer wealth to protect those who cannot fend for themselves?"

Here is the short answer to these questions: Make your first priorities your children's and grandchildren's financial security in retirement, their education, and their health. If you can afford to help them out in these matters, they will have more freedom to take risks as entrepreneurial stewards or to pursue vitally important career paths that are less swayed by economic imperatives. They will have added incentive to pursue careers in religious life, medicine, the arts, or in teaching, like my brother and brother-in-law who are both outstanding primary school teachers.

Making these transfers of wealth requires no legal documents, no complex disclosures on your tax returns, and no incursion of estate or transfer tax. Here's how you do it:

Funding Your Heirs' Retirement

In 2012, you and your spouse are each allowed to give away up to $13,000 (a total of $26,000) to as many individuals as you wish without incurring tax. This is called the Annual Exclusion gift. If you and your spouse have three children and you together give each of them $26,000 per year for 30 years, you can give away $2.34 million! It's difficult to tell what will happen to the Annual Exclusion in future years. If Congress does nothing, it will shrink in 2013. But, over the longer term, it might rise above $13,000, making the gift potential even greater.

Taking this example a step further, if your kids marry and have a total of seven grandchildren among them, you can add Annual Exclusion gifts to all your relations over another 20 years, with the total dollars given away reaching $9.1 million!

These are pretty generous gifts if you can afford them, because all told, those children, spouses, and grandchildren are receiving $338,000 per year from you!

Let's look at this from the recipient's perspective to fully understand the power behind these simple gifts. At birth, a lucky baby receives $13,000 from each of his or her parents and two of four grandparents for a total of $52,000. The child receives similar gifts for each of the next 20 years. Starting at age 20 and continuing until age 50, this person continues to receive $26,000 from his parents, but nothing from grandparents because they are presumed to have died in this example. If the assets are invested in an equity index fund and it generates a 5% after-tax annual return (significantly below the long-term historic average) over that 50-year period, this lucky person will have accumulated $10 million just from Annual Exclusion gifts! Even if the recipient's parents do not make gifts in some years, the blend of regular gifts, prudent management, and compounding are still enormously powerful...if the gifts are invested and not spent.

If you are concerned about your children's financial discipline, you can make the gifts into a simple trust and stipulate in the trust that the assets cannot be distributed until your child reaches a certain age. If your children have good discipline, let them manage the assets directly. If you're not certain, do a little of both.

Now, let me add another wrinkle to further increase the power of Annual Exclusion gifts. At age 20, the fortunate beneficiary in this example earns enough salary that he or she qualifies to sock away $13,000 per year, pretax, into a tax-deferred retirement account.

Many young people, of course, can't afford (or choose not) to save for retirement aggressively in their early years. But this forward-thinking person does put the $13,000 from his salary into the retirement plan. He does so because his enlightened parents give him $13,000 in the form of an Annual Exclusion gift. Now his taxable income each year is reduced $13,000 by the retirement plan contribution, and he saves $13,000 each year courtesy of his parents' gift. And his retirement assets can grow on a tax-deferred basis for the next 50 years.

But it gets even better. Because his taxable income is reduced by $13,000, he does not incur a federal income tax liability on this amount, which could total $4,500 or more. He can spend this "saved" amount or put it in an Individual Retirement Account or a Roth IRA. Investing through an IRA would further lower his taxable income and increase the dollars that are compounding tax-deferred. In the Roth IRA, income tax is paid on the earned income but then the asset grows tax free and distributions upon retirement are also tax free, a nice hedge on rising tax rates.

By receiving Annual Exclusion gifts, this person can benefit in two big ways: spending more of his salary than he could before, and putting away lots of money for retirement early in his career and watching it compound over the decades. Eventually, because of his good discipline, he might need to save less for retirement later in life and can use the extra money to give away to his children in the same manner that his parents did to him. And so the cycle continues: perpetual transfer of substantial wealth, no gift taxes, deferred income taxes, no big legal fees, and a simple investment strategy. It can work if your children are business tycoons, dancers, artists, or academics.

Funding Your Heirs' Education

Do you want to do even more, like pay for your children's and/or your grandchildren's education? Here's how:

When you make payments directly to the relevant educational institutions, these payments do not count as gifts and are exempt from gift tax. Again, these are expenses your heirs do not have to incur, and this results in the student graduating debt free. To exit our educational system with no debts is a real gift.

Many people have established so-called "529 plans" to help fund their children's and grandchildren's college educations. Unlike direct payments for education, contributions to 529 plans are considered gifts and are subject to gift tax and the per-beneficiary gift-tax exclusion. In addition, contributions to a 529 plan are subject to income tax. But, once inside the plan, they grow tax-deferred and distributions for the beneficiaries' college expenses are exempt from tax. In addition, if the benefits are not used by a named beneficiary, you may designate other family members. Another advantage is that although the assets are no longer in your gross estate, you can still maintain substantial control over them. If you subsequently want the contributions back, you can get them without tax. You can also access the gains, but tax and a 10% penalty apply. Depending on how Congress changes the estate and gift tax, 529 plans might be an attractive estate planning tool as well as a means to support the education of future generations of family members. Check with your financial and tax advisors. When thinking about 529 plans, remember though that the costs and providers vary from state to state. Do your homework and remember to keep your costs as low as possible. At least right now, Utah has the lowest costs around, but if your home state gives tax benefits and is low-cost as well, you might want to stay closer to home.

Funding Your Heirs' Healthcare

Do you want to do even more, like pay for your children's and/or your grandchildren's healthcare costs? Here's how:

Again, if you make payments directly to medical service providers (hospitals and the like), these payments don't count as gifts and are exempt from gift tax. A benefit of this approach is that you can help your kids save money on their health insurance by having them raise their deductibles—thereby lowering their insurance premiums—while you take responsibility for making up the difference in covered costs should major medical bills arise.

I know what you're thinking. What happens if these lucky recipients of your generosity get used to your paying private-school tuition, or medical bills, and they spend the money that would otherwise be earmarked for these purposes on different things?

If you are concerned about this issue, I recommend that you require them to save a portion of the money that would otherwise go toward these expenses. Put it in writing and have them sign a pledge. It will confirm the seriousness and significance of what you are doing and also give them experience with entering into a contract. Your generosity is contingent upon certain behavior on their part.

Funding Your Heirs' First Home Purchase

You might want to help your children buy their first house. Houses have been great investments in the past and, in part because of the financial and housing crisis, they might be again. A bigger house means a larger investment and more potential appreciation. A bigger house can also mean a bigger mortgage deduction if your children borrow the money to finance the purchase. The mortgage deduction is a great perk, if you continue to be eligible. Other than accruing taxes on unrealized gains, it is about the best tax benefit around.

My one reservation here is that you would be doing your children a disservice if you helped them buy a house that they can't afford to maintain properly. Make sure that your son or daughter has budgeted all the costs of home ownership and can afford them before going ahead. If you don't, instead of giving them a gift, you have saddled them with an albatross.

By now, you have noticed that all the recommendations in Step 2 involve delayed gratification. Many of the benefits are deferred decades into the future, or they simply reduce or eliminate debt that would otherwise be owed. They also require that the beneficiaries of your generosity generate their own earned income to meet their living expenses. They must budget carefully and invest prudently. Admittedly, they do get some current benefit because they don't have to save for retirement, repay loans, or pay private-school tuition. But these are all secondary benefits that are predicated on their own ability to earn a living.

Step #3: Deal with Family Houses and Other "Legacy Assets"

Though real estate is not often thought of as a "negative cash flow" item on the family balance sheet, it can be. Primary homes, secondary/vacation homes, and a few other assets—like an art collection or a special boat—can be integral to a family's identity, purpose, and traditions. They can also be costly to maintain. People want to keep them in the family, but they are expensive luxuries. As families grow across generations, family members will have varying degrees of interest in these family assets and differing desires or financial resources to manage them.

Children sometimes want to hold onto the family homestead in which they were raised. My wife and I ran across this a few years ago when we bought a house from a couple who wanted to downsize and move into the "doorman phase" of their lives. One of this couple's grown sons liked visiting and staying in the room in which he grew up, and he put pressure (unsuccessfully) on his parents to hold onto the house. Eventually, practicality won out over sentimentality.

Likewise, many adult children want to hold onto family vacation homes because of the happy memories they have of those homes from their days as kids. With the rapid rise in values of highly coveted vacation properties around the world, it might tempt a family (or family member) to consider selling a longtime vacation property to make a healthy profit. Yet sentimentality often keeps the home in the family, and with that comes a whole host of financial and logistical challenges. How do you split time spent at the house among two or more adult children and their families? How do you share expenses and handle issues such as maintenance and taxes? It takes a lot of communication, teamwork, and goodwill to figure out all of this in a multigenerational scenario.

Sentimentality aside, there are various legal techniques you can employ to execute intergenerational transfers of real estate, and these can be highly tailored to your individual circumstances. One of the most common is a Qualified Personal Residence Trust. A "QPRT" ("*Cue*-purt"), as it's commonly called, lets you make a gift of your house at its current value some years into the future. Several features of the QPRT have the effect of lowering the value of the home for gift-tax purposes. There are also some risks with the strategy, most notably that the donor has to be alive on the date the trust terminates. If you predecease the term of the QPRT, the house reverts to your estate and is subject to estate tax at its value at the time of your death. For a more detailed evaluation of QPRTs and related strategies, you should seek good legal advice to help you explore your options.

I have two practical recommendations to make if you want to transfer your family vacation home to your children. First, before your kids inherit or buy the house from you, get them to prepare a written operating agreement that spells out how they will handle the expenses, operations, decorating decisions, scheduling, and potential sale of the house. Is it something that just your children should own, or should spouses become owners too? How can they come to a fair agreement if some kids like to use the house but others don't? We've come to terms with all these issues, and so can you.

Second, try to shift their mentality from one of ownership to one of stewardship. A trust or limited liability partnership can be a helpful tool, especially if you can fund the entity not only with the house itself but also with an "endowment" to fund the house's operating expenses. Adding an "endowment" takes the financial pressure off of your children, especially those who are not big wage earners, to cover the operating costs of the house. You could also restrict how interests in the entity can be transferred. This eliminates economic pressure on people to fund expenses they can't afford or would prefer to allocate elsewhere.

Your children can then think of the property as a luxury to share rather than an asset to manage. There is no requirement to use the house and no economic burden. Even with all this planning, it might come to pass that the house is no longer practical or pleasurable to retain. Then it's time to convert the luxury to cash. At that point, a majority, a supermajority, or all the children (or grandchildren) can agree to sell the house. One sibling can buy out the others. They can all choose to sell and then buy another one that better suits them. Or they can distribute all the proceeds from the house sale and the endowment and liquidate the trust or partnership.

Step #4: Perpetuate the Family's Economic Engine

Successful businesses, unlike houses, usually have existing or antici-pated positive cash flow. Through astute estate planning, you can either transfer a family business from one generation to the next or provide financial support to your child or grandchild who wants to start or buy a business (or other income-producing asset), thereby maintaining the family's spirit of entrepreneurial stewardship and its wealth-building capabilities across generations.

Under most circumstances, I am not an advocate of significant leverage when managing family wealth. But when it comes to promoting entre-preneurial stewardship through estate planning, my view is the opposite with regard to one particular kind of leverage: intergenerational family lending. In fact, I think it is one of the best estate planning techniques around. And it really gets to the heart of strategic wealth management. Let's look at two examples so that you can see what I mean.

Transferring the Family Business

First, let's take the case of a family business that is to be transferred from one generation to the next. For simplicity's sake, assume that both ownership and management control are being passed simultaneously. In this case, the technique is really nothing more than an intergenera-tional leveraged buyout, known in some circles as a "freeze" because it freezes the value of the company for one generation and allocates any additional value to the next one. The idea is to get an appropriate value for the company. Let's call it $1 million, based on annual pretax profits of $100,000. The parents agree to sell the business to their adult children (the "kids") for this amount, but they provide seller financing for 90% of the amount. There are specific IRS regulations that stipulate the rate of interest that intrafamily loans must use to avoid being subject to gift tax, but the rates are quite attractive to the borrower, especially in a low-interest-rate environment. Using today's rates, the company profits in this example could more than pay the interest and still leave money to reinvest in the business.

The kids, having accumulated a number of Annual Exclusion gifts over the years, have savings in excess of $100,000 to purchase the equity. So now the parents have transferred the family business to the next generation without incurring any estate tax.

Now let's look at what happens going forward. The kids own the business and are now running it. They are under pressure to make the interest payments and eventually pay off the loan to their parents. They have real economic incentives to perform. Let's assume that the company was well positioned at the time of sale, the kids are good managers, and economic conditions are favorable. In the early years, things are tight because after payments on the loan and the business's capital requirements there is no extra cash. But in ten years, the kids have paid off the loan, the company has grown to be worth $10 million, and it's generating a million dollars a year of profit. This is clearly a good outcome. The entrepreneurial skills of the kids have paid off handsomely, and the parents get their money out of the business, plus interest too, to do with as they please.

But what happens if the business hits a roadblock? Then the debt covenants give the parents several options. If the kids are managing well but the company is experiencing a cyclical downturn, the parents might choose to accrue any interest and principal payments that are due and ride out the storm. If the kids are not managing well, the parents can regain control over the company and manage it back to health. If the company is just a dud, the parents have a problem, especially if the sale proceeds from the company are a substantial portion of their net worth. But this is a problem they would have had anyway. A freeze gone wrong can also have some adverse tax consequences if loans are forgiven by the parents. Such forgiveness could be deemed a constructive gift for tax purposes. The moral of the last outcome is "Don't sell the duds to relatives!"

Family Funding of Business Ventures

Another type of intergenerational lending occurs when an entrepreneur wants to start or buy a company and approaches his parents for financial support. The parents have at least three options. They can lend the money directly to the project (on a nonrecourse basis), much as was done in the preceding example. They can provide financial guarantees to a third-party lender that lower the cost of borrowing for their kid.

Finally, they can make a personal loan to their kid to buy the company's equity and secure the loan with the stock (and only the stock). In some cases, it makes sense to buy preferred stock in the company instead of making or guaranteeing a loan. The option you choose depends on the specific circumstances.

I like using intrafamily loans and leveraged buyouts for several reasons:

- The technique is relatively simple to structure, and it remains flexible in the face of unforeseen future circumstances. Even if multiple siblings are involved, you can split operational and ownership interests equally or unequally, depending on how many family members are involved in the business. If the parent(s) dies while still holding the note on the business, one can often document a strong case as to why the paper is worth significantly less than 100 cents on the dollar, making it possible to transfer the asset out of the decedent's estate more efficiently.

- The risk of the deal is separated from its potential upside benefits. I assume that if parents are trying to transfer wealth to their kids in this manner, they don't need more money. Yet they still capture cash value for the company as the loan is paid off. I also hope they have diversified their assets, because they are taking most of the risk when structuring a freeze or intergenerational loan. At least in a worst-case scenario, if their loan is a write-off, it creates a good tax deduction, which they are more likely to be able to use than the kids.

The kid(s) gets most of the economic benefit if the business is a success, yet faces a significant disincentive with a loss of equity if it fails. With the right economic incentives in place, the parents can step back and let those in the next generation prove themselves.

- The structure encourages entrepreneurial instincts and it rewards success in the next generation. The next generation has a leveraged opportunity to generate a substantial return with limited risk. Empowerment encourages success and success translates into wealth creation. Does this create incentives to be entrepreneurial? You bet!

Still, there is cause to be cautious. First, hire a good lawyer to set up the appropriate structure. There are a lot of rules about making loans to related parties, and you want to make sure you follow them. Second, by using this structure, you are artificially lowering the downside risk for your children (and you are taking disproportionate risk relative to your potential reward). Without the downside risk, your children might become overly eager to take more risk than they should.

If you want to fund the next generation's business ventures, I encourage you to establish an advisory board or some other independent mechanism to assess the viability of new business propositions that are brought to you by your children. Going through a rigorous vetting process will benefit all parties involved. Maybe you should consider allowing members of the advisory board to invest in a portion of the equity (with real money) as compensation for their expertise. This would go a long way toward aligning everyone's interests.

Step #5: Prepare Estate Plans to Create Income Streams

In Step #2, I talked about making gifts to fund your children's retirement. In that case, you created an income stream that they could tap into 20, 30, or 40 years in the future. But if you have the financial scale, you might want to create income streams for your children and grandchildren that start sooner than that. You can do so using retirement plans, irrevocable trusts, family companies, family partnerships, or other means. Sometimes the income stream gets transferred on the death of the benefactor. Other times it kicks in when the beneficiary reaches a certain age or milestone. Some benefactors create these income streams to protect the financial security of someone who cannot fend for himself or herself. Others want simply to do something generous for people they care about. The income gives the beneficiary a wine collection, an annual trip, a monthly evening out for dinner, or the money to buy new furniture. The assets have to get quite large before the income stream threatens to become demotivating. And if the family has a financial goal of maintaining real per capita wealth across generations, they cannot afford to distribute a lot and will have to work hard to keep the economic engine firing on all cylinders.

Retirement Plans

Everyone who has a 401k, an IRA, or another retirement plan should designate beneficiaries and responsible stewards of the assets in case of death. It's possible, but not necessary, for the beneficiary and the steward to be the same person. If you use retirement plans as vehicles to pass wealth from one generation to the next, make sure that you get good legal advice on how to properly structure such transfers. You should also analyze whether the cost and tax structure of a retirement plan are the most economic ways to pass assets. Such bequests can be lucrative for the beneficiary, but they can also reinforce family purpose, or simply facilitate a little fun. Let me give you an example from my own life. Ten years ago, my Uncle John passed away. He had a modest estate, no wife or children, and he was kind enough to bequeath to me part of his IRA. The $40,000 was a lot of money to him, he was very proud that he enriched my life with it, and I am very grateful for his generosity. Each year, I am required by law to withdraw roughly $2,000. For a year or so, I contemplated how to honor this money as a gift and to reflect on his memory. After a while, I hit on an answer. Because I enjoy good wine, I've decided that each year after getting my distribution, I will buy one or two cases of wine and build the John B. Lucas collection. His collection is segregated from my other wine, but I've opened a few bottles for special occasions. Using his bequest in this way allows me to think of him during my annual pilgrimage to the wine store, when I uncork the bottle, when I enjoy the bouquet and flavor of the wine, and even when I go past his collection to get a more commonplace bottle of what the British call "plonk."

I will treasure Uncle John's gift to me for a lifetime, and many years from now I hope to pass to my kids, and even grandchildren, some well-aged bottles from the John B. Lucas collection.

Irrevocable Trusts

An irrevocable trust is a more effective way than retirement plans for passing assets to future generations. An irrevocable trust is a vehicle to hold your assets and manage and distribute them in specified ways. Although it might be self-evident, the terms of an irrevocable trust cannot be changed after it is established. One or several trustees must be designated to manage the affairs of the trust, but neither you nor your spouse nor any other current beneficiary of the trust should be trustee. This helps to protect the assets within the trust from creditor claims, including bankruptcy, lawsuits, divorce, and liens.

The trustee of the irrevocable trust is responsible for managing the trust according to the law and the terms of the trust document. Finding a responsible trustee usually involves finding someone who combines traits of professionalism with the ability to say no if and when beneficiaries want to change the terms of the trust in ways the grantor did not intend. That said, it is equally important for there to be a separate individual, a "trust protector," who can review the performance of a trustee and, if necessary, remove him or her.

Sidebar 11.1: When Structural Rigidity in Wealth Management Planning Is Good

Most rules have their exceptions and mine do too. In the trust world, an element of rigidity is good. I highly recommend that any irrevocable trust creator make five critical (and unchangeable) decisions when designing a trust:

1. Make the rate of trust distributions consistent with your long-term goals, but not rigid in number. For example, if you want the real asset value of the trusts to remain the same, distributing more than 2.0% to 2.5% in annual after-tax distributions will make the primary goal difficult to achieve. When your lawyer drafts the trust, you might want to include specific language to give trustees flexibility to distribute more or less than the designated amount. For example, the income beneficiary could have or develop special needs, due to a physical or mental disability, that require a larger payout. In contrast, the income beneficiary might today be a spendthrift who, given the chance, spends money in ways that are self-destructive or otherwise inappropriate, but tomorrow might develop greater discipline and control. There is precise legal terminology to deal with these issues that is well tested in the courts and is enforceable by a trustee.

2. Stipulate the age at which distributions begin. Distributions can be staged so that as your children get older, the size of the distribution grows.

3. Adopt a unitrust approach to calculate distributions. For many decades, common trust language talked about distributing the income from a trust. However, more and more states have legislated trusts (unitrusts) that distribute a certain percentage of assets rather than the income. The beauty of a unitrust format is that it allows the trust assets to be invested for total return, and it aligns more closely the interests of income and remainder beneficiaries. Income beneficiaries receive regular distributions as long as the trust is in force. Remainder beneficiaries receive the remaining trust assets upon termination. Both benefit if the assets grow in value and both suffer if they decline in value.

4. Stipulate the method of allocating assets within the family. Typically the choice will be *per stirpes* or *per capita*. *Per stirpes* means that assets are distributed equally to the children of each beneficiary; *per capita* means that assets are distributed equally to the people in each generation. If a trust creator has two children and one of those children has four children and the other has one child, the allocations are as follows. Under a per stirpes arrangement, in the third generation, four children each have a 12.5% interest in the trust and the fifth has a 50% interest. Under a per capita arrangement all five children have 20%. Under either scenario, the second generation shares the trust interests 50/50.

5. If you plan to hold a concentrated position, like shares in your family business, in the trust document include specific language to allow the trustees to retain it as a concentrated position indefinitely. Otherwise, they will feel considerable pressure to sell and diversify the position.

Beyond these selected decisions, the fewer decisions you can inscribe in the trust document and the more latitude you can offer a trustee, the better. However, in a separate, nonbinding letter, the trust creator should communicate his or her intentions with regard to these and any other issues of economic, philanthropic, philosophical, family, or personal importance as clearly as possible.

> Doing so can eliminate family friction later and ensure that a trust creator's intentions and wishes are judiciously applied as our personal journeys, and as the world, evolve in ever-changing and unpredictable ways.

Some irrevocable trusts have attractive generation-skipping attributes that reduce or eliminate estate taxes. These trusts can save you and your family millions of dollars in taxes over the long run, as well as create income flows for the benefit of family members.

Family Companies and Family Partnerships

Family companies and family partnerships are additional structures people use to transfer wealth and to create income streams for beneficiaries. In many cases, family companies and partnerships are designed to limit the liability of some or all participants. Unlike with irrevocable trusts, oversight and economic interests do not need to be separated in family companies or partnerships, but can be.

Let me explain. One of the benefits of family companies and partnerships is that management control, economic benefit, and oversight responsibility are changeable and can be easily tailored to specific circumstances. That makes it easier to delegate operating control to a management team, reward them with (tax-efficient) capital appreciation if they create wealth, and give family members the power to reassert control if they need to or choose to, simply by garnering the necessary votes to exercise their power. Another benefit of these structures is that the governing documents can be modified to suit changing circumstances.

Economic interests can also be bought and sold as well as gifted, subject to governing documents. The careful structuring of governing documents will affect the value of economic interests for gift-tax purposes. As a general rule, the less liquid an asset is and the less control an owner has, the less the asset is worth. The IRS periodically challenges use of these techniques in court, but well-structured and well-documented strategies have proven resilient to these challenges. These benefits are difficult, if not impossible, to achieve in an irrevocable trust structure.

Just like trusts, companies and partnerships can be designed to distribute income to partners or shareholders. Companies and partnerships can also distribute salaries and ownership interests. Although they are operationally more flexible than trusts, they do not have the generation-skipping tax characteristics of trusts. In addition, the responsibility of those who oversee companies and partnerships might not rise to the standard of trust fiduciary. The person or people who control a company can pay themselves salaries at whatever level they like regardless of whether the decision erodes the value of minority shareholder interests. In other words, there is not the same obligation to be equally fair to all shareholders or partners. These entities are great, but confidence in the skill and integrity of management is crucial to making them work well. So is having good governance to hold the managers accountable on a regular basis!

Many of the structures that wealth advisors promote are complex variations of the entities I've just described. In every case, you should compare the costs, risks, and benefits of these more complex structures against the simple ones I have described. In most cases, I think you'll find that simple is better.

One thing to evaluate very carefully when considering complex estate structures is how flexible they are. After they are put in place, complex estate plans can be hard or impossible to change. Do a number of different scenario analyses, even improbable ones, to see how well the strategy works. Ask yourself these questions:

- What if tax rates change?
- How will I or my heirs feel if my strategy is exposed on the front page of our local newspaper or the *Wall Street Journal*?
- What if the value of the investment declines precipitously?
- Do I have the ongoing administrative capabilities in place to execute the strategy?
- What if there is a death or a divorce in the family?
- What if more children arrive on the scene, either naturally or by adoption?
- What if the investment returns wildly exceed my expectations?

- What if my children who are managing the business aren't competent, get distracted, or suffer ill health?

- How much change can strategies withstand and still hold up? The more inflexible they are, the greater the risk and the more caution, analysis, and experience you should have in estate planning before you charge ahead.

It will be worth the money to hire someone who is very practical and who understands not only estate law, but also family dynamics. This professional can advise you on how to administer an estate for many decades—regardless of the structures you set up.

Step #6: Accomplish the Must-Dos

Throughout this book, I have provided options for accomplishing various goals. Now, at the very end, I am breaking with that tradition and stating, in the most declarative voice I can: Do these things or you will undermine everything else that you've accomplished!

Must-Do #1: Write a Will!!

A will enables you to

- State clearly your intentions for disposition of your nontrust property.

- Address specific personal matters.

- Designate your preferred legal guardian for your minor children if both parents die unexpectedly.

- Make direct outright gifts of money or property (jewelry, furniture, housewares, art, and so on) to specific individuals or institutions.

- Describe your wishes for a funeral.

Without a will

- The IRS could inherit half of your assets, and lawyers, accountants, and opportunists could inherit the other half.

- Beneficiaries of your estate can go on spending sprees, if they are unencumbered by any restrictions or guidelines in the will.

- Your estate will end up in probate. Probate is a court-supervised procedure for the distribution of a decedent's estate. It's an invasive, public process that bares the financial assets of the decedent for all to see and invites anyone who might have a claim against the estate to participate. It can even take place in the decedent's residence! All sorts of unexpected issues can arise that add costs and time to the estate settlement process, even if the issues are later deemed frivolous. Probate cannot be closed until all public claims are heard and rulings are made on each of them. And few distributions can be made to rightful heirs until probate closes.

Don't put off estate planning just because you are busy, are young, don't like paying lawyers, or have some other excuse to procrastinate!

Must-Do #2: Set Up a Revocable Trust

A revocable trust keeps most of your assets, and especially your financial assets, out of probate (make sure that you actually transfer your assets into the trust after you set it up). The revocable trust operates like a set of explicit written instructions clearly stating how you want its trust assets distributed upon your death.

Although creditors can still make a claim on your estate, they have to convince a judge to freeze the estate assets while their claim is argued. While the grantor (you) usually acts as trustee during your lifetime, the trust documents will name a trustee (often a spouse) who is responsible for the management of the trust after the grantor's death. You should review your revocable trust every five years or so to make sure it is still operating as expected. If, for whatever reason, you want to dissolve the trust or switch assets in or out of the trust, such actions are easy and inexpensive to undertake. It is a highly flexible structure.

Must-Do #3: Set Up a Marital Trust

A marital trust allows a spouse access to your assets after your death for specified purposes without actually giving him or her your estate. This helps to protect the spouse's financial security while allowing you to control the eventual distribution of the assets. It also allows you to fully use your estate tax exemption while still making it possible for your spouse to draw on the assets if needed. Be aware that the mechanics of setting up such trusts will differ by individual state and the rules governing this are continually changing. You'll have to investigate the rules for establishing a marital trust in the state where you reside.

Must-Do #4: Consider Giving Assets to Your Spouse

If you are married and one spouse controls most of your combined assets, you should consider redistributing the assets between you. You are allowed to transfer an infinite amount of assets to your spouse without adverse tax consequences. But each person is allowed to transfer only a specified amount of assets (above the Annual Exclusion gift) free of estate tax to others. This is called the Estate Tax Exemption, and in 2012, it was $5.1 million per person. (The size of exemption in 2013 and beyond is impossible at this point to predict.) This right is not transferable. So, if you and your spouse want to take full advantage of the Estate Tax Exemption, you need to make sure that each of your estates can take maximum use of it.

Must-Do #5: Consider Irrevocable Trusts

As part of your estate plan, consider setting up irrevocable trusts for your children so that when you (and your spouse) die, they will be provided for. In establishing the trusts, you will have to designate a trustee to be a responsible party. (You and your spouse should not be trustees.) Depending on your family dynamics and the complexity of the trusts, you might choose another family member, a close friend, or a corporate trustee. Especially if the assets in trust are, or will be, more than a few hundred thousand dollars, I encourage you to use a corporate trustee for reasons I explained in Sidebar 7.3, "The Case for Corporate Trustees."

In case you were to die unexpectedly, you can structure your estate to fully fund the trusts and provide financial security for your children. Some people who buy life insurance designate these irrevocable trusts as the beneficiaries of the policy. With a responsible trustee, you have the oversight in place to manage the assets and to control spending. This can be particularly important if your children are minors or young adults. You can design irrevocable trusts to give control of the assets to your children as they reach a certain age or some other milestone. Or you can establish the trusts as generation-skipping trusts that remain in trust for several generations and avoid several layers of estate tax.

Sidebar 11.2:   The Murky State of Estate Tax Laws

When Congress passed the Tax Reform Act of 2001, it created havoc for estate planners. Over the next several years, the Estate Tax Exemption bounced all over the place. It grew from $1,500,000 in 2005 to $3,500,000 in 2009. Then, in 2010, the estate tax was, to the surprise of most, repealed. Then, in 2011, it reverted to $5,000,000 per person. In 2013 and forward, your guess is as good as mine as to what will happen. This wild volatility creates a nightmare planning scenario.

In 1976, Congress also passed into law a "Lifetime Exemption" provision to close a loophole in the gift tax that had allowed people to give away assets during their lifetime without taxing them at Estate Tax rates. This exemption currently allows people to make gifts up to $5,100,000 over their lifetime, but it will likely change significantly in 2013. This is an aggregate amount per donor, not an amount per beneficiary. The Lifetime Exemption also forms part of the Estate Tax Exemption, so if you use a portion of your Lifetime Exemption, it reduces your Estate Tax Exemption by the same amount.

That is why, more than ever, you should put a premium on maintaining flexibility in your estate plans. Hopefully, in 2013 Congress will readdress the estate tax and clean up this mess. Many in the Republican Party want to eliminate the estate tax, but I think this is unlikely given the government's fiscal woes. There are many powerful countervailing voices, including Bill Gates, Sr., and Warren Buffett, who are lobbying against repeal of the estate tax. I happen to agree with these two that estate tax reform is needed but that eliminating the estate tax will not be beneficial to American society. Our country is strong because it rewards people who create wealth. Legislation that reinforces a permanent aristocracy of ultrawealthy people is not consistent with the Land of Opportunity.

Conclusion

Estate planning should focus on three issues. The first issue is fundamentals: planning and execution so that you can live the rest of your life feeling financially secure and well cared for and so that your heirs (and theirs) have good educations, adequate healthcare, and long-term financial security.

The second is family affinities and values. Working through how estate planning will affect the harmony and functionality of your family will prevent or minimize friction that, left unchecked, can undermine well-intended financial plans.

The third is empowerment of your family's human capital. How can you transfer your wealth so that it motivates and empowers your heirs rather than sapping their will to aspire and succeed?

If you succeed at these three fundamental issues, whatever you pay in estate tax is secondary. You will have created a great legacy because you will have nurtured and mentored people you love who are now prepared to accept the mantle of wealth with all its responsibilities and privileges. They might invest your wealth in ways that create even more wealth. Or, because they have financial stability, they might feel empowered to do other things, great and small, that are not motivated by money, but that are central to living a rich, useful, and productive life. Like my great-grandfather E. A. Stuart, my grandparents, and parents, I see this as the ultimate goal of strategic wealth management.

Chapter 11: Issues to Discuss with Your Family

1. Are you teaching all members of your family about wealth management? If not, what do you think is preventing you from doing so?

2. If you have held off talking to your family about your death, are you convinced now that it's important to open the discussion? If not, what additional information do you think would be helpful?

3. Do you have confidence that there is someone who will carry out your wishes in case of impairment or death? If so, does this person understand your wishes? Have you committed your wishes to paper?

4. Do you think that funding your heirs' education, retirement, and so forth has the potential to "spoil" them? How can you support them while still encouraging them to work hard and be successful in their own right?

5. How do you encourage your children and grandchildren to save for retirement early in their careers when the power of compounding has the greatest opportunity to work its magic?

6. Have you set up the management of family assets—like a vacation home—so that everyone clearly understands their rights, benefits, and obligations? Have you generated consensus around these issues? If you are the primary person responsible for managing these family assets today, how will you transfer these responsibilities over time, and to whom?

7. If you want to leave assets to your heirs, how much is enough? Too much? Why might you not want to leave most (or any) of your wealth to your family? Where else do you want your wealth to go?

8. Is an irrevocable trust a concept that you find easily understandable? If not, are you convinced of its merits enough to seek out additional professional assistance to learn more about it?

9. What if there isn't a Wealth Strategist in the next generation or if no consensus can be reached on who it should be? What are

the costs and benefits of fragmentation or, alternatively, forging a consensus?

10. Do you have a will and a revocable trust that you have properly funded? Have you considered transferring assets from one spouse to another for estate planning purposes?

Index

E

eat well/sleep well analogy (risk tolerance), 65-66

economic engine
    careers, 27
    family businesses, 25
    financial assets, 26
    overview, 24-27

economics and opportunistic investing, 202

education
    entrepreneurial stewardship, 287-289
    heirs, funding, 338-339

Eight Principles
    alignment of interests, 39-40
    benefits, 29
    culture of accountability, 40-41
    delegate, empower, and respect independence, 46-47
    diversification, 47-48
    family combined resources, 41-44
        cumulative advantages, 42-43
        inherited wealth, 44-46
    future family leaders, developing, 50-51
    listing of, 37-38
    simplicity, 49-50
    taking charge and doing it early, 38-39

emerging markets, 190

Employee Retirement Income Security Act. See ERISA

empowerment to serve others, 279

Enchanted Forest, 144-148
    advisors, 144-145
    Angel Investing, 146-147

clients, 144
    Country Club Gamblers, 145-146
    leaving, 152-153

entrepreneurial stewardship, 10-11
    benefits, 277
    children
        fairness, 300-301
        growing up in privilege, 286-287
        intrafamily business venture funding, 345-346
        nepotism, 299-300
        not being clients, 293-295
        parenting, 291-292
        risks, taking, 280-281
        selling the family business considerations, 281-284
        stewards, 276
        successful traits, 277
    distribution rates, selecting, 280
    education, 287-289
    empowerment to serve others, 279
    entrepreneurs, 276
    family
        culture, 278, 289-291
        leadership, 296-297, 299
        meetings, 293-296
    freedoms of wealth, 284-286

entrepreneurs, 276

ERISA (Employee Retirement Income Security Act), 129
    benefits, 129
    individual investor disadvantages, 135-136
    Prudent Investor Rule, 129-130

fees
asset-based, 231
firms, evaluating, 229-230
hidden compensation, 232
high management with low
returns, 266
profit participations, 232
retirement/tax-deferred
plans, 269
spread-based, 231
switching costs, 232
time-based, 231
transaction-based, 231
Fidelity FundsNetwork, 134
Financial Administrators. *See* FAs
financial modesty, 13
financial security in retirement,
maximizing, 58-59
financial windfalls through inheritance, marriage (divorce), and
adoption growth factor, 100-101
FINRA (Financial Industry Regulatory Authority), 143
firms. *See also* industry (wealth
management)
choosing, 137, 139-143
classic approach to wealth
management, 19-21
FA, selecting, 228
*active alpha investing skill/
experience requirements,
229-230*
*administrative infrastructure,
233-234*
*fee structure, evaluating,
229-230*
*how FAs measured/incentiv-
ized by firms, 234-237*

*index investing skill/experience
requirements, 228-229*
language, 19-20
Foundation Source website, 315
foundations, 315
donor intent, 322
family, 326-327
governance, 322-323
limited versus perpetual lives,
320-321
Four A's of investing, 131-132
access, 131
accountability, 132
acumen, 131
alignment of interests, 131
FOX (Family Office Exchange)
Advisor Directory, 238
framework (strategic wealth management), 22-28
economic engine, 24-27
family purpose, 23-24
leakage management, 27-28
virtuous circles, building, 28
freedoms of wealth, 284-286
funds-of-funds, 193
future family leaders, developing,
50-51
future financial worth of careers,
97-98
future tax rates, 268

G

*Getting to Giving: Fundraising the
Entrepreneurial Way* (Stevenson),
317
gift giving, 63
global economic views, identifying,
71-72

J-K

L

right growth assets, targeting, 172-173
rigidity (trusts), 348-350
risks
    downside protection, 256-258
    leverage, 176
    mitigation, 53-54
    taking, 280-281
    tolerance, 65-66
Roth IRA, 265
Rothschild dynasty, 67

S

Sarbanes-Oxley Law, 323
saving early, 264-265
scale of wealth
    advantages, 116-118
    regulatory issues, 119
Schwab, Charles, 134
SEC (Securities and Exchange Commission), 119
    advisor fiduciary duty to clients, 143
    scale, 119
Secret Society, 148-150
selling the family business considerations, 281-284
senior living, researching, 334
simplicity (Eight Principles), 49-50
social capital, acquiring, 308-309
social responsibility, 308
Soros, George, 200-201
specialists, coordinating, 217-219
spending
    cash flows relative to objectives, measuring, 215
    goals, 60

growing wealth while, 112-114
    tax rate, lowering, 260
spread-based compensation model, 231
stable income, maintaining, 87-88
Stevenson, Howard, 292, 317
stewards, 276
strategic wealth management
    benefits, 23
    defined, 22
    Eight Principles
        alignment of interests, 39-40
        benefits, 29
        culture of accountability, 40-41
        delegate, empower, and respect independence, 46-47
        diversification, 47-48
        family combined resources, 41-44
        future family leaders, developing, 50-51
        listing of, 37-38
        simplicity, 49-50
        taking charge and doing it early, 38-39
    framework, 22-28
        economic engine, 24-27
        family purpose, 23-24
        leakage management, 27-28
        virtuous circles, building, 28
    introducing, 8-9
    stewards of wealth, 9
    taking control, 10
strategies (investment)
    active alpha, 177-178
        alternative investments, 181-193
        defined, 177

FINANCIAL TIMES

In an increasingly competitive world, it is quality
of thinking that gives an edge—an idea that opens new
doors, a technique that solves a problem, or an insight
that simply helps make sense of it all.

We work with leading authors in the various arenas
of business and finance to bring cutting-edge thinking
and best-learning practices to a global market.

It is our goal to create world-class print publications
and electronic products that give readers
knowledge and understanding that can then be
applied, whether studying or at work.

To find out more about our business
products, you can visit us at www.ftpress.com.